M000209980

CONAN DOYLE'S
WIDE WORLD

CONAN DOYLE'S WIDE WORLD

Sherlock Holmes and Beyond

ANDREW LYCETT

TAURIS PARKE
Bloomsbury Publishing Plc
50 Bedford Square, London, WC1B 3DP, UK
1385 Broadway, 5th Floor, New York, NY

BLOOMSBURY, TAURIS PARKE and the TAURIS PARKE logo are trademarks
of Bloomsbury Publishing Plc

First published in Great Britain by Bloomsbury Publishing Plc in 2020
This edition published in 2020

Andrew Lycett has asserted his right under the Copyright, Designs and
Patents Act, 1988, to be identified as Author of this work

SHERLOCK HOLMES® and  are trademarks of the
Conan Doyle Estate Ltd®

Bloomsbury Publishing Plc does not have any control over, or responsibility for, any
third-party websites referred to or in this book. All internet addresses given in this
book were correct at the time of going to press. The author and publisher regret
any inconvenience caused if addresses have changed or sites have ceased to exist,
but can accept no responsibility for any such changes

A catalogue record for this book is available from the British Library

Library of Congress Cataloguing-in-Publication data has been applied for

ISBN: HB: 978-1-7883-1206-6; eBook: 978-1-7867-2573-8

2 4 6 8 10 9 7 5 3 1

Typeset in Perpetua by Deanta Global Publishing Services, Chennai, India
Printed and bound in the United Kingdom by CPI Group (UK) Ltd,
Croydon, CR0 4YY

FSC
www.fsc.org
MIX
Paper from
responsible sources
FSC® C020471

To find out more about our authors and books visit www.bloomsbury.com
and sign up for our newsletters

The glamour and mystery of the place, with its sinister atmosphere of forgotten nations, appealed to the imagination of my friend.

Arthur Conan Doyle,
'The Adventure of the Devil's Foot'

CONTENTS

INTRODUCTION

Sherlock Holmes wasn't the mirror image of his creator; he was more cerebral and introverted than Sir Arthur Conan Doyle, for a start. But the two men shared the same restless energy which spurred the fictional consulting detective to rouse himself from his cocaine-induced reveries in Baker Street and launch into a criminal investigation, while the famously robust Conan Doyle would regularly up sticks to take part in some demanding physical activity – often involving sport (particularly his favourite game of cricket), but also girding himself for lengthy periods of travel, as he ventured abroad in Europe, Africa, North America and Australasia.

Along with their driven natures, Holmes and Conan Doyle were professional observers of people and their environments. The former's livelihood depended on his ability to interpret seemingly trivial aspects of the world around him. The latter had trained as a doctor in his home town of Edinburgh, where his professor, Joseph Bell, drilled into him the importance of examining his patients in order to determine their illnesses.

Conan Doyle brought this skill to all areas of his life and work, including his writing. He took pains to scrutinise his surroundings, as much as the individuals who inhabited them. He added an innate artist's sense of composition which allowed him to paint a scene with colour and economy. (Fittingly he came from a notable artistic family – a background he shared with Sherlock Holmes who said, 'Art in the blood is liable to take the strangest forms.')

Such attributes helped make Conan Doyle a formidable author of travel pieces, as well as of fiction. Wherever he was, he could summon the essential features of a place in a few well-chosen words. This talent lasted throughout his life, from his evocations of the eerie silences of the Artic when he was twenty, to his account of a harrowing journey through an African swamp almost half a century later.

It's no coincidence that the Holmes 'canon' started with a man (Dr John Watson) who had spent time in distant Afghanistan. At this stage Conan Doyle himself was living in Southsea, 'a brand new fashionable watering-place, resplendent with piers, parades and hotels', beside the naval stronghold of Portsmouth, 'a grim old fortified town, grey with age and full of historical reminiscences', as he noted in one of his pieces collected here. Southsea attracted many retired people who had travelled the globe as servants of the British Empire, then in its heyday.

Starting with *A Study in Scarlet* (published in 1887), Conan Doyle imbued his Sherlock Holmes stories with a strong sense of place. After a brief recapitulation of his time on the north-west frontier, referring to Candahar (sic) and his wounding at the Battle of Maiwand, Dr Watson was introduced in St Bartholomew's Hospital in London. After deciding to room with Sherlock Holmes in Baker Street, he and his new companion were soon winging their ways across the British capital by cab. 'A minute later we were both in a hansom, driving furiously for the Brixton Road. It was a foggy, cloudy morning, and a dun-coloured veil hung over the housetops, looking like the reflection of the mud-coloured streets beneath'.

Places in London abound in the Sherlock Holmes stories – from opium dens of the East End that featured in 'The Man with the Twisted Lip' (1891) to Hampstead, where the 'king of the blackmailers', Charles Augustus Milverton, lived ('The Adventure of Charles Augustus Milverton', 1904). Further afield Holmes went to Herefordshire ('The Boscombe Valley Mystery', 1891) and Sussex ('The Adventure of Black Peter', 1904) where Conan Doyle's reference to Forest Row, on the edge of Ashdown Forest, betrayed a knowledge of the area that came from his illicit love affair with Jean Leckie.

Holmes's trips were aided by his close knowledge of the railways: not just their timetables, but their infrastructure, so a journey from Woking, reaching Waterloo at 3.23 p.m., could allow him to take 'a hasty lunch in the buffet' before pushing on to Scotland Yard ('The Adventure of the Naval Treaty', 1893). When Holmes ventured abroad after his apparent demise at the Reichenbach Falls, his journey took him to Tibet, Persia, (Saudi) Arabia, Sudan and France, as chronicled in 'The Adventure of the Empty House' (1903). Many characters in the stories either came from overseas, like the 'adventuress' Irene Adler, who had been born in New Jersey, in 'A Scandal in Bohemia' (1891), or spent time there, such as Leon Sterndale, the famous African explorer in 'The Adventure of the Devil's Foot' (1910).

Holmes's investigation of the murder in *A Study in Scarlet* largely took place in London, but it was complemented by a back story in the American state of Utah, taking in the great Mormon trek across the great plains to the Rockies, a setting which had excited Conan Doyle since, as a boy, he had read about it in the novels of Thomas Mayne Reid.

This was where his love of travel and adventure began. Before he was ten, he wrote his first book (which he illustrated himself), about a man's encounter with a tiger. He told his mother it was easy to get his characters into scrapes, but more difficult to get them out, and that, 'is surely the experience of every writer of adventures'.

That sense of adventure permeated all he wrote. His autobiography was called *Memories and Adventures*; his first collection of stories about his fictional consulting detective was *The Adventures of Sherlock Holmes* (1892). Even earlier he had published a book of non-Sherlockian stories called *Mysteries and Adventures* (1889).

He felt the world was a place to be discovered and enjoyed. Like most people of his era, he was excited by the possibilities of boundaries to be crossed and new territories opened up. Paradoxically, he would later admit his disappointment when explorers ventured to the furthest ends of the earth because this had the effect of limiting the scope of his imagination.

Along with the thrill of adventure, his travel writing often showed a moral earnestness and sense of purpose that reflected his personality and age. It also incorporated his historical vision, with a particular reverence for medievalism and its tradition of chivalry. As is well known, Conan Doyle quickly tired of writing Sherlock Holmes stories, because his main literary ambition was to write a great historical novel in the romantic tradition of Walter Scott or Victor Hugo. It was partly so he could fulfil this aim that he appeared to kill off Holmes at the Reichenbach Falls.

He brought his historical awareness to his view of the world, which was also proudly patriotic, in a way only possible of an Irishman born in Scotland and living in England. These features were accentuated by the accident of his mid-Victorian birth, which meant that he reached maturity at the height of the British Empire – a project to which he lent his enthusiastic (if often discriminating) support.

Again, this stemmed from his restlessness and curiosity – the same sort of energy which led him to embark on another more personal journey, as an ardent follower of and propagandist for spiritualism. As a lapsed Roman Catholic, he retained a sense that there was a state of being beyond everyday reality.

However, Conan Doyle was also a realist. He couldn't discard the vestiges of his scientific training as a doctor. So, his waking days were spent trying to square the demands of his lofty idealism with those of the physical world. The resulting tension helped make Sherlock Holmes (and Conan Doyle himself) such intriguing and lasting characters. It suffused his personal struggle as he tried to reconcile his sense of the numinous with his rational education. And it made for an individual, sometimes even idiosyncratic, style of reflection about his globe-trotting, as he tried to match his efforts to record what he came across with his sense of a deeper historical or even spiritual purpose.

Indeed, his later journeys to far-off lands were often undertaken as part of his crusade to tell the world about the benefits of spiritualism, the creed he had espoused during the First World War after many years of dabbling with it, but rejecting it on scientific grounds.

In this respect, his travel writing, with its undertow of romanticism and exploration, sometimes seemed like a branch of quest literature. It is no coincidence that one of his books (from 1914) bears the title *In Quest of Truth*, while his later works include *Western Wanderings* (about a visit to North America, published in 1915) and *The Wanderings of a Spiritualist* (mainly about his journey to Australasia, which came out in 1921).

However, one shouldn't be deflected by such considerations. In simple terms Conan Doyle was an astute, vivid and often witty travel writer who brought his great historical knowledge to his output. As Dr John Watson said of Sherlock Homes in '*The Adventure of the Devil's Foot*': 'The glamour and mystery of the place, with its sinister atmosphere of forgotten nations, appealed to the imagination of my friend.' The location didn't have to be sinister, of course. But in this respect, Conan Doyle was certainly very similar to his literary creation.

Andrew Lycett, London, April 2019

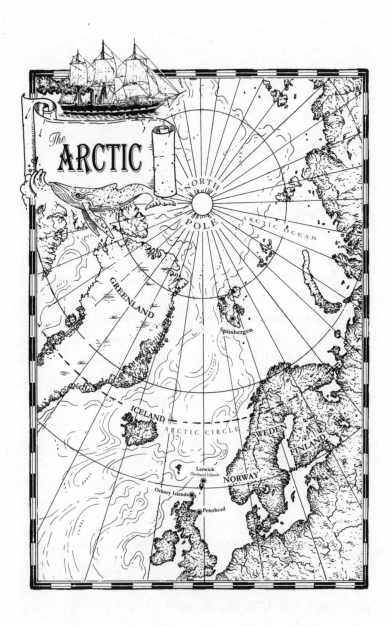

The ARCTIC

NORTH POLE

ARCTIC OCEAN

GREENLAND

Spitsbergen

ICELAND

ARCTIC CIRCLE

SWEDEN

FINLAND

Lerwick
Shetland Islands

NORWAY

Orkney Islands

Peterhead

THE ARCTIC

Among the Whales and Ice-fields

Conan Doyle's travels started young. When he was only eight he experienced the solitary nature of journeying long distances when he was forced to make the day-long trek by train from his home town of Edinburgh to his boarding school, Stonyhurst, in Lancashire. He described how he 'felt very lonesome and wept bitterly upon the way', and even after he had arrived at Preston, the nearest station to the school, he still had a twelve-mile drive in a trap before he reached his destination. It was such an arduous trip in fact that often he didn't go home for the holidays, even for Christmas.

But, somehow, the experience helped spark a life-long taste for travel and discovery (the other significant factor was the boy's enthusiasm for reading adventure stories and historical novels). In 1875, he decided to take what we would now call a gap year at Stella Matutina, a Jesuit school associated to Stonyhurst, which was situated at Feldkirch in Western Austria. After gaining a taste for long walks in the mountains, he returned on his own via Lake Constance, Basel, Strasbourg and Paris, where he stayed with his Irish godfather and great uncle, Michael Conan.

He recalled how, after a 'rather lively supper at Strasburg' (sic), he reached the French capital with two pence in his pocket, and had to walk all the way from the Gare de l'Est to his uncle's apartment in Avenue de Wagram, off the Champs-Elysées.

Having opted to read medicine at Edinburgh University, Conan Doyle was able to spend leisure hours exploring unknown parts of Scotland, such as the island of Arran. He was still only twenty when, in February 1880, he took six months off from his studies to work as a locum doctor on an Arctic trawler, the 575-ton SS *Hope*, which sailed out of Peterhead in Aberdeenshire. He wrote about this formative experience in a number of places, including letters to his mother, a personal illustrated diary, his own memoirs, several articles, and even a fictional account in one his first published stories, '*The Captain of the Pole-Star*', in January 1883. Here is an extract from his article 'The Glamour of the Arctic', a later reflective piece which conveys his distinctive style, which mixed acute observation, great background knowledge and flashes of humour. It provides an excellent introduction to his travel writing.

It is a strange thing to think that there is a body of men in Great Britain, the majority of whom have never, since their boyhood, seen the corn in the fields. It is the case with the whale-fishers of Peterhead. They began their hard life very early as boys or ordinary seamen, and from that time onward they leave home at the end of February, before the first shoots are above the ground, and return in September, when only the stubble remains to show where the harvest has been.

I have seen and spoken with many an old whaling-
man to whom a bearded ear of corn was a thing to be
wondered over and preserved.

The trade which these men follow is old and
honourable. There was a time when the Greenland
seas were harried by the ships of many nations, when
the Basques and the Biscayens were the great fishers
of whales, and when Dutchmen, men of the Hansa
towns, Spaniards, and Britons, all joined in the great
blubber hunt. Then one by one, as national energy
or industrial capital decreased, the various countries
tailed off, until, in the earlier part of this century, Hull,
Poole, and Liverpool were three leading whaling-ports.
Again the trade shifted its centre. Scoresby was the
last of the great English captains, and from his time
the industry has gone more and more north, until the
whaling of Greenland waters came to be monopolised
by Peterhead, which shares the sealing, however,
with Dundee and with a fleet from Norway. But now,
alas! The whaling appears to be upon its last legs; the
Peterhead ships are seeking new outlets in the Antarctic
seas, and a historical training-school of brave and hardy
seamen will soon be a thing of the past.

It is not that the present generation is less persistent
and skilful than its predecessors, nor is it that the
Greenland whale is in danger of becoming extinct;
but the true reason appears to be, that Nature, while
depriving this unwieldy mass of blubber of any weapons,
has given it in compensation a highly intelligent brain.
That the whale entirely understands the mechanism of
his own capture is beyond dispute. To swim backward

and forward beneath a floe, in the hope of cutting the rope against the sharp edge of the ice, is a common device of the creature after being struck. By degrees, however, it has realised the fact that there are limits to the powers of its adversaries, and that by keeping far in among the icefields it may shake off the most intrepid of pursuers. Gradually the creature has deserted the open sea, and bored deeper and deeper among the ice barriers, until now, at last, it really appears to have reached inaccessible feeding grounds; and it is seldom, indeed, that the watcher in the crow's-nest sees the high plume of spray and the broad black tail in the air which sets his heart a-thumping.

But if a man has the good fortune to be present at a 'fall', and, above all, if he be, as I have been, in the harpooning and in the lancing boat, he has a taste of sport which it would be ill to match. To play a salmon is a royal game, but when your fish weighs more than a suburban villa, and is worth a clear two thousand pounds; when, too, your line is a thumb's thickness of manilla rope with fifty strands, every strand tested for thirty-six pounds, it dwarfs all other experiences. And the lancing, too, when the creature is spent, and your boat pulls in to give it the *coup de grâce* with cold steel, that is also exciting! A hundred tons of despair are churning the waters up into a red foam; two great black fins are rising and falling like the sails of a windmill, casting the boat into a shadow as they droop over it; but still the harpooner clings to the head, where no harm can come, and with the wooden butt of the twelve-foot lance against his stomach, he presses it home until the long struggle is finished, and the black back rolls over to expose the livid, whitish surface beneath. Yet amid all the excitement – and no one who has not held an oar in such a scene can tell how exciting it is – one's sympathies lie with the poor hunted creature. The whale has a small eye, little larger than that of a bullock; but I cannot easily forget the mute expostulation which I read in one, as it dimmed over in death within hand's touch of me. What could it guess, poor creature, of laws of supply and demand; or how could it imagine that when Nature placed an elastic filter inside its mouth, and when man discovered that the plates of which it was composed were the most pliable and yet durable things in creation, its death-warrant was signed?

Of course, it is only the one species, and the very rarest species, of whale which is the object of the fishery. The common rorqual or finner, largest of creatures upon this planet, whisks its eighty feet of worthless tallow round the whaler without fear of any missile more dangerous than a biscuit. This, with its good-for-nothing cousin, the hunchback whale, abounds in the Arctic seas, and I have seen their sprays on a clear day shooting up along the horizon like the smoke from a busy factory. A stranger sight still is, when looking over the bulwarks into the clear water, to see, far down, where the green is turning to black, the huge, flickering figure of a whale gliding under the ship. And then the strange grunting, soughing noise which they make as they come up, with something of the contented pig in it, and something of the wind in the chimney! Contented they well may be, for the firmer has no enemies, save an occasional sword-fish; and Nature, which in a humorous mood has in the case of the right whale affixed the smallest of gullets to the largest of creatures, has dilated the swallow of its less valuable brother, so that it can have a merry time among the herrings.

The gallant seaman, who in all the books stands in the prow of a boat, waving a harpoon over his head, with the line snaking out into the air behind him, is only to be found now in Paternoster Row. The Greenland seas have not known him for more than a hundred years, since first the obvious proposition was advanced that one could shoot both harder and more accurately than one could throw. Yet one clings to the ideals of one's infancy, and I hope that another century may have elapsed before the brave fellow disappears from the frontispieces, in which he still throws his outrageous weapon an impossible distance. The swivel gun, like a huge horse-pistol, with its great oakum wad, and twenty-eight drams of powder, is a more reliable, but a far less picturesque object.

But to aim with such a gun is an art in itself, as will be seen when one considers that the rope is fastened to the neck of the harpoon, and that, as the missile flies, the downward drag of this rope must seriously deflect it. So difficult is it to make sure of one's aim, that it is the etiquette of the trade to pull the boat right on to the creature, the prow shooting up its soft, gently-sloping side, and the harpooner firing straight down into its broad back, into which not only the four-foot harpoon, but ten feet of the rope behind it, will disappear. Then, should the whale cast its tail in the air, after the time-honoured fashion of the pictures, that boat would be in evil case; but, fortunately, when frightened or hurt, it does no such thing, but curls its tail up underneath it, like a cowed dog, and sinks like a stone. Then the bows splash back into the water, the harpooner hugs his own soul, the crew light their pipes and keep their legs apart, while the line runs merrily down the middle of the boat and over the bows. There are two miles of it there, and a second boat will lie alongside to splice on if the first should run short, the end being always kept loose for that purpose. And now occurs the one serious danger of whaling. The line has usually been coiled when it was wet, and as it runs out it is very liable to come in loops which whizz down the boat between the men's legs. A man lassoed in one of these nooses is gone, and fifty fathoms deep, before the harpooner has time to say, 'Where's Jock?' Or if it be the boat itself which is caught, then down it goes like a cork on a trout-line, and the man who can swim with a whaler's high boots on is a swimmer indeed. Many a whale has had a Parthian revenge in this fashion. Some years ago a man was whisked over with a bight of rope round his thigh. 'George, man, Alec's gone!' shrieked the boat-steerer, heaving up his axe to cut the line. But the harpooner caught his wrist. 'Na, na, mun,' he cried, 'the oil money'll be a good thing for the widdie.' And so it was arranged, while Alec shot on upon his terrible journey.

That oil money is the secret of the frantic industry of these seamen, who, when they do find themselves taking grease aboard, will work day and night, though

night is but an expression up there, without a thought
of fatigue. For the secure pay of officers and men is low
indeed, and it is only by their share of the profits that
they can hope to draw a good cheque when they return.
Even the new-joined boy gets his shilling in the ton, and
so draws an extra five pounds when a hundred tons of
oil are brought back. It is practical socialism, and yet a
less democratic community than a whaler's crew could
not be imagined. The captain rules the mates, the mates
the harpooners, the harpooners the boat-steerers, the
boat-steerers the line-coilers, and so on in a graduated
scale which descends to the ordinary seaman, who, in
his turn, bosses it over the boys. Every one of these has
his share of oil money, and it may be imagined what
a chill blast of unpopularity blows around the luckless
harpooner who, by clumsiness or evil chance, has
missed his whale. Public opinion has a terrorising effect
even in those little floating communities of fifty souls. I
have known a grizzled harpooner burst into tears when
he saw by his slack line that he had missed his mark, and
Aberdeenshire seamen are not a very soft race either.

Though twenty or thirty whales have been taken in
a single year in the Greenland seas, it is probable that
the great slaughter of last century has diminished their
number until there are not more than a few hundreds in
existence. I mean, of course, of the right whale; for the
others, as I have said, abound. It is difficult to compute
the numbers of a species which comes and goes over
great tracts of water and among huge icefields; but the
fact that the same whale is often pursued by the same
whaler upon successive trips shows how limited their

number must be. There was one, I remember, which was conspicuous through having a huge wart, the size and shape of a beehive, upon one of the flukes of its tail. 'I've been after that fellow three times,' said the captain, as we dropped our boats. 'He got away in '61. In '67 we had him fast, but the harpoon drew. In '76 a fog saved him. It's odds that we have him now!' I fancied that the betting lay rather the other way myself, and so it proved; for that warty tail is still thrashing the Arctic seas for all that I know to the contrary.

I shall never forget my own first sight of a right whale. It had been seen by the lookout on the other side of a small icefield, but had sunk as we all rushed on deck. For ten minutes we awaited its re-appearance, and I had taken my eyes from the place, when a general gasp of astonishment made me glance up, and there was the whale in the air. Its tail was curved just as a trout's is in jumping, and every bit of its glistening lead-coloured body was clear of the water. It was little wonder that I should be astonished, for the captain, after thirty voyages, had never seen such a sight. On catching it, we discovered that it was very thickly covered with a red, crab-Like parasite, about the size of a shilling, and we conjectured that it was the irritation of these creatures which had driven it wild. If a man had short, nailless flippers, and a prosperous family of fleas upon his back, he would appreciate the situation.

When a fish, as the whalers will forever call it, is taken, the ship gets alongside, and the creature is fixed head and tail in a curious and ancient fashion, so that by slacking or tightening the ropes, each part of the

vast body can be brought uppermost. A whole boat may
be seen inside the giant mouth, the men hacking with
axes, to slice away the ten-foot screens of bone, while
others with sharp spades upon the back are cutting off
the deep great-coat of fat in which kindly Nature has
wrapped up this most over-grown of her children. In a
few hours all is stowed away in the tanks, and a red islet,
with white projecting bones, lies alongside, and sinks
like a stone when the ropes are loosed. Some years ago,
a man, still lingering upon the back, had the misfortune
to have his foot caught between the creature's ribs, at
the instant when the tackles were undone. Some aeons
hence those two skeletons, the one hanging by the foot
from the other, may grace the museum of a subtropical
Greenland, or astonish the students of the Spitzbergen
Institute of Anatomy.

Apart from sport, there is a glamour about those
circumpolar regions which must affect everyone who
has penetrated to them. My heart goes out to that old,
gray-headed whaling-captain who, having been left for
an instant when at death's door, staggered off in his night
gear, and was found by his nurses far from his house,
and still, as he mumbled, 'pushing to the norrard'. So
an Arctic fox, which a friend of mine endeavoured to
tame, escaped, and was caught many months afterwards
in a gamekeeper's trap in Caithness. It also was pushing
'norrard', though who can say by what strange compass
it took its bearings? It is a region of purity, of white
ice, and of blue water, with no human dwelling within
a thousand miles to sully the freshness of the breeze
which blows across the icefields. And then it is a region

of romance also. You stand on the very brink of the unknown, and every duck that you shoot bears pebbles in its gizzard which come from a land which the maps know not.

These whaling-captains profess to see no great difficulty in reaching the Pole. Some little margin must be allowed, no doubt, for expansive talk over a pipe and a glass, but still there is a striking unanimity in their ideas. Briefly they are these:

What bars the passage of the explorer as he ascends between Greenland and Spitzbergen is that huge floating ice-reef which scientific explorers have called 'the palmocrystic sea', and the whalers, with more expressive Anglo-Saxon, 'the barrier'. The ship which has picked its way among the great ice-floes finds itself, somewhere about the eighty-first degree, confronted by a single mighty wall, extending right across from side to side, with no chink or creek up which she can push her bows. It is old ice, gnarled and rugged, and of an exceeding thickness, impossible to pass, and nearly impossible to travel over, so cut and jagged is its surface. Over this it was that the gallant Parry struggled with his sledges in 1827, reaching a latitude (about 82° 30°, if my remembrance is correct) which for a long time was the record. As far as he could see, this old ice extended right away to the Pole.

Such is the obstacle. Now for the whaler's view of how it may be surmounted.

This ice, they say, solid as it looks, is really a floating body, and at the mercy of the water upon which it rests. There is in those seas a perpetual southerly drift, which weakens the cohesion of the huge mass; and when, in addition to this, the prevailing winds happen to be from the north, the barrier is all shredded out, and great bays and gulfs appear in its surface. A brisk northerly wind, long continued, might at any time clear a road, and has, according to their testimony, frequently cleared a road, by which a ship might slip through to the Pole. Whalers fishing as far north as the eighty-second degree have in an open season seen no ice, and, more important still, no reflection of ice in the sky to the north of them. But they are in the service of a company; they are there to catch whales, and there is no adequate inducement to make them risk themselves, their vessels, and their cargoes, in a dash for the north.

The matter might be put to the test without trouble or expense. Take a stout wooden gunboat, short and strong, with engines as antiquated as you like, if they be but a hundred horse-power. Man her with a sprinkling of Scotch and Shetland seamen from the Royal Navy, and let the rest of the crew be lads who must have a training-cruise in any case. For the first few voyages carry a couple of experienced ice-masters, in addition to the usual naval officers. Put a man like Markham in command. Then send this ship every June or July to inspect the barrier, with strict orders to keep out of the heavy ice unless there were a very clear water-way. For six years she might go in vain. On the seventh you might have an open season, hard, northerly winds, and a clear sea. In any case no expense or danger is incurred, and there could be no better training for young seamen. They will find the Greenland seas in summer much more healthy and pleasant than the Azores or Madeira, to which they are usually despatched. The whole expedition should be done in less than a month.

Singular incidents occur in those northern waters, and there are few old whalers who have not their queer yarn, which is sometimes of personal and sometimes of general interest. There is one which always appeared to me to deserve more attention than has ever been given to it. Some years ago, Captain David Gray of the *Eclipse*, the doyen of the trade, and the representative, with his brothers John and Alec, of a famous family of whalers, was cruising far to the north, when he saw a large bird flapping over the ice. A boat was dropped, the bird shot, and brought aboard, but no man there could say what manner of fowl it was. Brought home, it was at once identified as being a half-grown albatross, and now stands in the Peterhead Museum, with a neat little label to that effect between its webbed feet.

Now the albatross is an Antarctic bird, and it is quite unthinkable that this solitary specimen flapped its way from the other end of the earth. It was young, and possibly giddy, but quite incapable of a wild outburst of that sort. What is the alternative? It must have been a southern straggler from some breed of albatrosses farther north. But if there is a different fauna farther north, then there must be a climatic change there. Perhaps Kane was not so far wrong after all in his surmise of an open Polar sea. It may be that that flattening at the poles of the earth, which always seemed to my childhood's imagination to have been caused by the finger and thumb of the Creator, when he held up this little planet before he set it spinning, has a greater influence on climate than we have yet ascribed to it. But if so, how simple would the task of our exploring ship become when a wind from the north had made a rift in the barrier!

There is little land to be seen during the seven months of a whaling-cruise. The strange solitary island of Jan Meyen may possibly be sighted, with its great snow-capped ex-volcano jutting up among the clouds. In the palmy days of the whale-fishing the Dutch had a boiling-station there, and now great stones with iron rings let into them and rusted anchors lie littered about in this absolute wilderness as a token of their former presence. Spitzbergen, too, with its black crags and its white glaciers, a dreadful looking place, may possibly be seen. I saw it myself, for the first and last time, in a sudden rift in the drifting wrack of a furious gale, and for me it stands as the very emblem of stern grandeur. And then towards the end of the season the whalers come south to the seventy-second degree, and try to bore in towards the coast of Greenland, in the south-eastern corner; and if you then, at the distance of eighty miles, catch the least glimpse of the loom of the cliffs, then, if you are anything of a dreamer, you will have plenty of food for dreams, for this is the very spot where one of the most interesting questions in the world is awaiting a solution.

Of course, it is a commonplace that when Iceland was one of the centres of civilisation in Europe, the Icelanders budded off a colony upon Greenland, which throve and flourished, and produced sagas of its own, and waged war upon the Skraelings or Esquimaux, and generally sang and fought and drank in the bad old, full-blooded fashion. So prosperous did they become, that they built them a cathedral, and sent to Denmark for a bishop, there being no protection for local industries at that time. The bishop, however, was prevented from reaching his see by some sudden climatic change which brought the ice down between Iceland and Greenland, and from that day (it was in the fourteenth century) to this no one has penetrated that ice, nor has it ever been ascertained what became of that ancient city, or of its inhabitants. Have they preserved some singular civilisation of their own, and are they still singing and drinking and fighting, and waiting for the bishop from over the seas? Or have they been destroyed by the hated Skraelings? Or have they, as is more likely, amalgamated with them, and produced a race of tow-headed, large-limbed Esquimaux? We must wait until some Nansen turns his steps in that direction before we can tell. At present it is one of those interesting historical questions, like the fate of those Vandals who were driven by Belisarius into the interior of Africa, which are better unsolved. When we know everything about this earth, the romance and the poetry will all have been wiped away from it. There is nothing so artistic as a haze.

There is a good deal which I had meant to say about bears, and about seals, and about sea-unicorns, and sword-fish, and all the interesting things which combine to throw that glamour over the Arctic; but, as the genial critic is fond of remarking, it has all been said very much better already. There is one side of the Arctic regions, however, which has never had due attention paid to it, and that is the medical and curative side. Davos Platz has shown what cold can do in consumption, but in the life-giving air of the Arctic Circle no noxious germ can live. The only illness of any consequence which ever attacks a whaler is an explosive bullet. It is a safe prophecy, that before many years are past, steam yachts will turn to the north every summer, with a cargo of the weak-chested, and people will understand that Nature's ice-house is a more healthy place than her vapour-bath.

'The Glamour of the Arctic', *The Idler* (July 1892),
McClure's Magazine (March 1894)

He recalled this formative time in the Arctic in another piece for *The Strand Magazine* a few years later.

What surprised me most in the Arctic regions was the rapidity with which you reach them. I had never realised that they lie at our very doors. I think that we were only four days out from Shetland when we were among the drift ice. I awoke of a morning to hear the bump, bump of the floating pieces against the side of the ship, and I went on deck to see the whole sea covered with them to the horizon. They were none of them large, but they lay so thick that a man might travel far by springing from one to the other. Their dazzling whiteness made the sea seem bluer by contrast, and with a blue sky above, and that glorious Arctic air in one's nostrils, it was a morning to remember. Once, on one of the swaying, rocking pieces we saw a huge seal, sleek, sleepy, and imperturbable, looking up with the utmost assurance at the ship, as if it knew that the close time had still three weeks to run. Further on we saw on the ice the long, human-like prints of a bear. All this with the snowdrops of Scotland still fresh in our glasses in the cabin.

I have spoken about the close time, and I may explain that, by an agreement between the Norwegian and the British Governments, the subjects of both nations are forbidden to kill a seal before the 3rd of April. The reason for this is that the breeding season is in March, and if the mothers should be killed before the young are able to take care of themselves, the race would soon become extinct. For breeding purposes, the seals all come together at a variable spot, which is evidently pre-arranged among them, and as this place may be anywhere within many hundreds of square miles of floating ice, it is no easy matter for the fisher to find it. The means by which he sets about it are simple but ingenious. As the ship makes its way through the loose ice-streams, a school of seals is observed travelling through the water. Their direction is carefully taken by compass and marked upon the chart. An hour afterwards perhaps another school is seen. This is also marked. When these bearings have been taken several times, the various lines upon the chart are prolonged until they intersect. At this point, or near it, it is likely that the main pack of the seals will be found.

When you do come upon it, it is a wonderful sight. I suppose it is the largest assembly of creatures upon the face of the world – and this upon the open ice-fields hundreds of miles from the Greenland coast. Somewhere between 71 deg. and 75 deg. is the rendezvous, and the longitude is even vaguer; but the seals have no difficulty in finding the address. From the crow's-nest at the top of the main-mast, one can see no end of them. On the furthest visible ice one can still see that sprinkling of pepper grains. And the young lie everywhere also, snow-white slugs, with a little black nose and large, dark eyes. Their half-human cries fill the air; and when you are sitting in the cabin of a ship which is in the heart of the seal-pack, you would think you were next door to a monstrous nursery.

The *Hope* was one of the first to find the seal-pack that year, but before the day came when hunting was allowed, we had a succession of strong gales, followed by a severe roll, which tilted the floating ice and launched the young seals prematurely into the water. And so, when the law at last allowed us to begin work, Nature had left us with very little work to do. However, at dawn upon the third, the ship's company took to the ice, and began to gather in its murderous harvest. It is brutal work, though not more brutal than that which goes on to supply every dinner-table in the country. And yet those glaring crimson pools upon the dazzling white of the ice-fields, under the peaceful silence of a blue Arctic sky, did seem a horrible intrusion. But an inexorable demand creates an inexorable supply, and the seals, by their death, help to give a living to the long line of seamen, dockers, tanners, curers, triers, chandlers, leather merchants, and oil-sellers, who stand between this annual butchery on the one hand, and the exquisite, with his soft leather boots, or the savant using a delicate oil for his philosophical instruments, upon the other ...

This April sealing is directed against the mothers and young. Then, in May, the sealer goes further north; and about latitude 77 deg. or 78 deg. he comes upon the old male seals, who are by no means such easy victims. They are wary creatures, and it takes good long-range shooting to bag them. Then, in June, the sealing is over, and the ship bears away further north still until in the 79th or 80th degree she is in the best Greenland whaling latitudes. There she remains for three months or so, and if she is fortunate she may bring back 300 or 400 per cent to her owners, and a nice little purse full for every man of her ship's company. Or if her profits be more modest, she has at least afforded such sport that every other sport is dwarfed by the comparison.

It is seldom that one meets anyone who understands the value of a Greenland whale. A well-boned and large one as she floats is worth to-day something between two and three thousand pounds. This huge price is due to the value of whalebone, which is a very rare commodity, and yet is absolutely essential for some trade purposes. The price tends to rise steadily, for the number of the creatures is diminishing. In 1880, Captain Gray calculated that there were probably not more than 300 of them left alive in the whole expanse of the Greenland seas, an area of thousands of square miles. How few there are is shown by the fact that he recognised individuals amongst those which we chased. There was one with a curious wart about the size of a beehive upon his tail which he had remembered chasing when he was a lad on his father's ship. Perhaps other generations of whalers may follow that warty tail, for the whale is a very long-lived creature. How long they live has never been ascertained; but in the days when it was customary to stamp harpoons with the names of vessels, old harpoons have been cut out of whales bearing names long forgotten in the trade, and all the evidence goes to prove that a century is well within their powers.

It is exciting work pulling on to a whale. Your own back is turned to him, and all you know about him is what you read upon the face of the boat-steerer. He is staring out over your head, watching the creature as it swims slowly through the water, raising his hand now and again as a signal to stop rowing when he sees that the eye is coming round, and then resuming the stealthy approach when the whale is end on. There are so many floating pieces of ice, that as long as the oars are quiet the boat alone will not cause the creature to dive. So you creep slowly up, and at last you are near that the boat-steerer knows that you can get there before the creature has time to dive – for it takes some little time to get that huge body into motion. You see a sudden gleam in his eyes, and a flush in his cheeks, and it's 'Give way, boys! Give way, all! Hard!'

Click goes the trigger of the big harpoon gun, and the foam flies from your oars. Six strokes, perhaps, and then with a dull, greasy squelch the bows run upon something soft, and you and your oars are sent flying in every direction. But little you care for that, for as you touched the whale you have heard the crash of the gun, and know that the harpoon has been fired point-blank into the huge, lead-coloured curve of its side. The creature sinks like a stone, the bows of the boat splash down into the water again, but there is the little red Jack flying from the centre thwart to show that you are fast, and there is the line whizzing swiftly under the seats and over the bows between your outstretched feet.

And there is the one element of danger — for it is rarely indeed that the whale has spirit enough to turn upon its enemies. The line is very carefully coiled by a special man named the line-coiler, and it is warranted not to kink. If it should happen to do so, however, and if the loop catches the limbs of any one of the boat's crew, that man goes to his death so rapidly that his comrades hardly know that he has gone. It is a waste of fish to cut the line, for thy victim is already hundreds of fathoms deep.

'Life on a Greenland Whaler',
The Strand Magazine, January 1897

As was often the case, Conan Doyle recycled such material in his fiction — in this instance, his Artic experiences were evident in one of his early fictional stories, 'The Captain of the Pole-Star', which appeared in *Temple Bar* magazine in January 1883.

September 11th — Lat. 81° 40° N.; long. 2° E. Still lying-to amid enormous ice fields. The one which stretches away to the north of us, and to which our ice-anchor is attached, cannot be smaller than an English county.

To the right and left unbroken sheets extend to the horizon. This morning the mate reported that there were signs of pack ice to the southward. Should this form of sufficient thickness to bar our return, we shall be in a position of danger, as the food, I hear, is already running somewhat short. It is late in the season, and the nights are beginning to reappear. This morning I saw a star twinkling just over the fore-yard, the first since the beginning of May. There is considerable discontent among the crew, many of whom are anxious to get back home to be in time for the herring season, when labour always commands a high price upon the Scotch coast. As yet their displeasure is only signified by sullen countenances and black looks, but I heard from the second mate this afternoon that they contemplated sending a deputation to the Captain to explain their grievance. I much doubt how he will receive it, as he is a man of fierce temper, and very sensitive about anything approaching to an infringement of his rights. I shall venture after dinner to say a few words to him upon the subject. I have always found that he will tolerate from me what he would resent from any other member of the crew. Amsterdam Island, at the north-west corner of Spitzbergen, is visible upon our starboard quarter – a rugged line of volcanic rocks, intersected by white seams, which represent glaciers. It is curious to think that at the present moment there is probably no human being nearer to us than the Danish settlements in the south of Greenland – a good nine hundred miles as the crow flies. A captain takes a great responsibility upon himself when he risks his vessel under such circumstances. No whaler has ever remained in these latitudes till so advanced a period of the year.

...

September 14th – Sunday, and a day of rest. My fears have been confirmed, and the thin strip of blue water has disappeared from the southward. Nothing but the great motionless ice fields around us, with their weird hummocks and fantastic pinnacles. There is a deathly silence over their wide expanse which is horrible. No lapping of the waves now, no cries of seagulls or straining of sails, but one deep universal silence in which the murmurs of the seamen, and the creak of their boots upon the white shining deck, seem discordant and out of place. Our only visitor was an Arctic fox, a rare animal upon the pack, though common enough upon the land. He did not come near the ship, however, but after surveying us from a distance fled rapidly across the ice. This was curious conduct, as they generally know nothing of man, and being of an inquisitive nature, become so familiar that they are easily captured. Incredible as it may seem, even this little incident produced a bad effect upon the crew. 'Yon puir beastie kens mair, ay, an' sees mair nor you nor me!' was the comment of one of the leading harpooners, and the others nodded their acquiescence. It is vain to attempt to argue against such puerile superstition.

'The Captain of the Pole-Star',
Temple Bar, January 1883

Great Britain & Ireland

Isle of May

Edinburgh

Arran

Wigtownshire

Stonyhurst

Waterford

Cambridge

Youghal

LONDON

Hankley Down
Winchester
Lyndhurst

Crowborough

Southsea

CELTIC SEA

DARTMOOR

ISLE OF WIGHT

Poldhu Bay

Proposed Channel Tunnel

FRANCE

GREAT BRITAIN AND IRELAND

From Youthful Forays to Sherlock Holmes

Edinburgh – Isle of May – Arran – Wigtownshire – Youghal – Southsea – Isle of Wight – London – Railways – Dartmoor – Cornwall – Sussex – Hampshire – Surrey

Conan Doyle wrote little about his native city of Edinburgh. It is only mentioned once in his Sherlock Holmes stories, and then only in passing. Scotland fares little better, making its only regular appearance in front of the word 'Yard'. His main published reference to Edinburgh is in his non-Sherlockian novel *The Firm of Girdlestone*.

Edinburgh

Better weather could not have been desired. The morning had been hazy, but as the sun shone out the fog had gradually risen, until now there remained but a suspicion of it, floating like a plume, above the frowning walls of Edinburgh Castle, and twining a fairy wreath round the unfinished columns of the national monument upon the Calton Hill. The broad stretch of the Prince's Street Gardens, which occupy the valley between the old town and the new, looked green and spring-like, and their fountains sparkled merrily in the sunshine. Their wide expanse, well-trimmed and bepathed, formed a strange contrast to the rugged piles of grim old houses which bounded them upon the other side and the massive grandeur of the great hill beyond, which lies like a crouching lion keeping watch and ward, day and night, over the ancient capital of the Scottish kings. Travellers who have searched the whole world round have found no fairer view.

The Firm of Girdlestone, London and New York, 1890

While an undergraduate, he became an enthusiastic amateur photographer – a hobby which called for elaborate safaris to remote parts of Scotland and further afield. He often wrote about these trips in enthusiastic essays which, while full of detail for camera lovers, also provide excellent introductions to several places. The Scottish countryside is eagerly evoked here in two of his youthful pieces for the *British Journal of Photography* which refer to journeys to the Isles of May and Arran. The former, now a National Nature Reserve, stands off Anstruther in the county of Fife at the eastern end of the Firth of Forth; the latter, much larger and inhabited, is technically in the Firth of Clyde in North Ayrshire.

Isle of May

Before us stretched the long line of the Fifeshire coast, while behind, wreathed in the morning mist, lay the modern Athens – Arthur's Seat, like a crouching lion, looming above the great sea of vapour. As the sun rose in the heavens, spire after spire and tier upon tier of houses pierced the pall that hid them from our view, and ere we had reached mid channel we could see the grim old city standing out sharp and clear against the morning sky ...

Midday and a flowing tide took us into the little harbour of Anstruther ...

A smart four-mile drive, varied by occasional glimpses of the German Ocean, brought us to the ancient and honourable Burgh of Crail. The coachman drew up his smoking steed in front of the Golf Inn, and one by one we alighted from our perches. The quaint little hostelry looked pre-eminently homely and comfortable, while a savoury smell of beefsteaks and onions from a kitchen door left artfully ajar whetted an appetite already painfully keen. Dinner was speedily ordered, and in the interval of its preparation 'Chawles' and I decided upon having 'a dip', leaving the Doctor extended upon the solitary sofa. Passing down the main street, which, to quote Mark Twain, is 'not quite as straight as a rainbow nor as crooked as a corkscrew' (a merciful dispensation of Providence to a not too sober population), we headed for the beach. There, apparently less than half its real distance from the land, lay the island which was the goal of our expedition. We both gazed at its basalt cliffs, flecked with white, but with very different sentiments ...

We retired early to 'roost' as it had been settled that we were to sail for the May early the following morning ...

It had been arranged that we were to commence operations upon the cliffs. As there are no inhabitants upon the island, except the keepers of the lighthouse, we had only our own convenience to consult. Springing ashore we made our way up the rough pathway which leads past the lighthouse.

On coming down to the beach on the southern side of the island a beautiful spectacle met my eyes. Nine fine yachts of the Forth Club were rounding the point of the island, each under a cloud of canvas and lying well over, for the breeze was beginning to freshen. They looked like some great flock of sea birds as they rose and fell on the crests of the waves ...

The weather next morning was certainly not calculated to make us prolong our stay. There was a heavy Scotch mist, and a thin drizzle of rain which soaked through an Ulster far more rapidly than an ostentatious downpour. Sport and photography were alike out of the question. It was then that the Doctor showed the stuff that was in him. He cheered us with song after song and depressed us with riddle after riddle, so that the time passed wonderfully until Sinbad looked in and announced that the tide was right for sailing. We bade adieu to our worthy friends in the lighthouse; and, having got my implements and specimens from the game bag aboard, we shoved our little craft off, and another hour saw us once more in the dissipated town of Crail. We made for our former quarters at the Golf Inn, and after drying ourselves and having some refreshments proceeded to take our places in the Anstruther coach ...

British Journal of Photography, 17 July 1885

Arran

The island of Arran may be said to be the epitome of
the whole of Scotland, just as the Isle of Wight is an
England in miniature. Within the narrow bounds of
Arran – it is some ten miles across and from fifteen
to twenty in length – there is every variety of scenery.
There are smiling lowlands and rugged highlands, wild
woods, and barren heaths. Nowhere can the wandering
photographer find in such a small compass so many
varying beauties upon which to exercise his skill, and it
is an important matter that members of the fraternity
should know of such places ...

Having made up our mind for a holiday, and chosen
Arran as the scene of our labour, my friend and I
consumed the 'midnight oil' in poring over guide-books
and *Bradshaws* in order to get some information as to
how we were to reach our destination. Let me publish
the result of our researches, in case anyone should
follow in our footsteps. The first stage, then, is to get
to Glasgow. From Glasgow one must travel by train to
a small port named Ardrossan, the distance being about
twenty miles. Ardrossan is situated exactly opposite the
island, and steamers ply between two or three times
a day to the two chief centres of Arran – Brodick and
Lamlash.

My friend was of a statistical and economical turn
of mind. 'We ought to do it on three pound ten each,'
he remarked. 'Put it down at a "fiver",' I suggested.
'Fiver be hanged!' he roared, with the indignation of an
outraged financier. 'How can you spend five pounds if

you are moderately careful? A return ticket to Glasgow won't cost more than thirty shillings, if you choose your time. Trains to Ardrossan (say) four shillings the return, and the boat to Arran you may put at another four shillings. Thirty-eight shillings for travelling.' 'Cabs,' I suggested, in a still, small voice. 'Well; say two pounds five all included,' continued the Chancellor of the Exchequer. 'Then there is our board and lodging in a cottage for three days. What else is there?' 'Casual drinks,' I replied. 'Let us have one,' said the wearied economist, and we relapsed.

With our hands full of gear then, and our heads full of figures, we found our way to Glasgow, travelling during the night so as to catch the early train for Ardrossan. There is a boat which waits for this train, so that we had no time to wait in the quaint little Scottish port, but found ourselves and belongings within five minutes upon the deck of a smart little steamer, and in another five minutes were steaming out of the harbour in company with forty or fifty fellow passengers.

The view of Arran as one approaches it is magnificent. A ring of yellow sand runs round the greater portion of the island, behind which rise up sloping green braes and dark fir forests. Behind these again are the rugged group of mountains, which form the north and centre of the island, the whole culminating in the majestic Goatfell, which towers up to nearly three thousand feet. The mist of morning was still rising, and the sunlight upon it gave the mountains that peculiar purple tinge which is characteristic of highland scenery, and which Horatio McCulloch and Waller Paton knew so well how to imitate. It might have been some enchanted island which floated upon the calm azure sea. Behind us was the long line of the Scottish coast, with the one great gap which indicated the mouth of the Clyde, and away to the north the long, jagged ridge of the Argyleshire hills. To the south stretched the Irish sea, broken only by the tall, white dome-like summit of Ailsa Craig, the strange solitary rock which stands out like a gigantic Druidical monolith amid the waste of waters.

Any romantic feelings which may have been aroused by the appearance of Arran were rudely dispelled by the demand for twopence each from the official who guards the pier at Brodick, and levies a tax upon all invaders. 'Every prospect pleases and only man is vile,' my friend quoted, as we trudged along the road which leads from the pier to the little township. There is a very fair hotel there, but we had determined to put up at a cottage kept by Mrs. Fullarton, with whom some friends of ours had boarded upon a previous occasion. We were aware that this good woman lived somewhere in the vicinity of Brodick, but we had lost her exact address. 'Can you tell me where any one of the name of Fullarton lives?' we asked an aged islander. The veteran smiled pensively. It appears from his statement that the whole population of the island are, with some few exceptions, all called 'Fullarton'. Eventually, however, by an ingenious cross-examination, and a happy recollection on the part of my friend that the woman in question had a lame leg, we succeeded in obtaining directions which led us to a little farmhouse, which proved to be the abode of the individual whom we were in search of.

Anyone who ventures into Arran must be prepared to rough it in the matter of edibles. Meat is a rare and scarce commodity. Bacon and eggs can generally be relied on, and fish are usually to be had. There are plenty of potatoes, and with a little butter the traveller can generally manage to arrange a succulent and nutritious meal without the aid of a butcher. Prices are extremely reasonable, and our board and lodging – we had a large room, which combined sitting-room and bedroom – only cost us a few shillings a day.

We had arranged to make no very long excursions upon the next day, but contented ourselves with wandering down to the village with our cameras, and as it was a beautifully bright morning we were rewarded by several excellent places. The broad stretch of Brodick Bay, with the Scotch coast in the background, formed a beautiful seascape, and the inland view, including the magnificent castle of the Duke of Hamilton, which peeps from among the trees at the base of the hills, was equally effective.

In the afternoon we wandered along the seashore as far as the little fishing hamlet of Corrie, some five miles from Brodick. The whole distance was one suggestion of magnificent 'bits', had we only had plates enough to do them justice. As it was, our carriers were soon filled, and we abandoned our gear at a fisherman's cottage, and picked it up again on our return. From Corrie a grand view is to be seen of the mountains and beautiful glens of Glen Sannox and Glen Ross, which intervene between them.

A local curiosity was pointed out to us in the shape of a rock called the 'Giant's Harp', on account of some resemblance which it was supposed to bear to the instrument. As a matter of fact, anything more elaborately unlike a harp it would be impossible to conceive. There used to be a rocking boulder in this neighbourhood, which, although it weighed several tons, was so delicately balanced that the slightest pressure would cause it to rock backwards and forwards. An officer and some seamen from a man-of-war, however, levered it over into the sea one day, for which piece of senseless Vandalism they were, I am glad to say, heavily mulct in a lawsuit taken against them by the islanders, on the ground that they had deprived them of one of the attractions which used to draw tourists to the place. After a most pleasant and profitable day we returned to our farm, and agreed over our evening pipe that it was a pity that we had not three weeks instead of three days to devote to the island and its beauties.

Next day we were up betimes, and made the pleasing discovery that there were two stout hobbledehoys attached to the establishment, who were ready for a small consideration to carry our impedimenta in any given direction for any given time. With these retainers in our rear we set off for a walk across the island. The path was desolate enough, running over a barren heather-covered heath, with an occasional gaunt telegraph post to break the monotony. We were rewarded, however, when we reached the other side by some beautiful scenery. It was an exceptionally clear day, and we could distinctly see the north end of Ireland, lying like a dark line upon the water. The chief object of curiosity was a cave, which is pointed out as being the one in which King Robert the Bruce observed the manoeuvres of the persevering but weak-minded spider, which endeavoured to swarm up a thread when it ought to have crawled up the wall ...

The next day was the last and the most important of our little holiday. We had determined to ascend Goatfell — a feat which seemed a great thing to my companion, who had done little mountaineering in the course of his life. We started at about seven in the morning, after a substantial porridge breakfast, with our two faithful followers bearing our camera-cases and plate-carriers. We ourselves were burdened with knapsacks containing provisions for the day. The morning was bright, but a chilliness in the air warned us that summer had fled. As we emerged from the forests of the Duke of Hamilton (in which the red deer swarmed upon every side, and climbed the sloping uplands beyond) the view was a marvellous one. From Bute and the Mull of Cantire, in the north almost as far as Wigtownshire, in the south the whole coast line of Scotland lay revealed. Down beneath us the blue ocean was flecked with the white sails of yachts and fishing boats, while here and there a dark cloud showed where some great steamer was ploughing its way to the great Scotch seaport.

The declivity is not very steep until the last few hundred yards when it becomes almost precipitous, but we managed, thanks to our young islanders, to convey

not only ourselves but our instruments also in safety
to the summit. To the north the country seemed a very
abomination of desolation — a world of wild peaks, of
rugged chasms, and brown gnarled rocks, all inextricably
jumbled together. I have been up several of the Alps,
but have never seen a grander mountain view than is
to be seen from the summit of Goatfell. The Carline's
Leap, a great double-peaked mountain, within a few
hundred feet of the same height as the one on which we
stood was the nearest of the rocky family. It derives its
name, as one of our youths informed us, from the fact
that there is a legend in the island which sets it down
as the site of a witch's revel or Walpurgis' Nacht, and it
is said that on certain nights the old sinners are still to
be seen mounted upon the conventional broomstick and
skimming across from one peak to the other ...

'Arran in Autumn',
British Journal of Photography, 17 July 1885

He also incorporated some other parts of Scotland (but
not the Highlands) in his early fiction. Wigtownshire
in the south west, bordering the Irish Sea, provided the
backdrop for his melodramatic novel about reincarnation,
The Mystery of Cloomber, for example.

Wigtownshire

Branksome might have appeared a poor dwelling-place
when compared with the house of an English squire,
but to us, after our long residence in stuffy apartments,
it was of regal magnificence.

The building was broad-spread and low, with red-tiled roof, diamond-paned windows, and a profusion of dwelling rooms with smoke-blackened ceilings and oaken wainscots. In front was a small lawn, girt round with a thin fringe of haggard and ill grown beeches, all gnarled and withered from the effects of the sea-spray. Behind lay the scattered hamlet of Branksome-Bere — a dozen cottages at most — inhabited by rude fisher-folk who looked upon the laird as their natural protector.

To the west was the broad, yellow beach and the Irish Sea, while in all other directions the desolate moors, greyish-green in the foreground and purple in the distance, stretched away in long, low curves to the horizon.

Very bleak and lonely it was upon this Wigtown coast. A man might walk many a weary mile and never see a living thing except the white, heavy-flapping kittiwakes, which screamed and cried to each other with their shrill, sad voices.

Very lonely and very bleak! Once out of sight of Branksome and there was no sign of the works of man save only where the high, white tower of Cloomber Hall shot up, like a headstone of some giant grave, from amid the firs and larches which girt it round.

This great house, a mile or more from our dwelling, had been built by a wealthy Glasgow merchant of strange tastes and lonely habits, but at the time of our arrival it had been untenanted for many years, and stood with weather-blotched walls and vacant, staring windows looking blankly out over the hill side.

Empty and mildewed, it served only as a landmark to the fishermen, for they had found by experience that by keeping the laird's chimney and the white tower of Cloomber in a line they could steer their way through the ugly reef which raises its jagged back, like that of some sleeping monster, above the troubled waters of the wind-swept bay.

The Mystery of Cloomber, *Pall Mall Gazette*,
10–28 September 1888

Conan Doyle first visited Ireland with his mother when he was seven. They were visiting relations in King's County, now County Offaly, where the young boy was discomfited by his sight of a band of Fenians. He returned soon after university in 1881, visiting additional family members in Waterford and Cork.

Youghal

A single ticket from Edinburgh right through to Glasgow, and thence by boat to Waterford, touching at Dublin, came to something well under a pound. I may add that starting from the other end of the chain the boats run from London, via Portsmouth, Southampton, and Plymouth, to Waterford, and so on to Glasgow, and I have no doubt that the fare from London to Waterford would be even less than that quoted. For some time I had been intending to give myself a holiday, and when would I get better opportunity? ...

We took our through tickets at Cook's tourist office, by which a further saving was effected. The mild-eyed clerk who dispenses them looked at us curiously and remarked that he had not sold many that year, for they were dangerous times in Ireland, and there was little inducement for the Saxon tourist unless he hankered for the absorbing but brief excitement of having his head battered in or otherwise tampered with by the 'down-trodden Clan-na-Gael'. Every day brought a grim list across the sea of midnight visits, maimed cattle, half-murdered bailiffs, and ruined landlords. These things, however, rather served to inflame our

fanatical photographic propensities than to allay them.
We saw a glorious vista of character portraits and
other novelties stretching out before us. The 'foinest
pisant in the world', or rather an assorted set of
samples of that individual – a rack-rent landlord in a
state of bloated impecuniosity ('lack-rent' would be
a better name for the class) – an agent, or as much
of one as the aborigines had left together by the time
of our arrival – these and all the other curiosities of
Irish life should adorn our collections. Then in still life
there would be the ruined homestead, the caretaker's
hut, and other signs of the times. It seemed to us,
as we stepped gaily into the train at the Caledonian
Station and deposited our traps under the seats, that
apart from the scenery our trip could hardly fail to
have interesting results ...

As the sun sank down towards the horizon we had got
well out to the mouth of the Clyde. The water was as
calm as a mill pond and reflected the scarlet tinge of the
clouds. Away to the north were the rugged mountains
of Argyleshire and of the great islands, wrapped in that
purple evening mist which Waller Paton loves. Ahead of
us was Arran, whose beauties my friend Dr. Thompson
has already recounted in this Journal, with its great
peak of Goat Fell enveloped in fleecy clouds. To the
south the strange precipitous upheaval called Ailsa
Crag reared itself out of the ocean – a grim looking
place, which has been the last spot upon earth that
the eyes of many a drowning man have rested on. The
whole scene was as beautiful a one as an artist could
love to dwell upon. Ramsay produced his paint-box,

and certainly put our whites and greys to shame for the nonce with his purples and vermillions. We passed Ailsa Crag before it was quite dark, but it was too late by that time for us to do it justice in a plate. However, we had succeeded in several distant views, so we had no cause to be discontented. As we passed the captain ordered the steam-whistle to be blown, which had the effect of sending up an innumerable cloud of sea-birds from their nests on the rock. For some minutes the air was simply alive with kittiwakes, gulls, solan geese, gannets, blackbacks, and other birds, whose screams and cries drowned every other sound. Then we steamed on, and the great Crag was left far astern until it was simply a dark loom in the darkness ...

Next morning – a Tuesday, if I remember right – found us steaming into the Bay of Dublin with the long line of the Irish coast on each side of us, and a single hill in front which marked the position of the city. As we approached it we expended a couple of plates upon the scene; but Dublin from the seaside is neither picturesque nor impressive. Steaming up the Liffey we threw out our warps at the North Wall, and found that six hours would elapse before the unloading of the cargo and the state of the tide would allow us to pursue our journey. We spent this time in rambling over the Irish metropolis, and were surprised at the civility we met with and at the order of the streets. The newspapers had prepared us to find it in a state of semi-rebellion; but, as a matter of fact, everything was quiet enough. The only bad symptom we could see was the great number of big, hulking fellows lounging about without employment – 'corner boys' they are named there – apparently ripe for any mischief …

We slept that night at Waterford, and set off the next day for the above mentioned port. By the way, it was at Waterford that we first began to see those seditious notices of which we had so often read. Just opposite our steamer, I remember, as we came off there was a tremendous placard imploring the citizens of the county to assemble in their millions (the census returns only account for about a hundred and fifty thousand), and to hold their crops, whatever that might mean. We also saw the traditional Irish peasant, whom I had always imagined to be a myth invented for music-hall purposes. There he was, however, as large as life, with corduroy knee-breeches, blue stockings, and a high, soft hat with a pipe stuck in the side of it. The delusion was so strong with us all, however, that we always had an inclination to assemble round each one we met and wait for a song. Truly travel enlarges men's minds.

Youghal is only a short distance from Waterford as the crow flies, but it is a formidable journey by rail. However, even an Irish train reaches its destination at last, and we found ourselves next day in the old Irish seaport. Here the Blackwater river opens out into a considerable estuary, which in turn opens out into the Irish Sea. The town itself is a quaint, old-fashioned place, with an amphibious population who live principally by fishing for the salmon as they try to ascend the Blackwater, and capturing them in long drift-nets.

The cousin of our friend Smith had been as good as his word, and his yacht was waiting for us in the harbour, a fine, roomy, old-fashioned craft, broad in the beam, with a cabin which would hold the whole of us. She was well provided with nets and trawling gear, the latter being a favourite amusement of her proprietor. We only made an experimental cruise that day, standing off and on the land, outside the harbour. We got several excellent views of the town from the sea face, but others were complete failures; for we soon found the difference in working on the broad deck of a steamer and on a tossing little cockle-shell. On landing, however, we were amply recompensed by a series of views of the antiquities of the little place taken in the evening, after which we adjourned to a popular concert, where the chief hit seemed to be a topical song with frequent allusions to 'Buckshot Forster', which never failed to bring down the house. We put up at the 'Crown' Hotel, where we met with the greatest kindness and comfort, and can conscientiously recommend it to any other of the fraternity who may find themselves in that quarter.

Next morning with 'a wet sheet and a flowing sea' – Cunningham suggested 'a wet blanket' – we scudded out of Youghal harbour, threading our way amongst fishing boats and drift nets. There was a slight chopping sea on, which made photography almost an impossibility for the time; so all hands devoted themselves, heart and soul, to drinking bottled beer and trawling. The great net with its big iron sinkers, or 'otters' as they are called, was lowered overboard and we dragged it behind us for half-an-hour or so. Our worthy host, who was an accomplished yachts-man, seemed considerably amused by our complete ignorance of boats and everything pertaining thereto. As Mark Twain said – the information which we did not possess would make a good-sized volume. Ramsay was the most erudite among us, but even he seemed to have a general impression that the flying jib was connected in some way with the tiller. 'It's been out long enough now!' cried our skipper; 'haul away at the line.' We all began to haul away at various lines with desperate eagerness until by objurgation and example, he concentrated us upon the right one. There is an excited cry of 'it's heavy – awfully heavy!' Up it comes through the blue water. We can see the bag of it flickering upwards, much distended apparently. 'It's nothing but seaweed!' roars one. 'I see a fish!' yells another. 'Lots of them!' gasps a third. 'Pull, boys, pull!' and then with a heavy splash down comes the net upon the deck, and next moment the whole place seems alive with flapping tails and waving fins and silver bellies and great red gills opening and shutting. It is a case of minding your ankles while a dogfish snaps at one side of the little deck and a conger eel both barks and bites at the other. However, all are successfully knocked on the head and we are able to classify our victims. There is a variety with a vengeance – hake, ling, rockcod, gurnard, red and grey mullet, eels, skate, crabs, octopi, the dogfish, and molluscs galore. Now was the time for photography to assert itself and come to the front. The net is piled tastefully in the sheets for a background; then with a little judicious selection a graceful and natural pile of fish are arranged in front, and we have a triumphal plate to remind us of our great haul ...

Behind the village there is the most perfect specimen in Ireland of that mysterious edifice known as the round tower. This one was about seventy feet high, built very much like a modern lighthouse. Though its erection is entirely pre-historic, the mortar between the stones is as firm now as ever, and the stones themselves do not show the least symptoms of decay. We took several views of this interesting building. What the original object of the round thought towers was is a puzzle to antiquaries. Some have thought that they were temples erected in honour of the sun god; and this seems to have been the idea among the early Christians, for a church has been erected beside the tower, apparently to act as an antidote to it. The church, however, is now reduced to a crumbling ruin, while the old heathen tower is as erect and defiant as ever. Others have thought that they were watch towers, but that is negatived by the fact that this one is built at the foot of a hill, which would be rather an unnatural situation for a watch tower. Altogether the building and its uses were 'the sort of thing no fellah would understand', so we contented ourselves with photographing it without indulging in further speculation.

'To the Waterford Coast and Along It',
British Journal of Photography, 17, 24 August 1883

After graduating from Edinburgh University, Conan Doyle spent a few months as the doctor on a steamer travelling to West Africa (see p.157). Following this voyage he decided, in January 1882, to pick up his medical career by working as a GP. First, briefly, in Plymouth and then more permanently in Southsea, a fashionable resort, contiguous with the old naval town of Portsmouth.

Southsea

Once again, he didn't write much about the place he lived in. He mentioned Southsea in one Sherlock Holmes story, 'The Adventure of the Cardboard Box', where Dr Watson admits he yearns for 'the glades of the New Forest or the shingle of Southsea'. Otherwise he limited himself to another photographic essay, 'Southsea: Three Days in Search of Effects', and a fictional representation where Southsea becomes Birchespool in his 1895 novel *The Stark Munro Letters*. The photography piece:

> ... Southsea is a geographical expression which it might puzzle a good many people to define. That it is a watering-place within an attainable distance of London is generally known, but its exact size is vaguely appreciated save by those who have had the pleasure of visiting it; and this vagueness is intensified when the inquirer demands his railway ticket and finds that none are issued to any place of the name. As a matter of fact, Southsea is an offshoot of Portsmouth, and has not been honoured by an independent station, although in point of size it is second only to Brighton, and when taken in conjunction with Portsmouth very much surpasses

it. There is something piquant and interesting in this union between a grim old fortified town, grey with age and full of historical reminiscences, and a brand new fashionable watering-place, resplendent with piers, parades and hotels. Apart from sentiment, it promises a variety to the vagrant photographer which can hardly be matched by any single town of my acquaintance ...

The morning was a bright and cheerful one, with just enough of cloud piled up in the horizon to make an effective seascape, in which each of the party immediately indulged. The broad Solent, with its three circular forts, its fleets of yachts, and its sullen-looking men-of-war, all backed up by the long slopes of the Isle of Wight, made as pretty a picture as an artist's eye could desire. Our next attempt was on the Ryde steamer, which came ploughing along in the fair-way about a couple of hundred yards from the shore, the decks black with excursionists, and the foam flying from the paddles ...

Running down to Spithead we cruised round the three forts erected by Lord Palmerston – two of which are iron-clad, and have fresh coatings of metal added on to meet every increase of armour upon any foreign man-of-war. These forts command the only channel by which Portsmouth can be approached, and, being supported by others on the shore, render the place impregnable upon the sea side. Passing the forts we ran out as far as the light-ship, where the isolated keepers seemed delighted to see us and threw us out their letters, ingeniously sandwiched in between biscuits so as to convert them into convenient missiles. Night was

falling, and a purple haze lying over the Isle of Wight, in
gorgeous contrast with the deep scarlet bands left by the
setting sun, before we found ourselves once more upon
Southsea beach. There, bidding adieu to the melancholy
mariner, we made our way back to headquarters in a
ravenous condition, which considerably astonished
'The Doctor's' house-keeper ...

'Southsea: Three Days in Search of Effects',
British Journal of Photography, 22 June 1883

And the fiction, which recalled his first few days in the
town:

Birchespool is really a delightful place, dear Bertie; and
I ought to know something about it, seeing that I have
padded a good hundred miles through its streets during
the last seven days. Its mineral springs used to be quite
the mode a century or more ago; and it retains many
traces of its aristocratic past, carrying it with a certain
grace, too, as an émigré countess might wear the faded
dress which had once rustled in Versailles. I forget the
new roaring suburbs with their out-going manufactures
and their incoming wealth, and I live in the queer health-
giving old city of the past. The wave of fashion has long
passed over it, but a deposit of dreary respectability
has been left behind. In the High Street you can see
the long iron extinguishers upon the railings where
the link-boys used to put out their torches, instead of
stamping upon them or slapping them on the pavement,
as was the custom in less high-toned quarters. There
are the very high curbstones too, so that Lady Teazle or

Mrs. Sneerwell could step out of coach or sedan chair without soiling her dainty satin shoes ...

I wrote to you last on the night that I reached here. Next morning I set to work upon my task. You would be surprised (at least I was) to see how practical and methodical I can be. First of all I walked down to the post-office and I bought a large shilling map of the town. Then back I came and pinned this out upon the lodging-house table. This done, I set to work to study it, and to arrange a series of walks by which I should pass through every street of the place. You have no idea what that means until you try to do it. I used to have breakfast, get out about ten, walk till one, have a cheap luncheon (I can do well on three-pence), walk till four, get back and note results. On my map I put a cross for every empty house and a circle for every doctor. So at the end of that time I had a complete chart of the whole place, and could see at a glance where there was a possible opening, and what opposition there was at each point.

...

Well, when I had finished my empty-house-and-doctor chart, I found that there was one villa to let, which undoubtedly was far the most suitable for my purpose. In the first place it was fairly cheap – forty pounds, or fifty with taxes. The front looked well. It had no garden. It stood with the well-to-do quarter upon the one side, and the poorer upon the other. Finally, it was almost at the intersection of four roads, one of which was a main artery of the town. Altogether, if I had ordered a house for my purpose I could hardly have got anything better, and I was thrilled with apprehension lest someone should get before me to the agent. I hurried round and burst into the office with a precipitancy which rather startled the demure clerk inside.

His replies, however, were reassuring. The house was still to let. It was not quite the quarter yet, but I could enter into possession. I must sign an agreement to take it for one year, and it was usual to pay a quarter's rent in advance ...

I did so, and drew my hind foot across the Rubicon. The die was cast. Come what might, 1 Oakley Villas was on my hand for a twelve-month.

'Would you like the key now?'

I nearly snatched it out of his hands. Then away I ran to take possession of my property. Never shall I forget my feelings, my dear Bertie, when the key clicked in the lock, and the door flew open. It was my own house – all my very own! I shut the door again, the noise of the street died down, and I had, in that empty, dust-strewn hall, such a sense of soothing privacy as had never come to me before. In all my life it was the first time that I had ever stood upon boards which were not paid for by another.

Then I proceeded to go from room to room with a delicious sense of exploration. There were two upon the ground floor, sixteen feet square each, and I saw with satisfaction that the wall papers were in fair condition. The front one would make a consulting room, the other a waiting room, though I did not care to reflect who was most likely to do the waiting. I was in the highest spirits, and did a step dance in each room as an official inauguration.

Then down a winding wooden stair to the basement, where were kitchen and scullery, dimly lit, and asphalt-floored. As I entered the latter I stood staring. In every corner piles of human jaws were grinning at me. The place was a Golgotha! In that half light the effect was sepulchral. But as I approached and picked up one of them the mystery vanished. They were of plaster-of-Paris, and were the leavings evidently of the dentist, who had been the last tenant. A more welcome sight was a huge wooden dresser with drawers and a fine cupboard in the corner. It only wanted a table and a chair to be a furnished room.

Then I ascended again and went up the first flight of stairs. There were two other good-sized apartments there. One should be my bedroom, and the other a spare room. And then another flight with two more. One for the servant, when I had one, and the other for a guest.

From the windows I had a view of the undulating gray back of the city, with the bustle of green tree tops. It was a windy day, and the clouds were drifting swiftly across the heavens, with glimpses of blue between. I don't know how it was, but as I stood looking through the grimy panes in the empty rooms a sudden sense of my own individuality and of my responsibility to some higher power came upon me, with a vividness which was overpowering. Here was a new chapter of my life about to be opened. What was to be the end of it? I had strength, I had gifts. What was I going to do with them? All the world, the street, the cabs, the houses, seemed to fall away, and the mite of a figure and the unspeakable

Guide of the Universe were for an instant face to face.
I was on my knees – hurled down all against my own
will, as it were.

The Stark Munro Letters, London and New York, 1895

From Southsea he was able to slip across the Solent to the
Isle of Wight.

Isle of Wight

Perhaps there is no tract of land in the world which
compresses into such a small space so many diversities
of configuration as the Isle of Wight. It is a miniature
of the great country from which it has been separated.
There are moors and fells as bleak as those of
Cumberland or the West Riding; chalk downs which
recall Kent and Sussex; wooded undulating plains like
those of Hampshire; and great stretches of rich arable
land as fertile and as cultivated as any in Leicestershire.
Amid such a variety of scenery, with the sea continually
presenting itself as a background, and historical
reminiscences upon every side, the amateur would be
hard to please indeed who did not find subjects enough
to gratify his photographic propensities ...

The journey to Portsmouth occupies about two hours
and a-half, and the traveller is eventually deposited
upon the harbour pier, alongside which the fine, roomy
'Victoria' is snorting impatiently out of its two funnels,
and in full readiness for its short voyage ...

In the foreground lie three great three-deckers –
the 'Victory' (the old historical flagship of Nelson),

the 'Duke of Wellington', and the 'St. Vincent'. Beside these great floating monsters is moored a tiny gunboat – a representative of the modern tendency of naval architecture as compared with the ancient. By the side of its companions it looks like a duckling among swans; yet in its very insignificance lies its strength, since it offers no target for an enemy's shot. Around and between these vessels a swarm of steam launches, yachts, and shore boats fill in the scene, while behind it all the quaint little town of Gosport lines the water's edge and forms a background to the picture ...

And now the good ship 'Victoria' gives a final snort of expostulation, and churns up the water impatiently with her paddles. 'All aboard!' shouts the captain. The warps are thrown off, and the vessel steams slowly out of the harbour, passing under frowning batteries, where the black-mouthed cannon peep sullenly out, as though sulky at having no more honourable task than the firing of salutes for so many hundreds of years. The channel here seems to the uninitiated to lie dangerously near the shore, even the largest ships passing within a stone's throw of the beach. There is a story, indeed, that on the occasion of some great wooden man-of-war going out in the beginning of the century she ran her bowsprit through the coffee-room window of the Blue Posts Hotel, considerably to the astonishment of some gentlemen who were dining therein. How far this is legendary and how far true is for some local historian to decide.

After touching at Southsea Pier the steamer stood right across for 'the Island'. Finer views could hardly be obtained than those of receding Southsea, with its charming variety of colour, white and red alternating in the houses, and the long line of shingle with the waves breaking merrily against it, or of the approaching shores of the Isle of Wight, with its undulating wooded hills, and the towers of Osborne peeping above the trees on the extreme right. Both were transferred to the plates of the photographers, together with a beautiful seascape of the Solent, with a solitary man-of-war lying at anchor at Spithead, and the three marine forts which stand out of the water like so many gigantic cheese-boxes, and command the winding channel which leads to the harbour. As the light was somewhat glaring the sky-shade was used in taking these views.

The Solent is five miles broad between Portsmouth and Ryde, so that twenty-five minutes of steaming brings the travellers across. Johnson's train has landed him on the pier at ten o'clock, and it is now hardly eleven, so that our excursionists have still a long day before them. Ryde pier is a very long one. As Johnson remarked, if it were a little longer there would be no need for any steamers at all. Happily there is a steam tramway which runs down it, and saves the necessity of trudging over half-a-mile of planking. The town itself is a decidedly hilly one. It is not so steep as the side of a house, but considerably more so than the roof. If you slip anywhere within half-a-mile or so you run a chance of reaching the beach in a shorter time than ever you took to traverse the same distance before. This is when you do not happen to bump into an inhabitant. In that case it is the inhabitant who gyrates down to the shore. If balloons were substituted for cabs in this town it would allow some small degree of comfort during the short time which will elapse before the whole thing goes adrift and slides majestically into the sea. I could say several ill-natured things of Ryde, but I refrain ...

To follow our travellers, however: the first move after getting into the town of Ryde is to repair to a large horse-and-trap agency there, and to engage an open carriage for the day — a matter which is not a very expensive one. Thus provided, the whole island is at their command. Should their tastes lie in the direction of Royalty, it is but six miles from the palace, where there are many beautiful views to be had; and just beyond lies the quaint old town of Cowes, with the many studies of the finest yachts in England which can be obtained there. If, however, the artist be of a historical and archaeological turn, then he should wend his way to the little town of Newport, the capital of the island, where, besides its many inherent beauties, there is the opportunity of viewing and photographing the venerable castle of Carisbrooke, in which Charles I was imprisoned before being taken to London and tried by the Parliament.

To confine myself to actual facts, however, the travellers, after a council of war with their driver, decided upon a somewhat more ambitious scheme than either of those indicated above. This was to drive right across the island, after first inspecting the Roman antiquities which have been lately unearthed at Brading. Brading is about four miles from Ryde, and as the road runs along the hills overlooking the sea the view was a beautiful one.

Brading is a pleasant little spot, and derives its principal importance from the magnificent specimen of a Roman villa which has been dug up in the immediate vicinity. From a short distance this interesting relic looks more like a quarry than anything else; and, alas! the operations of the photographer are confined to a distance, since the picturing of the tessellated pavement and other remains are a monopoly which the vagrant artist is not allowed to infringe upon. The tourists had to content themselves, therefore, with this general treatment of the subject, and then, after being divorced from their cameras, were led through the different chambers by a remorseless guide who explained the habits and customs of the 'hancient Romans' in a manner which was more amusing than trustworthy.

The road from Brading leads to Newport, but there is a side road which opens into the highway between Ryde and Ventnor, and this was selected by the driver. This main road, which runs from north to south across the island, passes over a succession of undulating hills, from the summit of every one of which a magnificent view is to be obtained. Curious features on the scenery are the numerous monoliths — long perpendicular stones erected upon the summits of these hills, either as landmarks or for some other purpose. These abound in the Isle of Wight. A succession of little villages were passed through on the way, offering as fine a selection of rural 'bits' as could be found anywhere — the little wayside cottage with thatched roof, diamond-paned windows, and clematis or Virginia creeper fringing the doorway; or, perhaps, the grizzled, round-shouldered proprietor, with his black pipe in his mouth, sitting *sub tegmine fagi*, densely unconscious that he is about to be endowed with a franchise, and that the press of the country are clamouring about his wrongs. There is often more interest in a little scene of this sort, selected artistically and well worked out, than in the broadest and most ambitious rendering of the beauties of nature.

Ventnor is about twelve miles from Ryde. As you plunge into the heart of the country the sea disappears entirely, and you might imagine yourself in one of the midland counties of England. About three miles from Ventnor there is a large inn on one side of the road and a wicket gate on the other. Here the coach-man pulls up with decision. At first, knowing the habits and customs of coachmen, our travellers imagine the inn to be the reason of this peremptory halt; but the landlord quickly sets them right, and they learn that the wicket gate is the attraction. Passing through it, camera in hand, they pick their way down a winding path and then across a brawling torrent. From there the path runs down a thickly-wooded valley, the trees meeting overhead so as to hide the sky, and the stream gurgling among the bracken far beneath. This is the famous Shanklin Chine, and certainly a more beautiful or fairy-like scene could hardly be conceived ...

Leaving the Chine behind, the carriage rolled over a tolerably-level road a couple of miles in length, terminating in a steep hill, which was rather a pull for the tired horse. Up to this, as I have said, there were no signs of the sea, but on reaching the crest of the hill a wonderful view lay before the party. Almost directly beneath was the ocean, stretching right away in every direction to the horizon. Coming so unexpectedly I know of no view in the world which gives such an idea of an infinite expanse. Here and there one looks straight down on the deck of some steamer or sailing ship, ploughing across to St. Malo or tacking along to Southampton. They look like toy vessels – mere specks in the enormous stretch of water around them ...

When one leaves Ryde he fancies that he has seen the steepest town in the world, but his mind broadens when he comes to Ventnor. It is very much steeper, and gives the impression of being a little more than perpendicular. It is the fact of being built on the side of this hill that gives the place its great reputation as a resort for consumptives. No wind but the balmy south one can get near it. Still there are draw-backs, and when a consumptive falls out of his front door down the High-street and into the sea his language is just as virulent as that of any healthy man.

'A Day on "The Island"', *British Journal of Photography*, 25 April 1884

While living in Southsea he decided he wasn't satisfied writing occasional stories, but wanted to see his name 'on the back of a volume'. So he turned his hand to detective fiction, initially in the novel *A Study in Scarlet*, written in 1886 and published the following year. The Sherlock Holmes stories, of which this was the first, offer a wide range of fine descriptions of place, which can broadly be included under the rubric of travel writing.

Along with Holmes and his companion, the third character in several of the stories is the great capital city of London. Conan Doyle is entranced by the excitement and bustle of a place where people from all corners of the globe make their ways through the all-encroaching fog by foot, cab, tube and rail. Dr Watson sets the tone in *A Study in Scarlet* where he describes London as 'that great cesspool into which all the loungers and idlers of the Empire are irresistibly drained'.

London

Under such circumstances I naturally gravitated to London, that great cesspool into which all the loungers and idlers of the Empire are irresistibly drained. There I stayed for some time at a private hotel in the Strand, leading a comfortless, meaningless existence, and spending such money as I had, considerably more freely than I ought. So alarming did the state of my finances become, that I soon realised that I must either leave the metropolis and rusticate somewhere in the country, or that I must make a complete alteration in my style of living. Choosing the latter alternative, I began by making up my mind to leave the hotel, and take up my quarters in some less pretentious and less expensive domicile.

On the very day that I had come to this conclusion, I was standing at the Criterion Bar, when someone tapped me on the shoulder, and turning round I recognised young Stamford, who had been a dresser under me at Bart's. The sight of a friendly face in the great wilderness of London is a pleasant thing indeed to a lonely man. In old days Stamford had never been a particular crony of mine, but now I hailed him with enthusiasm, and he, in his turn, appeared to be delighted to see me. In the exuberance of my joy, I asked him to lunch with me at the Holborn, and we started off together in a hansom.

A Study in Scarlet, London 1888, New York 1890

London's astonishing energy becomes even more apparent in Conan Doyle's second Sherlock Holmes novel, *The Sign of Four*, published in 1890.

It was a September evening, and not yet seven o'clock, but the day had been a dreary one, and a dense drizzly fog lay low upon the great city. Mud-coloured clouds drooped sadly over the muddy streets. Down the Strand the lamps were but misty splotches of diffused light which threw a feeble circular glimmer upon the slimy pavement. The yellow glare from the shop-windows streamed out into the steamy, vaporous air, and threw a murky, shifting radiance across the crowded thoroughfare. There was, to my mind, something eerie and ghost-like in the endless procession of faces which flitted across these narrow bars of light – sad faces and glad, haggard and merry. Like all human kind, they flitted from the gloom into the light, and so back into the gloom once more. I am not subject to impressions, but the dull, heavy evening, with the strange business upon which we were engaged, combined to make me nervous and depressed. I could see from Miss Morstan's manner that she was suffering from the same feeling.

Holmes alone could rise superior to petty influences. He held his open note-book upon his knee, and from time to time he jotted down figures and memoranda in the light of his pocket-lantern.

At the Lyceum Theatre the crowds were already thick at the side-entrances. In front a continuous stream of hansoms and four-wheelers were rattling up, discharging their cargoes of shirt-fronted men and beshawled, bediamonded women. We had hardly reached the third pillar, which was our rendezvous, before a small, dark, brisk man in the dress of a coachman accosted us.

'Are you the parties who come with Miss Morstan?' he asked.

'I am Miss Morstan, and these two gentlemen are my friends,' said she.

He bent a pair of wonderfully penetrating and questioning eyes upon us. 'You will excuse me, miss,' he said with a certain dogged manner, 'but I was to ask you to give me your word that neither of your companions is a police-officer.'

'I give you my word on that,' she answered.

He gave a shrill whistle, on which a street Arab led across a four-wheeler and opened the door. The man who had addressed us mounted to the box, while we took our places inside. We had hardly done so before the driver whipped up his horse, and we plunged away at a furious pace through the foggy streets.

The situation was a curious one. We were driving to an unknown place, on an unknown errand. Yet our invitation was either a complete hoax, which was an inconceivable hypothesis – or else we had good reason to think that important issues might hang upon our journey. Miss Morstan's demeanour was as resolute and collected as ever. I endeavoured to cheer and amuse her by reminiscences of my adventures in Afghanistan; but, to tell the truth, I was myself so excited at our situation and so curious as to our destination that my stories were slightly involved. To this day she declares that I told her one moving anecdote as to how a musket looked into my tent at the dead of night, and how I fired a double-barrelled tiger cub at it. At first I had some idea as to the direction in which we were driving; but soon, what with our pace, the fog, and my own limited knowledge of London, I lost my bearings, and knew nothing, save that we seemed to be going a very long way. Sherlock Holmes was never at fault, however, and he muttered the names as the cab rattled through squares and in and out by tortuous by-streets.

'Rochester Row,' said he. 'Now Vincent Square. Now we come out on the Vauxhall Bridge Road. We are making for the Surrey side, apparently. Yes, I thought so. Now we are on the bridge. You can catch glimpses of the river.'

We did indeed get a fleeting view of a stretch of the Thames with the lamps shining upon the broad, silent water; but our cab dashed on, and was soon involved in a labyrinth of streets upon the other side.

'Wordsworth Road,' said my companion. 'Priory Road. Lark Hall Lane. Stockwell Place. Robert Street. Cold Harbour Lane. Our quest does not appear to take us to very fashionable regions.'

We had, indeed, reached a questionable and forbidding neighbourhood. Long lines of dull brick houses were only relieved by the coarse glare and tawdry brilliancy of public houses at the corner. Then came rows of two-storied villas each with a fronting of miniature garden, and then again interminable lines of new staring brick buildings, the monster tentacles which the giant city was throwing out into the country. At last the cab drew up at the third house in a new terrace. None of the other houses were inhabited, and that at which we stopped was as dark as its neighbours, save for a single glimmer in the kitchen window. On our knocking, however, the door was instantly thrown open by a Hindoo servant clad in a yellow turban, white loose-fitting clothes, and a yellow sash. There was something strangely incongruous in this Oriental figure framed in the commonplace door-way of a third-rate suburban dwelling-house.

'The Sahib awaits you,' said he, and even as he spoke there came a high piping voice from some inner room. 'Show them in to me, khitmutgar,' it cried. 'Show them straight in to me.'

The Sign of Four, London 1890, New York 1891

This short novel offers a lively account of the River Thames acting as the backdrop to a dramatic police chase. This was the first instance of what has become a regular feature of thrillers, both in print and on film – the river pursuit.

While this conversation had been proceeding, we had been shooting the long series of bridges which span the Thames. As we passed the City the last rays of the sun were gilding the cross upon the summit of St. Paul's. It was twilight before we reached the Tower.

'That is Jacobson's Yard,' said Holmes, pointing to a bristle of masts and rigging on the Surrey side. 'Cruise gently up and down here under cover of this string of lighters.' He took a pair of night-glasses from his pocket and gazed some time at the shore. 'I see my sentry at his post,' he remarked, 'but no sign of a handkerchief.'

'Suppose we go down-stream a short way and lie in wait for them,' said Jones, eagerly. We were all eager by this time, even the policemen and stokers, who had a very vague idea of what was going forward.

'We have no right to take anything for granted,' Holmes answered. 'It is certainly ten to one that they go down-stream, but we cannot be certain. From this point we can see the entrance of the yard, and they can hardly see us. It will be a clear night and plenty of light. We must stay where we are. See how the folk swarm over yonder in the gaslight.'

'They are coming from work in the yard.'

'Dirty-looking rascals, but I suppose everyone has some little immortal spark concealed about him. You would not think it, to look at them. There is no a priori probability about it. A strange enigma is man!'

...

'And there is the *Aurora*,' exclaimed Holmes, 'and going like the devil! Full speed ahead, engineer. Make after that launch with the yellow light. By heaven, I shall never forgive myself if she proves to have the heels of us!'

She had slipped unseen through the yard-entrance and passed behind two or three small craft, so that she had fairly got her speed up before we saw her. Now she was flying down the stream, near in to the shore, going at a tremendous rate. Jones looked gravely at her and shook his head.

'She is very fast,' he said. 'I doubt if we shall catch her.'

'We MUST catch her!' cried Holmes, between his teeth. 'Heap it on, stokers! Make her do all she can! If we burn the boat we must have them!'

We were fairly after her now. The furnaces roared, and the powerful engines whizzed and clanked, like a great metallic heart. Her sharp, steep prow cut through the river-water and sent two rolling waves to right and to left of us. With every throb of the engines we sprang and quivered like a living thing. One great yellow lantern in our bows threw a long, flickering funnel of light in front of us. Right ahead a dark blur upon the water showed where the *Aurora* lay, and the swirl of white foam behind her spoke of the pace at which she was going. We flashed past barges, steamers, merchant-vessels, in and out, behind this one and round the other. Voices hailed us out of the darkness, but still the *Aurora* thundered on, and still we followed close upon her track.

'Pile it on, men, pile it on!' cried Holmes, looking down into the engine-room, while the fierce glow from below beat upon his eager, aquiline face. 'Get every pound of steam you can.'

'I think we gain a little,' said Jones, with his eyes on the *Aurora*.

'I am sure of it,' said I. 'We shall be up with her in a very few minutes.'

At that moment, however, as our evil fate would have it, a tug with three barges in tow blundered in between us. It was only by putting our helm hard down that we avoided a collision, and before we could round them and recover our way the *Aurora* had gained a good two hundred yards. She was still, however, well in view, and the murky uncertain twilight was setting into a clear starlit night. Our boilers were strained to their utmost, and the frail shell vibrated and creaked with the fierce energy which was driving us along. We had shot through the Pool, past the West India Docks, down the long Deptford Reach, and up again after rounding the Isle of Dogs. The dull blur in front of us resolved itself now clearly enough into the dainty *Aurora*. Jones turned our search-light upon her, so that we could plainly see the figures upon her deck. One man sat by the stern, with something black between his knees over which he stooped. Beside him lay a dark mass which looked like a Newfoundland dog. The boy held the tiller, while against the red glare of the furnace I could see old Smith, stripped to the waist, and shovelling coals for dear life. They may have had some doubt at first as to whether we were really pursuing them, but now as we followed every winding and turning which they took there could no longer be any question about it. At Greenwich we were about three hundred paces behind them. At Blackwall we could not have been more than two hundred and fifty. I have coursed many creatures in many countries during my chequered career, but never did sport give me such a wild thrill as this

mad, flying man-hunt down the Thames. Steadily we
drew in upon them, yard by yard. In the silence of
the night we could hear the panting and clanking of
their machinery. The man in the stern still crouched
upon the deck, and his arms were moving as though
he were busy, while every now and then he would
look up and measure with a glance the distance which
still separated us. Nearer we came and nearer. Jones
yelled to them to stop. We were not more than four
boat's lengths behind them, both boats flying at a
tremendous pace. It was a clear reach of the river,
with Barking Level upon one side and the melancholy
Plumstead Marshes upon the other. At our hail the
man in the stern sprang up from the deck and shook
his two clinched fists at us, cursing the while in a
high, cracked voice. He was a good-sized, powerful
man, and as he stood poising himself with legs astride
I could see that from the thigh downwards there was
but a wooden stump upon the right side. At the sound
of his strident, angry cries there was movement in
the huddled bundle upon the deck. It straightened
itself into a little black man – the smallest I have ever
seen – with a great, misshapen head and a shock of
tangled, dishevelled hair. Holmes had already drawn
his revolver, and I whipped out mine at the sight of
this savage, distorted creature. He was wrapped in
some sort of dark ulster or blanket, which left only his
face exposed; but that face was enough to give a man
a sleepless night. Never have I seen features so deeply
marked with all bestiality and cruelty. His small eyes
glowed and burned with a sombre light, and his thick

lips were writhed back from his teeth, which grinned and chattered at us with a half animal fury.

'Fire if he raises his hand,' said Holmes, quietly. We were within a boat's-length by this time, and almost within touch of our quarry. I can see the two of them now as they stood, the white man with his legs far apart, shrieking out curses, and the unhallowed dwarf with his hideous face, and his strong yellow teeth gnashing at us in the light of our lantern.

It was well that we had so clear a view of him. Even as we looked he plucked out from under his covering a short, round piece of wood, like a school-ruler, and clapped it to his lips. Our pistols rang out together. He whirled round, threw up his arms, and with a kind of choking cough fell sideways into the stream. I caught one glimpse of his venomous, menacing eyes amid the white swirl of the waters. At the same moment the wooden-legged man threw himself upon the rudder and put it hard down, so that his boat made straight in for the southern bank, while we shot past her stern, only clearing her by a few feet. We were round after her in an instant, but she was already nearly at the bank. It was a wild and desolate place, where the moon glimmered upon a wide expanse of marsh-land, with pools of stagnant water and beds of decaying vegetation. The launch with a dull thud ran up upon the mud-bank, with her bow in the air and her stern flush with the water. The fugitive sprang out, but his stump instantly sank its whole length into the sodden soil. In vain he struggled and writhed. Not one step could he possibly take either forwards or backwards. He yelled in impotent rage, and kicked frantically into the mud with his other foot, but his struggles only bored his wooden pin the deeper into the sticky bank. When we brought our launch alongside he was so firmly anchored that it was only by throwing the end of a rope over his shoulders that we were able to haul him out, and to drag him, like some evil fish, over our side. The two Smiths, father and son, sat sullenly in their launch, but came aboard meekly enough when commanded. The *Aurora* herself we hauled off and made fast to our stern. A solid iron chest of Indian workmanship stood upon the deck. This, there could be no question, was the same that had contained the ill-omened treasure of the Sholtos. There was no key, but it was of considerable weight, so we transferred it carefully to our own little cabin. As we steamed slowly up-stream again, we flashed our search-light in every direction, but there was no sign of the Islander. Somewhere in the dark ooze at the bottom of the Thames lie the bones of that strange visitor to our shores.

'See here,' said Holmes, pointing to the wooden hatchway. 'We were hardly quick enough with our pistols.' There, sure enough, just behind where we had been standing, stuck one of those murderous darts which we knew so well. It must have whizzed between us at the instant that we fired. Holmes smiled at it and shrugged his shoulders in his easy fashion, but I confess that it turned me sick to think of the horrible death which had passed so close to us that night.

The Sign of Four, London 1890, New York 1891

Although frequently mentioned in earlier Sherlock Holmes stories, the London tube train system featured at the centre of 'The Adventure of the Bruce-Partington Plans', written in 1908. There Holmes used his knowledge of the underground system to deduce that the dead Cadogan West could not have been killed where he was found close to Aldgate Station, since his body had clearly been dumped on the roof of a train as far back as Gloucester Road.

However, with his copy of Bradshaw to hand, Holmes was generally more at home on the railways. Take this piece from 'The Adventure of the Copper Beeches', written in June 1892:

Railways

'There is a train at half-past nine,' said I, glancing over my Bradshaw. 'It is due at Winchester at 11:30.'

'That will do very nicely. Then perhaps I had better postpone my analysis of the acetones, as we may need to be at our best in the morning.'

By eleven o'clock the next day we were well upon our way to the old English capital. Holmes had been buried in the morning papers all the way down, but after we had passed the Hampshire border he threw them down and began to admire the scenery. It was an ideal spring day, a light blue sky, flecked with little fleecy white clouds drifting across from west to east. The sun was shining very brightly, and yet there was an exhilarating nip in the air, which set an edge to a man's energy. All over the countryside, away to the rolling hills around Aldershot, the little red and grey roofs of the farm-steadings peeped out from amid the light green of the new foliage.

'Are they not fresh and beautiful?' I cried with all the enthusiasm of a man fresh from the fogs of Baker Street.

But Holmes shook his head gravely. 'Do you know, Watson,' said he, 'that it is one of the curses of a mind with a turn like mine that I must look at everything with reference to my own special subject. You look at these scattered houses, and you are impressed by their beauty. I look at them, and the only thought which comes to me is a feeling of their isolation and of the impunity with which crime may be committed there.'

'Good heavens!' I cried. 'Who would associate crime with these dear old homesteads?'

'They always fill me with a certain horror. It is my belief, Watson, founded upon my experience, that the lowest and vilest alleys in London do not present a more dreadful record of sin than does the smiling and beautiful countryside.'

'You horrify me!'

'But the reason is very obvious. The pressure of public opinion can do in the town what the law cannot accomplish. There is no lane so vile that the scream of a tortured child, or the thud of a drunkard's blow, does not beget sympathy and indignation among the neighbours, and then the whole machinery of justice is ever so close that a word of complaint can set it going, and there is but a step between the crime and the dock. But look at these lonely houses, each in its own fields, filled for the most part with poor ignorant folk who know little of the law. Think of the deeds of hellish cruelty, the hidden wickedness which may go on, year in, year out, in such places, and none the wiser. Had this lady who appeals to us for help gone to live in Winchester, I should never have had a fear for her. It is the five miles of country which makes the danger. Still, it is clear that she is not personally threatened.'

'The Adventure of the Copper Beeches', *The Strand Magazine*, June 1892. Collected in *The Adventures of Sherlock Holmes*, London and New York, 1892

This seems to offer an unexpected insight into Conan Doyle's attitude to the English countryside, which he presents as threatening and isolating. But in real life he was a great lover of rural England. In this particular story he wrote about Jephro Rucastle, who, in encouraging Miss Violet Hunter to enter his employ as a governess, told her that his estate is situated in Hampshire. 'Charming rural place. The Copper Beeches, five miles on the far side of Winchester. It is the most lovely country, my dear young lady, and the dearest old country house.' Conan Doyle had a soft spot for Winchester, the old Saxon capital of England, which also featured in the later Sherlock Holmes story 'The Problem of Thor Bridge' (1922).

However, the author's topographical imagination was really engaged by the wilder open spaces in Dartmoor in Devon. He first wrote about this vast moor in one of his pieces, 'Dry Plates on a Wet Moor', for the *British Journal of Photography*. This appeared in November 1882, during a brief interlude in his career when he was working in Plymouth, which was neatly sketched in the opening paragraphs.

Dartmoor

When the Commodore strode into my apartment in the middle of August, and interrupted me in retouching a batch of plates, I knew that something was up. He is not a demonstrative man; on the contrary, his emotions are all deeply seated and seldom show upon the surface, but it was evident that he was in high spirits and bursting with some piece of information. I mischievously left him to simmer for some time upon a chair, while I finished my retouching.

'Well, Commodore,' I said at last, 'what is it?'

The murder was soon out. The office were to have a holiday after their ten months servitude at the desk — only for three days, it is true, but still a holiday. The Commodore had been brushing up his fossil apparatus, and was bent upon a short campaign among the wilds. He had come up to know if I would accompany him. Dartmoor was to be the destination, and the train started within an hour and a half.

'Awfully short notice,' he said, apologetically, 'but we weren't sure about it ourselves until this afternoon, and then I had to get my things together and put on my travelling togs.' The Commodore here waved his hand complacently to indicate the togs in question, the principal articles of which consisted of a broad-brimmed lawn-tennis hat and a pair of corduroy knickerbockers — a combination which suggested a cross between Oscar

Wilde and a gamekeeper, though the simple-minded wearer evidently regarded it as pregnant with danger to the susceptibilities of the opposite gender.

... In the first grey light of morning we found ourselves in the great Devonshire seaport [of Plymouth], and were conveyed with our 'belongings' to the Royal Hotel, where we turned in just as the other inmates were thinking of rising. A few hours' sleep proved a wonderful restorative, and when after a hearty breakfast, we sallied out to show ourselves upon the Hoe, we were hardly recognisable as the tired travellers of the morning. The Commodore stalked proudly along in that heart-breaking hat and the knickerbockers suggestive of blighted affections, while the Genius trotted by his side, pulling frantically at his incipient moustache, as if under the impression that it might be elongated by pure muscular exertion. I was the only one true to the objects of our journey, and lugged my camera along with me, to the undisguised disgust of my companions.

I was amply rewarded, however, for my disregard of public opinion. The lovely scene may still be imprinted upon the recollection of my companions – the deep blue of the harbour, the wooded slopes of Mount Edgecumbe, the rough outline of Drake's Island, and away beyond the breakwater the great stretch of ocean reaching to the horizon, where two dark pinnacles indicated the position of the Eddystone light. But the retina is a poor and fleeting receiver of impressions, while the scene which I carried off in my carrier will be before me for many a year to come.

But another and more expected photographic treat was in store for me. As we sauntered down in the direction of the dockyard we came across an excited crowd eagerly 'craning' their necks along the water's edge. Every fort and bastion and possible coigne of vantage was lined by spectators, and the crews of the 'Cambridge' and other old-fashioned line-of-battle ships clustered upon the yards. Before we could inquire the reason of this excitement a great prow came looming round the corner of the winding channel, and a glorious troopship, radiant in white and blue and gold, steamed slowly down the stream, with a knot of willing little tugs crowding and pushing in front of her, the tops of their funnels hardly level with the deck of their gigantic charge. The 'red-coats' clustered like bees upon the shrouds and their cheers were echoed back from the men-of-war and the crowds upon the shore ...

I should like to have spent the whole day in the old historical sea town, taking its curiosities and those numberless 'bits' in which it is richer than any town in the south of England. It was strange to see the very alehouses still standing upon the Barbican, in which the bearded and bejewelled filibusters of Drake and Hawkins had squandered the doubloons which they risked their lives for upon the Spanish Main. The Commodore, however, had no appreciation of the romance of history, and the Genius made dark innuendoes as to my real motives in lingering lovingly about the old 'pubs'; so, finding myself in a minority, I was compelled to withdraw my motion for prolonging our stay. We had luncheon at the hotel, and then, having strapped our impedimenta upon our shoulders, we struck out into the country with the air of men who were attempting to beat the six days' pedestrian record.

The pace was killing while it lasted, but, unfortunately, it only lasted for a mile and a-half, at the end of which time we all sat down simultaneously upon the slope of one of the outlying forts. My companions stared gloomily back at the city behind us; but a return would be too ignominious, so we proceeded to justify our halt by taking the view. It was a glorious seascape, with just a few bunches of gorse and heather upon the shoulder of the hill to serve as a foreground, while the coast line from the Eddystone to the Start lay like a map before us, framing in the broad stretch of ocean, clotted with sails. None of our results did justice to the exquisite original, though all were fairly good in their way. I see mine hanging upon the wall before me as I write. Clear enough it is, and accurate in detail; but, oh! the dismal greys and whites! Are we never to have the yellow of the sand and the green of the grass and the blue of the ocean transferred to our plates? It seems to me that a standing fund should be put by as a reward, to attract the researches of chemists and physicists in that direction, just as one awaits the fortunate discoverer of the Pole.

Stifling the unworthy temptation to return to our luxurious hotel, we strode sturdily northwards in the direction of the Moor. As we advanced the character of the scenery began to change. Rugged 'tors' and tangled masses of half-withered vegetation shut us in, and the narrow road wound through a wilderness in which the only living creatures seem to be a few half-starved Devonshire sheep, who eyed us curiously, as if speculating upon our motives for intruding upon their domains. Wild and stern as was the scene there was a certain rough beauty in it all, and several charming little nooks and corners were secured by our ever-watchful cameras. The enormous number of white sign posts fixed at the angle where every sheep-path departed from the main track told a grim story of the byegone dangers of the Moor – where men had wandered in circles until they had dropped dead of hunger and fatigue. Indeed, with all these precautions, during the last twelve months there have been at least three cases of individuals having met with a similar fate.

The long summer evening was drawing to a close before we trudged into the pretty little village of Roborough, where we had determined to put up for the night. The old English inn – with its signpost of Admiral Vernon and a kitchen door left artfully open to waft a savoury odour into the street – was so irresistible that I was fortunate we had pre-arranged to make it our head-quarters …

There was something in the old-world flavour of the whole place which was so congenial to the tastes of the conservative Commodore that I quite expected to hear him propose that our expedition should terminate there and then, and the remainder of the holiday be spent in this luxurious little wayside tavern. However, he rose superior to the temptation, and sketched out our programme for the morrow with the air of a man suffering for conscience sake.

...

There are disadvantages even in old-fashioned inns and antiquated four-post beds, as we found to our cost during the watches of the night. As the Genius expressed it, 'We felt a bit crowded at first, but there was more room when we had given the sheets a shaking.' However, the healthy exercise which we had taken triumphed eventually over every obstacle, and we strode forth in the morning like giants refreshed, bearing away in our knapsacks a goodly bottle of milk and a plentiful store of bread for our luncheon on the Moor.

Leaving Roborough behind us, we pushed steadily northward through a waste even more delicate than that which we traversed the day before. For ten miles neither house nor inhabitant met our eyes – nothing but a long, undulating plain covered with scanty vegetation; and intersected by innumerable peaty brooks, which meandered down to help to form the Plymouth 'leat', constructed by the great Sir Francis Drake, and still used as the only means of water supply. The scene, monotonous as it was, had an interest in my eye as being the seat of several of the incidents in Kingsley's *Westward Ho!* It was along one of these winding, uncertain tracts that Amyas Leigh rode across with his shipmates from Plymouth to Bideford, and the spot where Salvation Yeo slew the King of the Gubbins must have lain a very little to the northward. Now and again, as we reached the summit of some eminence, we had a magnificent view of the country we had passed through, stretching away down to the sea, while on the left the silver Tamar curled along between its thickly-wooded banks ...

Had we been told that those were to be the last efforts of our trip we should have laughed the idea to scorn; but alas! a change came over the spirit of our dream. A dusky cloud, which had lain low and threatening along the whole eastern horizon, began gradually to throw out long, ragged tentacles in our direction, which coalesced until they covered the whole heaven, and then with a swish down came a mighty torrent of rain, which soaked us through before we had time to remove our knapsacks and take shelter in our mackintoshes. It had evidently set in wet, so, with heads bowed to the blast and collars buttoned about our necks we staggered along in the direction in which we knew that Tavistock lay. I don't think any of us are ever likely to forget that eight-mile trudge. The thought of the 'I told you so's' of certain good friends who had seen us off at the station, and had warned us of the vicissitudes of the 'wet moor', added gall and wormwood to our sufferings. When we found ourselves at last in the streets of the picturesque town our plates were the only dry things in our possession, and three sorrier figures could not have been picked out in the length and breadth of England. The sight of the Commodore, with the water streaming down his rakish hat, and with the glory departed from the mud-bespattered knickerbockers, was almost enough to console the Genius and myself for all our misfortunes.

However, 'all's well that ends well'. A good dinner and a stiff glass of whisky and water – whisky without the water was suggested by the Genius, as our systems were already permeated by the milder liquid – soon set us on our legs again, and we retired to rest with great resolutions for the morrow. One glance at the streaming window panes in the morning dissipated every hope of being able to finish our third day. The rain was still pouring down in the way we knew so well. With heavy hearts we were forced to acknowledge that the game was up, and a hermetically-sealed four-wheeler bore us off with our effects to catch the midday train for home.

'Dry Plates on a Wet Moor', *British Journal of Photography*, 3 November 1882

Dartmoor of course acted as the setting for perhaps the best-known and best-loved Sherlock Holmes story, the novel *The Hound of the Baskervilles*. Conan Doyle skilfully conveyed the ambiguous appeal of the moor when Dr Watson first arrived at Baskerville Hall.

The train pulled up at a small wayside station and we all descended. Outside, beyond the low, white fence, a wagonette with a pair of cobs was waiting. Our coming was evidently a great event, for station-master and porters clustered round us to carry out our luggage. It was a sweet, simple country spot, but I was surprised to observe that by the gate there stood two soldierly men in dark uniforms who leaned upon their short rifles and glanced keenly at us as we passed. The coachman, a hard-faced, gnarled little fellow, saluted Sir Henry Baskerville, and in a few minutes we were flying swiftly down the broad, white road. Rolling pasture lands curved upward on either side of us, and old gabled houses peeped out from amid the thick green foliage, but behind the peaceful and sunlit countryside there rose ever, dark against the evening sky, the long, gloomy curve of the moor, broken by the jagged and sinister hills.

The wagonette swung round into a side road, and we curved upward through deep lanes worn by centuries of wheels, high banks on either side, heavy with dripping moss and fleshy hart's-tongue ferns. Bronzing bracken and mottled bramble gleamed in the light of the sinking sun. Still steadily rising, we passed over a narrow granite bridge and skirted a noisy stream which gushed swiftly down, foaming and roaring amid the gray boulders. Both road and stream wound up through a valley dense with scrub oak and fir. At every turn Baskerville gave an exclamation of delight, looking eagerly about him and asking countless questions. To his eyes all seemed beautiful, but to me a tinge of melancholy lay upon the countryside, which bore so clearly the mark of the waning year. Yellow leaves carpeted the lanes and fluttered down upon us as we passed. The rattle of our wheels died away as we drove through drifts of rotting vegetation – sad gifts, as it seemed to me, for Nature to throw before the carriage of the returning heir of the Baskervilles.

. . .

We had left the fertile country behind and beneath us. We looked back on it now, the slanting rays of a low sun turning the streams to threads of gold and glowing on the red earth new turned by the plough and the broad tangle of the woodlands. The road in front of us grew

bleaker and wilder over huge russet and olive slopes,
sprinkled with giant boulders. Now and then we passed
a moorland cottage, walled and roofed with stone, with
no creeper to break its harsh outline. Suddenly we
looked down into a cuplike depression, patched with
stunted oaks and firs which had been twisted and bent
by the fury of years of storm. Two high, narrow towers
rose over the trees. The driver pointed with his whip.

'Baskerville Hall,' said he.

The Hound of the Baskervilles,
London and New York, 1902

Conan Doyle exulted in the other-worldly nature of the
moor when covered with mist:

The night was clear and fine above us. The stars shone
cold and bright, while a half-moon bathed the whole
scene in a soft, uncertain light. Before us lay the
dark bulk of the house, its serrated roof and bristling
chimneys hard outlined against the silver-spangled
sky. Broad bars of golden light from the lower
windows stretched across the orchard and the moor.
One of them was suddenly shut off. The servants had
left the kitchen. There only remained the lamp in
the dining-room where the two men, the murderous
host and the unconscious guest, still chatted over
their cigars.

Every minute that white woolly plain which covered
one-half of the moor was drifting closer and closer to
the house. Already the first thin wisps of it were curling
across the golden square of the lighted window. The

farther wall of the orchard was already invisible, and
the trees were standing out of a swirl of white vapour.
As we watched it the fog-wreaths came crawling round
both corners of the house and rolled slowly into one
dense bank on which the upper floor and the roof
floated like a strange ship upon a shadowy sea. Holmes
struck his hand passionately upon the rock in front of us
and stamped his feet in his impatience.

'If he isn't out in a quarter of an hour the path will
be covered. In half an hour we won't be able to see our
hands in front of us.'

'Shall we move farther back upon higher ground?'

'Yes, I think it would be as well.'

So as the fog-bank flowed onward we fell back before
it until we were half a mile from the house, and still
that dense white sea, with the moon silvering its upper
edge, swept slowly and inexorably on.

The Hound of the Baskervilles,
London and New York, 1902

Conan Doyle penned similarly deft descriptions of the
English countryside in Sherlock Holmes stories such
as 'The Adventure of the Devil's Foot', which centred
on Cornwall, and *The Valley of Fear*, which was set in
Sussex.

Cornwall

Thus it was that in the early spring of that year we found
ourselves together in a small cottage near Poldhu Bay,
at the further extremity of the Cornish peninsula.

It was a singular spot, and one peculiarly well suited to the grim humour of my patient. From the windows of our little whitewashed house, which stood high upon a grassy headland, we looked down upon the whole sinister semicircle of Mounts Bay, that old death trap of sailing vessels, with its fringe of black cliffs and surge-swept reefs on which innumerable seamen have met their end. With a northerly breeze it lies placid and sheltered, inviting the storm-tossed craft to tack into it for rest and protection.

Then come the sudden swirl round of the wind, the blistering gale from the south-west, the dragging anchor, the lee shore, and the last battle in the creaming breakers. The wise mariner stands far out from that evil place.

On the land side our surroundings were as sombre as on the sea. It was a country of rolling moors, lonely and dun-coloured, with an occasional church tower to mark the site of some old-world village. In every direction upon these moors there were traces of some vanished race which had passed utterly away, and left as its sole record strange monuments of stone, irregular mounds which contained the burned ashes of the dead, and curious earthworks which hinted at prehistoric strife. The glamour and mystery of the place, with its sinister atmosphere of forgotten nations, appealed to the imagination of my friend, and he spent much of his time in long walks and solitary meditations upon the moor.

'The Adventure of the Devil's Foot', *The Strand Magazine*, December 1910. Collected in *His Last Bow*, London and New York, 1917

Sussex

The village of Birlstone is a small and very ancient cluster of half-timbered cottages on the northern border of the county of Sussex. For centuries it had remained unchanged; but within the last few years its picturesque appearance and situation have attracted a number of well-to-do residents, whose villas peep out from the woods around. These woods are locally supposed to be the extreme fringe of the great Weald forest, which thins away until it reaches the northern chalk downs. A number of small shops have come into being to meet the wants of the increased population; so there seems some prospect that Birlstone may soon grow from an ancient village into a modern town. It is the centre for a considerable area of country, since Tunbridge Wells, the nearest place of importance, is ten or twelve miles to the eastward, over the borders of Kent.

About half a mile from the town, standing in an old park famous for its huge beech trees, is the ancient Manor House of Birlstone. Part of this venerable building dates back to the time of the first crusade, when Hugo de Capus built a fortalice in the centre of the estate, which had been granted to him by the Red King. This was destroyed by fire in 1543, and some of its smoke-blackened corner stones were used when, in Jacobean times, a brick country house rose upon the ruins of the feudal castle.

The Manor House, with its many gables and its small diamond-paned windows, was still much as the builder had left it in the early seventeenth century. Of the double moats which had guarded its more warlike predecessor, the outer had been allowed to dry up, and served the humble function of a kitchen garden. The inner one was still there, and lay forty feet in breadth, though now only a few feet in depth, round the whole house. A small stream fed it and continued beyond it, so that the sheet of water, though turbid, was never ditchlike or unhealthy. The ground floor windows were within a foot of the surface of the water.

The only approach to the house was over a drawbridge, the chains and windlass of which had long been rusted and broken. The latest tenants of the Manor House had, however, with characteristic energy, set this right, and the drawbridge was not only capable of being raised, but actually was raised every evening and lowered every morning. By thus renewing the custom of the old feudal days the Manor House was converted into an island during the night – a fact which had a very direct bearing upon the mystery which was soon to engage the attention of all England.

The Valley of Fear, London and New York, 1915

Conan Doyle waxed lyrical about the English counties in his other fiction, with Hampshire providing much of the backdrop to his novel *The White Company* (1891), as does Surrey in his later work *Sir Nigel* (1905/6). He cannot quite make up his mind if the countryside is menacing (as in *The Hound of the Baskervilles*) or gloriously uplifting (as in most of his other work). Suffice it to say, it is not bustling, fog-ridden city. And it was in rural Surrey and, later, Sussex that he himself lived for most of his adult life.

Hampshire

The sun had risen over Ashurst and Denny woods, and was shining brightly, though the eastern wind had a sharp flavor to it, and the leaves were flickering thickly from the trees. In the High Street of Lyndhurst the wayfarers had to pick their way, for the little town was crowded with the guardsmen, grooms, and yeomen prickers who were attached to the King's hunt. The King himself was staying at Castle Malwood, but several of his suite had been compelled to seek such quarters as they might find in the wooden or wattle-and-daub cottages of the village. Here and there a small escutcheon, peeping from a glassless window, marked the night's lodging of knight or baron. These coats-of-arms could be read, where a scroll would be meaningless, and the bowman, like most men of his age, was well versed in the common symbols of heraldry.

'There is the Saracen's head of Sir Bernard Brocas,' quoth he. 'I saw him last at the ruffle at Poictiers some ten years back, when he bore himself like a man. He is the master of the King's horse, and can sing a right jovial stave, though in that he cannot come nigh to Sir John Chandos, who is first at the board or in the saddle. Three martlets on a field azure, that must be one of the Luttrells. By the crescent upon it, it should be the second son of old Sir Hugh, who had a bolt through his ankle at the intaking of Romorantin, he having rushed into the fray ere his squire had time to clasp his solleret to his greave. There too is the hackle which is the old device of the De Brays. I have served under Sir Thomas de Bray, who was as jolly as a pie, and a lusty swordsman until he got too fat for his harness.'

So the archer gossiped as the three wayfarers threaded their way among the stamping horses, the busy grooms, and the knots of pages and squires who disputed over the merits of their masters' horses and deer-hounds. As they passed the old church, which stood upon a mound at the left-hand side of the village street the door was flung open, and a stream of worshippers wound down the sloping path, coming from the morning mass, all chattering like a cloud of jays. Alleyne bent knee and doffed hat at the sight of the open door; but ere he had finished an ave his comrades were out of sight round the curve of the path, and he had to run to overtake them.

...

The path which the young clerk had now to follow lay through a magnificent forest of the very heaviest timber, where the giant bowls of oak and of beech formed long aisles in every direction, shooting up their huge branches to build the majestic arches of Nature's own cathedral. Beneath lay a broad carpet of the softest and greenest moss, flecked over with fallen leaves, but yielding pleasantly to the foot of the traveller. The track which guided him was one so seldom used that in places it lost itself entirely among the grass, to reappear as a reddish rut between the distant tree trunks. It was very still here in the heart of the woodlands. The gentle rustle of the branches and the distant cooing of pigeons were the only sounds which broke in upon the silence, save that once Alleyne heard afar off a merry call upon a hunting bugle and the shrill yapping of the hounds.

It was not without some emotion that he looked upon the scene around him, for, in spite of his secluded life, he knew enough of the ancient greatness of his own family to be aware that the time had been when they had held undisputed and paramount sway over all that tract of country. His father could trace his pure Saxon lineage back to that Godfrey Malf who had held the manors of Bisterne and of Minstead at the time when the Norman first set mailed foot upon English soil. The afforestation of the district, however, and its conversion into a royal demesne had clipped off a large section of his estate, while other parts had been confiscated as a punishment for his supposed complicity in an abortive Saxon rising. The fate of the ancestor had been typical of that of his descendants. During three hundred years their domains had gradually contracted, sometimes through royal or feudal encroachment, and sometimes through such gifts to the Church as that with which Alleyne's father had opened the doors of Beaulieu Abbey to his younger son. The importance of the family had thus dwindled, but they still retained the old Saxon manor-house, with a couple of farms and a grove large enough to afford pannage to a hundred pigs – *sylva de centum porcis* – as the old family parchments describe it. Above all, the owner of the soil could still hold his head high as the veritable Socman of Minstead – that is, as holding the land in free socage, with no feudal superior, and answerable to no man lower than the king. Knowing this, Alleyne felt some little glow of worldly pride as he looked for the first time upon the land with which so many generations of his ancestors had been associated. He pushed on the quicker, twirling his staff merrily, and looking out at every turn of the path for some sign of the old Saxon residence.

The White Company, London and New York, 1891

Surrey

Blind, frantic fury surged in the yellow horse's heart once more at this new degradation, this badge of serfdom and infamy. His spirit rose high and menacing at the touch. He loathed this place, these people, all and everything which threatened his freedom. He would have done with them forever; he would see them no more. Let him away to the uttermost parts of the earth, to the great plains where freedom is. Anywhere over the far horizon where he could get away from the defiling bit and the insufferable mastery of man.

He turned with a rush, and one magnificent deer-like bound carried him over the four-foot gate. Nigel's hat had flown off, and his yellow curls streamed behind him as he rose and fell in the leap. They were in the water-meadow now, and the rippling stream twenty feet wide gleamed in front of them running down to the main current of the Wey. The yellow horse gathered his haunches under him and flew over like an arrow. He took off from behind a boulder and cleared a furze-bush on the farther side. Two stones still mark the leap from hoof-mark to hoof-mark, and they are eleven good paces apart. Under the hanging branch of the great oak-tree on the farther side (that Quercus Tilfordiensis ordiensis is still shown as the bound of the Abbey's immediate precincts) the great horse passed. He had hoped to sweep off his rider, but Nigel sank low on the heaving back with his face buried in the flying mane. The rough bough rasped him rudely, but never shook his spirit nor his grip. Rearing, plunging and struggling, Pommers broke through the sapling grove and was out on the broad stretch of Hankley Down.

And now came such a ride as still lingers in the gossip of the lowly country folk and forms the rude jingle of that old Surrey ballad, now nearly forgotten, save for the refrain:

The Doe that sped on Hinde Head,
The Kestril on the winde,
And Nigel on the Yellow Horse
Can leave the world behind.

Before them lay a rolling ocean of dark heather, knee-deep, swelling in billow on billow up to the clear-cut hill before them. Above stretched one unbroken arch of peaceful blue, with a sun which was sinking down toward the Hampshire hills. Through the deep heather, down the gullies, over the watercourses, up the broken slopes, Pommers flew, his great heart bursting with rage, and every fiber quivering at the indignities which he had endured.

And still, do what he would, the man clung fast to his heaving sides and to his flying mane, silent, motionless, inexorable, letting him do what he would, but fixed as Fate upon his purpose. Over Hankley Down, through Thursley Marsh, with the reeds up to his mud-splashed withers, onward up the long slope of the Headland of the Hinds, down by the Nutcombe Gorge, slipping, blundering, bounding, but never slackening his fearful speed, on went the great yellow horse. The villagers of Shottermill heard the wild clatter of hoofs, but ere they could swing the ox-hide curtains of their cottage doors horse and rider were lost amid the high bracken of the Haslemere Valley. On he went, and on, tossing the miles behind his flying hoofs. No marsh-land could clog him, no hill could hold him back. Up the slope of Linchmere and the long ascent of Fernhurst he thundered as on the level, and it was not until he had flown down the incline of Henley Hill, and the gray castle tower of Midhurst rose over the coppice in front, that at last the eager outstretched neck sank a little on the breast, and the breath came quick and fast. Look where he would in woodland and on down, his straining eyes could catch no sign of those plains of freedom which he sought.

. . .

He saw no longer where he placed his feet, he cared no longer whither he went, but his one mad longing was to get away from this dreadful thing, this torture which clung to him and would not let him go. Through Thursley village he passed, his eyes straining in his agony, his heart bursting within him, and he had won his way to the crest of Thursley Down, still stung forward by stab and blow, when his spirit weakened, his giant strength ebbed out of him, and with one deep sob of agony the yellow horse sank among the heather. So sudden was the fall that Nigel flew forward over his shoulder, and beast and man lay prostrate and gasping while the last red rim of the sun sank behind Butser and the first stars gleamed in a violet sky.

Sir Nigel, London and New York, 1906

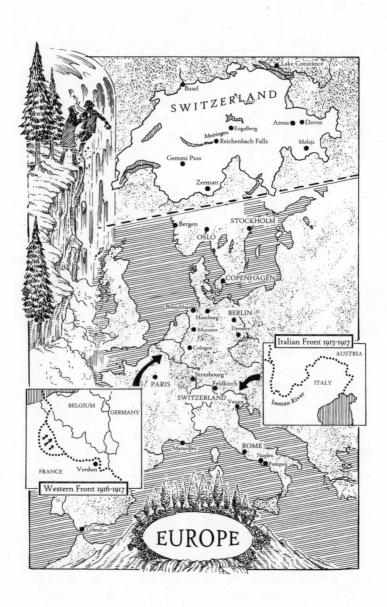

SWITZERLAND

Lake Constance

Basel

Arosa ● ● Davos

Engelberg
Meiringen ●
● Reichenbach Falls

Maloja

Gemmi Pass

Zermatt

Bergen

STOCKHOLM

OSLO

COPENHAGEN

Bremerhaven
Hamburg
Munster
Cologne

BERLIN
Dresden

Italian Front 1915-1917

AUSTRIA

ITALY

Isonzo River

Strasbourg
Feldkirch
PARIS
SWITZERLAND
Venice

BELGIUM
GERMANY

Marseilles

ROME

Naples
● Pompeii

FRANCE
Verdun

Western Front 1916-1917

Gibraltar

EUROPE

EUROPE

The Lure of the Alps

Reichenbach Falls — Davos and the Furka Pass —
The Alps — Paris — Flanders — Isonzo — Gibraltar —
Marseilles

In 1890 Conan Doyle decided to leave Southsea and
further his career in London. To do that successfully, he
felt he needed more specialised medical expertise. So,
in December that year he travelled to Berlin to study
tuberculosis at the feet of the renowned German physician
and microbiologist Robert Koch. The following month
he went to Vienna to conduct further research into
ophthalmology. He returned with his wife Louise via
Milan, Venice and Paris, and then set up his practice as
an eye specialist in Upper Wimpole Street. However his
sojourn there did not last long, as he was soon making a
huge success of his Sherlock Holmes stories for *The Strand
Magazine* and was able to give up medicine completely.

In August 1892 he holidayed with family and friends
(including Jerome K. Jerome) in Norway. Having
enjoyed the snow and mountains, he was happy the
following summer to accept an invitation to travel to
Lucerne in Switzerland, where he addressed a youth

camp organised by a crusading periodical called *The Young Man*. He took the opportunity to take long walks in the area, visiting Meiringen and the Reichenbach Falls. He also journeyed, partly by donkey, through the Gemmi Pass, which rises to heights of 2,332 metres and looks out on the Matterhorn, before proceeding to Zermatt.

His visit to Switzerland would have important consequences, for he was growing tired of writing Sherlock Holmes stories and wanted to get off what he regarded as the treadmill of regular monthly commitments. He had ambitions to write historical novels, which he regarded as proper literature. He realised that the Alps provided an ideal location to kill off Sherlock Holmes, or so it seemed. As recorded by Dr Watson, this act of (attempted) murder, carried out by Holmes's long-time nemesis, Professor James Moriarty, took place at the Reichenbach Falls.

Reichenbach Falls

For a charming week we wandered up the valley of the Rhone, and then, branching off at Leuk, we made our way over the Gemmi Pass, still deep in snow, and so, by way of Interlaken, to Meiringen. It was a lovely trip, the dainty green of the spring below, the virgin white of the winter above; but it was clear to me that never for one instant did Holmes forget the shadow which lay across him. In the homely Alpine villages or in the lonely mountain passes, I could still tell by his quick glancing eyes and his sharp scrutiny of every face that passed us, that he was well convinced that, walk where we would, we could not walk ourselves clear of the danger which was dogging our footsteps.

Once, I remember, as we passed over the Gemmi, and walked along the border of the melancholy Daubensee, a large rock which had been dislodged from the ridge upon our right clattered down and roared into the lake behind us.

In an instant Holmes had raced up on to the ridge, and, standing upon a lofty pinnacle, craned his neck in every direction. It was in vain that our guide assured him that a fall of stones was a common chance in the springtime at that spot. He said nothing, but he smiled at me with the air of a man who sees the fulfilment of that which he had expected. And yet for all his watchfulness he was never depressed. On the contrary, I can never recollect having seen him in such exuberant spirits. Again and again he recurred to the fact that if he could be assured that society was freed from Professor Moriarty he would cheerfully bring his own career to a conclusion.

'I think that I may go so far as to say, Watson, that I have not lived wholly in vain,' he remarked. 'If my record were closed to-night I could still survey it with equanimity. The air of London is the sweeter for my presence. In over a thousand cases I am not aware that I have ever used my powers upon the wrong side. Of late I have been tempted to look into the problems furnished by nature rather than those more superficial ones for which our artificial state of society is responsible. Your memoirs will draw to an end, Watson, upon the day that I crown my career by the capture or extinction of the most dangerous and capable criminal in Europe.'

I shall be brief, and yet exact, in the little which remains for me to tell. It is not a subject on which I would willingly dwell, and yet I am conscious that a duty devolves upon me to omit no detail.

It was on the third of May that we reached the little village of Meiringen, where we put up at the Englischer Hof, then kept by Peter Steiler the elder. Our landlord was an intelligent man and spoke excellent English, having served for three years as waiter at the Grosvenor Hotel in London. At his advice, on the afternoon of the fourth we set off together, with the intention of crossing the hills and spending the night at the hamlet of Rosenlaui. We had strict injunctions, however, on no account to pass the falls of Reichenbach, which are about halfway up the hills, without making a small detour to see them.

It is, indeed, a fearful place. The torrent, swollen by the melting snow, plunges into a tremendous abyss, from which the spray rolls up like the smoke from a burning house. The shaft into which the river hurls itself is an immense chasm, lined by glistening coal-black rock, and narrowing into a creaming, boiling pit of incalculable depth, which brims over and shoots the stream onward over its jagged lip. The long sweep of green water roaring forever down, and the thick flickering curtain of spray hissing forever upward, turn a man giddy with their constant whirl and clamour. We stood near the edge peering down at the gleam of the breaking water far below us against the black rocks, and listening to the half-human shout which came booming up with the spray out of the abyss.

The path has been cut halfway round the fall to afford a complete view, but it ends abruptly, and the traveller has to return as he came. We had turned to do so, when we saw a Swiss lad come running along it with a letter in his hand. It bore the mark of the hotel which we had just left and was addressed to me by the landlord. It appeared that within a very few minutes of our leaving, an English lady had arrived who was in the last stage of consumption. She had wintered at Davos Platz and was journeying now to join her friends at Lucerne, when a sudden haemorrhage had overtaken her. It was thought that she could hardly live a few hours, but it would be a great consolation to her to see an English doctor, and, if I would only return, etc. The good Steiler assured me in a postscript that he would himself look upon my compliance as a very great favour, since the lady absolutely refused to see a Swiss physician, and he could not but feel that he was incurring a great responsibility.

The appeal was one which could not be ignored. It was impossible to refuse the request of a fellow-countrywoman dying in a strange land. Yet I had my scruples about leaving Holmes. It was finally agreed, however, that he should retain the young Swiss messenger with him as guide and companion while I returned to Meiringen. My friend would stay some little time at the fall, he said, and would then walk slowly over the hill to Rosenlaui, where I was to rejoin him in the evening. As I turned away I saw Holmes, with his back against a rock and his arms folded, gazing down at the rush of the waters. It was the last that I was ever destined to see of him in this world.

'The Adventure of the Final Problem', *The Strand Magazine*, December 1893. Collected in *The Memoirs of Sherlock Holmes*, London and New York, 1894

Conan Doyle's trips to Norway and Switzerland gave him a taste for skiing. At one stage he even claimed to have introduced this sport to Switzerland. This was somewhat exaggerated, but he did help popularise it, particularly among British visitors. One method was his articles, such as this piece, 'An Alpine Pass on "Ski"', published in *The Strand Magazine* in December 1894, which gave a wonderful sense of the excitement he felt skiing in the mountains. It told of a lengthy 12-mile trek by ski over the 8,000-feet high Furka Pass from Davos to Arosa in Switzerland.

Davos and the Furka Pass

There is nothing peculiarly malignant in the appearance of a pair of ski. They are two slips of elm wood, eight feet long, four inches broad, with a square heel, turned-up toes, and straps in the centre to secure your feet. No one, to look at them, would guess at the possibilities which lurk in them. But you put them on and you turn with a smile to see whether your friends are looking at you, and then the next moment you are boring your head madly into a snow bank, and kicking frantically with both feet, and half-rising, only to butt viciously into that snow bank again, and your friends are getting more entertainment than they had ever thought you capable of giving.

That is when you are beginning. You naturally expect trouble then, and you are not likely to be disappointed. But as you get on a little, the thing becomes more irritating. The skis are the most capricious things upon the earth. One day you cannot go wrong with them; on another with the same weather and the same snow you cannot go right. And it is when you least expect it that things begin to happen. You stand on the crown of a slope, and you adjust your body for a rapid slide; but your ski stick motionless, and over you go on your face. Or you stand upon a plateau which seems to you to be as level as a billiard table, and in an instant, without cause or warning, away them shoot, and you are left behind, staring at the sky. For a person who suffers from too much dignity, a course in Norwegian snowshoes would have a fine moral effect.

Whenever you brace yourself for a fall, it never comes off. Whenever you think yourself absolutely secure, it is all over with you. You come to a hard ice slope at an angle of seventy-five degrees and you zigzag up it, digging the side of your ski into it, and feeling that if a mosquito settles upon you, you are gone. But nothing ever happens and you reach the top in safety. Then you stop upon the level to congratulate your companion, and you have just time to say, 'What a lovely view is this!' when you find yourself standing upon two shoulder-blades, with your ski tied tightly around your neck. Or again, you may have had a long outing without any misfortune at all, and as you shuffle back along the road, you stop for an instant to tell a group in the hotel veranda how well you are getting on.

Something happens – and they suddenly find that their congratulations are addressed to the soles of your ski. Then if your mouth is not full of snow, you find yourself muttering the names of a few Swiss villages to relieve your feelings. 'Ragatz' is a very handy word and may save a scandal.

But all this is in the early stage of skiing. You have to shuffle along the level, to zigzag, or move crab fashion, up the hills, to slide down without losing your balance, and above all to turn with facility. The first time you try to turn, your friends think it is part of your fun. The great ski flapping in the air has the queerest appearance – like an exaggerated negro dance. But this sudden whisk round is really the most necessary of accomplishments; for only so can one turn upon the mountain side without slipping down. It must be done without presenting one's heels to the slope, and this is the only way.

But granted that a man has perseverance, and a month to spare in which to conquer all these early difficulties, he will then find that skiing opens up a field of sport for him which is, I think, unique. This is not appreciated yet, but I am convinced that the time will come when hundreds of Englishmen will come to Switzerland for the skiing season, in March and April. I believe that I may claim to be the first save only two Switzers [the Branger brothers he writes about in this essay] to do any mountain work (though on a modest enough scale) on snow-shoes, but I am certain that I will not by many a thousand be the last.

The fact is it is easier to climb an ordinary peak, or to make a journey over the higher passes, in winter than in summer, if the weather is only set fair. In summer, you have to climb down as well as to climb up, and the one is as tiring as the other. In winter your trouble is halved, as most of your descent is a mere slide. If the snow is tolerably firm, it is much easier to zigzag up it on ski than to clamber over boulders ... Our project was to make our way from Davos to Arosa, over the Furka Pass, which is over nine thousand feet high [sic].

We were up before four in the morning, and had started at half past for the village of Frauenkirch, where we were to commence our ascent. A great pale moon was shining in a violet sky, with such stars as can only be seen in the tropics or the higher Alps. At quarter past five we turned from the road, and began to plod up the hillsides, over alternate banks of last year's grass, and slopes of snow. We carried our ski over our shoulders, and our ski-boots slung round our necks, for it was good walking where the snow was hard, and it was sure to be hard wherever the sun had struck it during the day. Here and there, in a hollow, we floundered into and out of a soft drift up to our waists; but on the whole it was easy going, and as much of our way led through fir woods, it would have been difficult to ski. About half-past six, after a long steady grind, we emerged from the woods, and shortly afterwards passed a wooden cow-house, which was the last sign of humans which we were to see until we reached Arosa.

The snow being still hard enough upon the slopes to give us a good grip for our feet, we pushed rapidly on, over rolling snow-fields with a general upward tendency. About half past seven the sun cleared the peaks behind us, and the glare upon the great expanse of virgin snow became very dazzling. We worked our way down a long slope, and then coming to the corresponding hill slope with a northern outlook, we found the snow as soft as powder, and so deep that we could touch no bottom with our poles. Here, then, we took to our snow-shoes, and zigzagged up over the long white haunch of the mountain, pausing at the top for a rest. They are useful things, the ski; for finding that the snow was again hard enough to bear us, we soon converted ours into a very comfortable bench, from which we enjoyed the view of a whole panorama of mountains, the names of which my readers will be relieved to hear I have completely forgotten.

The snow was rapidly softening now, under the glare of the sun, and without our ski all progress would have been impossible. We were making our way along the steep side of a valley with the mouth of the Furka Pass fairly in front of us. The snow fell away here at an angle of from fifty to sixty degrees, and as this steep incline, along the face of which we were shuffling, sloped away down until it ended in an absolute precipice, a slip might have been serious. My two more experienced companions walked below me for the half mile or so of danger, but soon we found ourselves upon a more reasonable slope, where one might fall with impunity. And now came the real sport of snow-shoeing. Hitherto, we had walked as fast as boots would do, over ground where no boots could pass. But now we had a pleasure which boots can never give. For a third of a mile we shot along over gently dipping curves, skimming down into the valley without a motion of our feet. In that great untrodden waste, with snow-fields bounding our vision on every side and no marks of life save the tracks of chamois and of foxes, it was glorious to whizz along in this easy fashion. A short zigzag at the bottom of the slope brought us, at half-past nine, into the mouth of the pass; and we could see the little toy hotels of Arosa, away down among the fir woods, thousands of feet beneath us.

Again we had half a mile or so, skimming along with our poles dragging behind us. It seemed to me that the difficulty of our journey was over, and that we had only to stand on our ski and let them carry us to our destination. But the most awkward place was yet in front. The slope grew steeper and steeper until it fell away into what was little short of being sheer precipices. But still that little, when there is soft snow upon it, is all that is needed to ring out another possibility of these wonderful slips of wood. The brothers Branger agreed that the slope was too difficult to attempt with the ski upon our feet. To me it seemed as if a parachute was the only instrument for which we had any use; but I did as I saw my companions do. They undid their ski, lashed the straps together, and turned them into a rather clumsy toboggan. Sitting on these, with our heels dug into the snow, and our sticks pressed hard down behind us, we began to move down the precipitous face of the pass. I think that both my comrades came to grief over it. I know that they were as white as Lot's wife at the bottom. But my own troubles were so pressing that I had no time to think of them. I tried to keep the pace within moderate bounds by pressing on the stick, which had the effect of turning the sledge sideways, so that one skidded down the slope. Then I dug my heels hard in, which shot me off backwards, and in an instant my two ski, tied together, flew away like an arrow from a bow, whizzed past the two Brangers, and vanished over the next slope, leaving their owner squatting in the deep snow.

It might have been an awkward accident in the upper fields, where the drifts are twenty or thirty feet deep. But the steepness of the place was an advantage now, for the snow could not accumulate to any great extent upon it. I made my way down in my own fashion. My tailor tells me that Harris tweed cannot wear out. This is a mere theory and will not stand a thorough scientific test. He will find samples of his wares on view from the Furka Pass to Arosa, and for the remainder of the day I was happiest when nearest the wall.

However, save that one of the Brangers sprained his ankle badly in the descent, all went well with us, and we entered Arosa at half-past eleven, having taken exactly seven hours over our journey. The residents of Arosa, who knew we were coming, had calculated that we could not possibly get there before one, and turned out to see us descend the steep pass just about the time when we were finishing a comfortable luncheon at the Seehof. I would not grudge them any innocent amusement, but still I was just as glad that my own little performance was over before they assembled with their opera-glasses.

'An Alpine Pass on "Ski"',
The Strand Magazine, December 1894

Conan Doyle was also a competent poet, his verse collected in *The Poems of Arthur Conan Doyle* (John Murray, 1922). His poem 'An Alpine Walk', with its reference to the popular Swiss resort of Engelberg, deserves a mention.

The Alps

Underneath the peaks of snow,
On the edge of nature's glacis,
Where the torrent far below
Ever rants, and roars and races,
And a man with just one slip
May come down a thousand paces;
So we walked from Engelberg
With the breeze upon our faces.

And we talked of many things
As we tramped through that oasis;
Of republics and of kings,
Of religion and its basis,
Of the patience of the poor,
Of the evil in high places,
So we walked from Engelberg
With the breeze upon our faces.

Then we spoke of England, too,
And the Anglo-Celtic races,
Also of the landlord crew
And our law and its disgraces,
With the selfishness of man
Which has left such evil traces;

So we walked from Engelberg
With the wind upon our faces.

And of grim Carlyle we spoke,
And of Froude's much argued cases,
How about the merest joke
He would pull the longest faces;
And of Madame, too, we talked,
Of her temper and her graces;
So we walked from Engelberg
With the wind upon our faces.

Spoke of Kipling – his command
Over life in all its phases,
How he held within his hand
All the cards from kings to aces.
Passing swift from passion's frown
Back to comedy's grimaces:
So we walked from Engelberg
With the wind upon our faces.

Well, it was a pleasant talk.
And perhaps in duller places
We may recollect that walk,
When with tightly fastened laces,
With our Alpenstocks in hand,
In that air which stirs and braces,
We three came from Engelberg
With the wind upon our faces.

'An Alpine Walk', *Independent*, 14 December 1893
(US) and *The Young Man*, January 1894 (UK)

Without the burden of writing monthly Sherlock Holmes stories, Conan Doyle now began to travel abroad more widely, particularly after his wife started to show manifest symptoms of tuberculosis. He saw it as his duty to take her to dry, healthy climes – notably Switzerland and further afield, in Egypt. Returning from the Swiss Alps in April 1894, he visited Paris where he stayed at the Hôtel Lord Byron and wrote this reflective piece:

Paris

It is a bold thing, on the strength of a few days' study of the Boulevards, to venture upon a comparison between two nations. Still it happens occasionally that in a flying visit one receives impressions more clearly than in a lengthy stay. Repetition blunts the effect. The most superficial observer cannot fail to be struck by the innumerable points of difference between our own ways and those of our neighbours, nor can he help weighing their respective advantages as judged from his own point of view. If these were drawn up in parallel columns, it would show, I think, that each nation has as much to teach as to learn.

To begin with the points which tell in favour of the French, their national temperance is the one which is most obvious and incontestable. In a day spent at a race-meeting we did not see one person the worse for drink. The general taste for light beers and wines, and the apparent impossibility of being served with spirits except in a liqueur glass, put a check on the abuse of stimulants. A French friend tells me that the working classes have taken to spirits of late years, but we saw no sums of it among them.

Then, of course, there is their unrivalled taste in the laying-out of their city and the beauty of their public buildings. Now that London has ceased to be a collection of vestry-governed villages, and has coalesced into a town, we shall no doubt, with our wealth and our energy, soon make up for past misgovernment. But a man must be blinded by prejudice if he can seriously claim that the streets of London are anything but squalid in comparison with those of Paris. And yet what fine opportunities we have! Fancy, for example, what an avenue a French architect would plan out from Trafalgar-square to the Houses of Parliament! How long would Parisian taste allow a sprinkling of dingy dwelling-houses and little cookshops to ruin what should be the central Street of London?

Again, at the risk of seeming unpatriotic, I cannot help thinking that the French are a cleaner and more tidy people than we are. From Calais to Nancy, right across the breadth of France, you look out of your carriage window and you always have that impression of neatness conveyed to you. Test the bed-linen of a London lodging-house against that of a French one – or the landlady's collar and cuffs, or the caps of the maids. I think they have the better of us there.

And again, to pass to a more contentious subject, their enjoyment of the Sunday seems to me infinitely more rational than our custom. Their picture galleries are as crowded on that day as our public-houses are. It

is surely the one day of the week on which everything
which is elevating and instructive should be put within
the reach of the people. They make it the brightest day,
and we make it the gloomiest – in which, by the way,
we differ from either the country of Luther or that of
Calvin. Another point to the credit of the French is
their management of the social evil. In our morality
we have made the streets of London the most openly
unmoral of those of any capital in Europe. I know no
other where it is difficult to take a lady out in some of
the principal streets at night. In France they recognise
that if an evil cannot be abolished it should be localised
and regulated.

Their law too is, as I am told, far cheaper and simpler
than ours. Of all things in the world surely justice is the
one which should be most within the reach of every
man. If it is so in France it is another immense advantage
which they have over us.

It is more pleasant to speak of the things in which
we can claim to be in front of them. In their view of
duelling and of war they seem to be 50 years behind
us. We look on fighting as an occasional unpleasant
necessity. The Frenchman seems to regard it as the grand
test of the worth of a nation. Battles and generals give
their names to the vast majority of streets and squares.
No doubt the military history of France is magnificent,
but she gives her soldiers an undue predominance over
her savants and her saints. We are far more humane
to animals. It is impossible to sit quietly behind some
of the French cabmen and see how they ill-treat their
over-worked, underfed horses. In our lover of outdoor

exercise and athletics we have a great advantage, though the French seem to be coming round to our view of the matter. The middle-aged Frenchman is very middle-aged indeed. It is seldom that you see among them any of those hard, grizzled-haired men who are common enough over here, where a man preserves some of his youthful habits long after his youth is past. The French generals will have some curious material to deal with when they call their reserves in.

The newspapers are astonishingly inaccurate as compared to ours. One of them sent us to a theatrical performance which had ceased a fortnight before. Such a thing would be inconceivable in London. The Legion of Honour seems to have become as much part of the equipment of a well-dressed Frenchman as his hat or his boots. We sat in the Grand Café of the Louvre, and tried to count the red-ribbon gentlemen as they passed. What can the value of a distinction be which is shared by so many? And what bitterness there must be amongst the excluded!

And then there is the position of woman, in which, again, I think that we are far in front of the French. The unmarried girl is still fenced round with restrictions which seem to us to be preposterous. And the lover arranges matters on a strictly cash basis with the parent or guardian. We met one young lady who had had three offers, all of which had fallen through because there was a difference between what the lover required and what the guardian could promise.

Such are a few of the impressions left upon my mind by what I saw and heard in Paris. They may at least serve

to give someone who knows more about it something
to contradict.

'Paris in 1894: A Superficial Impression',
The Speaker, 21 April 1894

He returned regularly to various countries in Europe,
often for holidays, over the next twenty years. Perhaps
the most unusual time he spent on the continent was in
July 1911 when he participated in the International Road
Competition organised by Prince Heinrich (or Henry) of
Prussia, the younger brother of Kaiser Wilhelm. Driving
a 16 horse-power Lorraine-Dietrich motor car, this
took him across a substantial area of Western Germany
(from Bad Homburg, through Cologne and Munster to
Bremerhaven) and Britain.

Denied once again the opportunity of signing up for
military service at the start of the First World War because
of his age, Conan Doyle nevertheless spent time in Europe
during the conflict, writing what were basically propaganda
reports of visits to various Allied fronts. These appeared in
June 1916, principally in the *Daily Chronicle* in the United
Kingdom and the *NewYork American* in the United States, and
were collected in his book *A Visit to Three Fronts* published
that same year. Although not travel pieces, he managed to
convey a good sense of place. The passage below describes
his time with British troops in Flanders.

Flanders

And now we are there – in what is surely the most
wonderful spot in the world, the front firing trench,

the outer breakwater which holds back the German tide. How strange that this monstrous oscillation of giant forces, setting in from east to west, should find their equilibrium here across this particular meadow of Flanders. 'How far?' I ask. '180 yards,' says my guide. 'Pop!' remarks a third person just in front. 'A sniper,' says my guide; 'take a look through the periscope.' I do so. There is some rusty wire before me, then a field sloping slightly upwards with knee-deep grass, then rusty wire again, and a red line of broken earth. There is not a sign of movement, but sharp eyes are always watching us, even as these crouching soldiers around me are watching them. There are dead Germans in the grass before us. You need not see them to know that they are there. A wounded soldier sits in a corner nursing his leg. Here and there men pop out like rabbits from dug-outs and mine-shafts. Others sit on the fire-step or lean smoking against the clay wall. Who would dream to look at their bold, careless faces that this is a front line, and that at any moment it is possible that a grey wave may submerge them? With all their careless bearing I notice that every man has his gas helmet and his rifle within easy reach.

...

One more experience of this wonderful day – the most crowded with impressions of my whole life. At night we take a car and drive north, and ever north, until at a late hour we halt and climb a hill in the darkness. Below is a wonderful sight. Down on the flats, in a huge semi-circle, lights are rising and falling. They are very brilliant, going up for a few seconds and then dying down. Sometimes a dozen are in the air at one time. There are the dull thuds of explosions and an occasional rat-tat-tat. I have seen nothing like it, but the nearest comparison would be an enormous ten-mile railway station in full swing at night, with signals winking, lamps waving, engines hissing and carriages bumping. It is a terrible place down yonder, a place which will live as long as military history is written, for it is the Ypres Salient. What a salient it is, too! A huge curve, as outlined by the lights, needing only a little more to be an encirclement. Something caught the rope as it closed, and that something was the British soldier. But it is a perilous place still by day and by night. Never shall I forget the impression of ceaseless, malignant activity which was borne in upon me by the white, winking lights, the red sudden glares, and the horrible thudding noises in that place of death beneath me.

. . .

The afternoon saw us in the Square at Ypres. It is the city of a dream, this modern Pompeii, destroyed, deserted and desecrated, but with a sad, proud dignity which made you involuntarily lower your voice as you passed through the ruined streets. It is a more considerable place than I had imagined, with many traces of ancient grandeur. No words can describe the absolute splintered wreck that the Huns have made of it. The effect of some of the shells has been grotesque. One boiler-plated water-tower, a thing forty or fifty feet high, was actually standing on its head like a great metal top. There is not a living soul in the place save a few pickets of soldiers, and a number of cats which become fierce and dangerous. Now and then a shell still falls, but the Huns probably know that the devastation is already complete.

We stood in the lonely grass-grown Square, once the busy centre of the town, and we marvelled at the beauty of the smashed cathedral and the tottering Cloth Hall beside it. Surely at their best they could not have looked more wonderful than now. If they were preserved even so, and if a heaven-inspired artist were to model a statue of Belgium in front, Belgium with one hand pointing to the treaty by which Prussia guaranteed her safety and the other to the sacrilege behind her, it would make the most impressive group in the world. It was an evil day for Belgium when her frontier was violated, but it was a worse one for Germany. I venture to prophesy that it will be regarded by history as the greatest military as well as political error that has ever been made. Had the great guns that destroyed Liège made their first breach at Verdun, what chance was there for Paris? Those few weeks of warning and preparation saved France, and left Germany as she now is, like a weary and furious bull, tethered fast in the place of trespass and waiting for the inevitable pole-axe.

We were glad to get out of the place, for the gloom of it lay as heavy upon our hearts as the shrapnel helmets did upon our heads. Both were lightened as we sped back past empty and shattered villas to where, just behind the danger line, the normal life of rural Flanders was carrying on as usual. A merry sight helped to cheer us, for scudding downwind above our heads

came a Boche aeroplane, with two British at her tail
barking away with their machine guns, like two swift
terriers after a cat. They shot rat-tat-tatting across the
sky until we lost sight of them in the heat haze over the
German line.

A Visit to Three Fronts,
London and New York, 1916

Isonzo
He also visited French troops in the Argonne (as close to
Verdun as he could get). But before then he made his way to
the Italian front where his reliably supportive journalistic
style was considered particularly necessary in an uncertain
period following the Italian army's retreat from Trentino
in May 1916.

My first experience of the Italian line was at the portion
which I have called the gap by the sea, otherwise the
Isonzo front. From a mound behind the trenches an
extraordinary fine view can be got of the Austrian
position, the general curve of both lines being marked,
as in Flanders, by the sausage balloons which float behind
them. The Isonzo, which has been so bravely carried
by the Italians, lay in front of me, a clear blue river, as
broad as the Thames at Hampton Court. In a hollow
to my left were the roofs of Gorizia, the town which
the Italians are endeavouring to take. A long desolate
ridge, the Carso, extends to the south of the town, and
stretches down nearly to the sea. The crest is held by
the Austrians and the Italian trenches have been pushed
within fifty yards of them. A lively bombardment was

going on from either side, but so far as the infantry goes there is none of that constant malignant petty warfare with which we are familiar in Flanders. I was anxious to see the Italian trenches, in order to compare them with our British methods, but save for the support and communication trenches I was courteously but firmly warned off.

A Visit to Three Fronts,
London and New York, 1916

Gibraltar

After the First World War, he ventured to other places, often on lecture tours promoting the spiritualist cause which he had espoused so passionately in the early years of the First World War. For three decades from his student days in Edinburgh he had maintained a scientist's scepticism towards paranormal affairs, but in 1916, following a series of deaths amongst his nearest and dearest, he changed his mind and became a fully fledged spiritualist. One such foreign trip was made to Australia from August 1920 to March 1921, when he was accompanied by his wife Jean, their three children, Adrian, Denis and Jean, a maid and his secretary Major Wood. The party travelled on the SS *Naldera* from Liverpool on 13 August 1920, reaching Gibraltar later that month:

We had a favourable journey across the Bay and came without adventure to Gibraltar, that strange crag, Arabic by name, African in type, Spanish by right, and British by might. I trust that my whole record has shown me to be a loyal son of the Empire, and I recognise that

we must have a secure line of communications with
the East, but if any change could give us Ceuta, on the
opposite African coast, instead of this outlying corner
of proud old Spain, it would be good policy as well as
good morality to make the change. I wonder how we
should like it if the French held a garrison at Mount St.
Michael in Cornwall, which would be a very similar
situation. Is it worth having a latent enemy who at
any time might become an active one, or is it wiser to
hold them to us by the memory of a great voluntary
act of justice? They would pay, of course, for all quays,
breakwaters and improvements, which would give
us the money to turn Ceuta into a worthy substitute,
which could be held without offending the pride of a
great nation, as old and proud as ourselves. The whole
lesson of this great war is that no nation can do what
is unjust with impunity, and that sooner or later one's
sin will find one out. How successful seemed all the
scheming of Frederick of Prussia! But what of Silesia
and of Poland now? Only on justice can you build with
a permanent foundation, and there is no justice in
our tenure of Gibraltar. We had only an hour ashore,
a great joy to the children, and carried away a vague
impression of grey-shirted Tommies, swarthy loungers,
one long, cobblestoned street, scarlet blossoms, and a
fine Governor's house, in which I picture that brave old
warrior, Smith-Dorrien, writing a book which will set
all the critics talking, and the military clubs buzzing a
year or two from now ...

The Wanderings of a Spiritualist,
London and New York, 1921

On this voyage he returned via the South of France:

Marseilles

> It was indeed wonderful to find ourselves at Marseilles once more, and, after the usual unpleasant douane formalities, which are greatly ameliorated in France as compared to our own free trade country, to be at temporary rest at the Hôtel du Louvre.
>
> ...
>
> I never take a stroll through a French town without appreciating the gulf which lies between us and them. They have the old Roman civilisation, with its ripe mellow traits, which have never touched the Anglo-Saxon, who, on the other hand, has his raw Northern virtues which make life angular but effective. I watched a scene to-day inconceivable under our rule. Four very smart officers, captains or majors, were seated outside a cafe. The place was crowded, but there was room for four more at this table on the sidewalk, so presently that number of negro privates came along and occupied the vacant seats. The officers smiled most good-humouredly, and remarks were exchanged between the two parties, which ended in the high falsetto laugh of a negro. These black troops seemed perfectly self-respecting, and I never saw a drunken man, soldier or civilian, during two days.
>
> *The Wanderings of a Spiritualist*,
> London and New York, 1921

His subsequent travels tended to be further afield but he returned to Europe in October 1929, shortly before his death, when he made his way to Scandinavia, passing through Holland, Netherlands, Denmark, Sweden and Norway. This was very much a spiritualist tour and he wrote nothing of note about the places he visited.

Constantinople

TURKEY

LIBYAN
DESERT

EGYPT

Cairo ☐ ☐ Suez Canal

ARABIA

Korosko ☐

Assouan ☐

Wadi Halfa ☐

Port Sudan ☐

Suakin ☐

Aden ☐

MIDDLE
EAST

MIDDLE EAST

The Libyan Desert – Upper Egypt (Assouan, Korosko, Wadi Halfa and the Nile Valley) – Nubia – Constantinople – Suez Canal – Aden

In November 1895 Conan Doyle took his ailing wife, Louise, to Egypt. They stayed at the Mena House Hotel, within walking distance of the Pyramids, seven miles southwest of Cairo. In search of winter sun, they then joined a cruise to Upper Egypt on the River Nile on the Thomas Cook company paddle-steamer *Nicrotis*. The whole trip lasted six months since, while he was there, he decided – with typical bravado – to sign up as the foreign correspondent for *The Westminster Gazette*. He reported on a British expedition against the Mahdi in Dongola (Sudan) and recalled these few months in his *Memories and Adventures*:

The Libyan Desert

I do not know how many temples we explored during that tour, but they seemed to me endless, some dating back to the mists of antiquity and some as recent as Cleopatra and the Roman period. The majestic continuity of Egyptian History seems to be its most remarkable feature. You examine the tombs of the First Dynasty at Abydos and there you see carved deep in the stone the sacred hawk, the goose, the plover, the signs of Horus and Osiris, of Upper and Lower Egypt. These were carved long before the Pyramids were built and can hardly be less ancient than 4000 B.C. Then you inspect a temple built by the Ptolemies, after the date of Alexander the Great, and there you see the same old symbols cut in the same old way. There is nothing like this in the world. The Roman and the British Empires are mushrooms in comparison. Judged by Egyptian standards the days of Alfred the Great would be next door to our own, and our customs, symbols and way of thinking the same. The race seems to have petrified, and how they could do so without being destroyed by some more virile nation is hard to understand.

Their arts seem to have been high but their reasoning power in many ways contemptible. The recent discovery of the King's tomb near Thebes — I write in 1924 — shows how wonderful were their decorations and the amenities of their lives. But consider the tomb itself. What a degraded intelligence does it not show! The idea that the body, the old outworn greatcoat which was once wrapped round the soul, should at any cost be preserved is the last word in materialism. And the hundred baskets of provisions to feed the soul upon its journey! I can never believe that a people with such ideas could be other than emasculated in their minds — the fate of every nation which comes under the rule of a priesthood.

It had been suggested that I should go out to the Salt Lakes in the Desert some 50 miles from Cairo, and see the old Coptic Monastery there. Those ancient monasteries, the abode alternately of saints and perverts – we saw specimens of each – have always aroused my keen interest, dating as they do to very early days of Christianity. Indeed, their date is often unknown, but everything betokens great age and the spirit which founded them seems to have been that of the hermits who in the third and fourth centuries swarmed in these wildernesses.

Leaving my wife at Mena, I went with Colonel Lewis of the Egyptian army, an excellent companion and guide. On arriving at a wayside station, we found a most amazing vehicle awaiting us, a sort of circus coach, all gilding and frippery. It proved to be the coach of state which had been prepared for Napoleon III on the chance that he would come to open the Suez Canal. It was surely a good bit of work, for here it was still strong and fit, but absurdly out of place in the majestic simplicity of the Libyan Desert.

Into this we got and set forth, the only guide being wheel-marks across the sand which in some of the harder places were almost invisible. The great sand waste rolled in yellow billows all around us, and far behind us the line of green trees marked the course of the Nile. Once a black dot appeared which, as it grew nearer, proved to be some sort of Oriental on foot. As he came up to us he opened a blackened mouth, pointed to it, and cried, 'Moya! Moya!' which means water. We had none and could only point encouragingly to the green belt behind us, on which with a curse he staggered upon his way.

A surprising adventure befell us, for the heavens suddenly clouded over and rain began to fall, an almost unknown thing in those parts. We lumbered on, however, with our two horses, while Colonel Lewis, who was keen on getting fit, ran behind. I remember saying to him that in my wildest dreams I never thought that I should drive across the Libyan Desert in an Emperor's coach with a full colonel as carriage dog. Presently in the fading light the horses slowed down, the Nubian driver descended, and began alternately scanning the ground and making gestures of despair. We realised then that he had lost the tracks and therefore that we had no notion where we were, though we had strong reasons to believe that we were to the south of the route. The difficulty was to know which was north and which south. It was an awkward business since we had no food or water and could see no end to our troubles. The further we moved the deeper we should be involved. Night had closed in, and I was looking up at the drifting scud above us when in the chink of two clouds I saw for an instant a cluster of stars, and made sure that they were the four wheels of Charles's Wain. I am no astronomer, but I reasoned that this constellation would lie to the north of us, and so it proved, for when we headed that way, examining the ground every hundred yards or so with matches, we came across the track once more.

Our adventures, however, were not over, and it was all like a queer dream. We had great difficulty in keeping the track in the darkness, and the absurd coach lumbered and creaked while we walked with lanterns ahead of it. Suddenly to our joy we saw a bright light in the gloom. We quickened our pace, and came presently to a tent with a florid bearded man seated outside it beside a little table where he was drawing by the light of a lamp. The rain had cleared now, but the sky was still overcast. In answer to our hail this man rather gruffly told us that he was a German surveyor at work in the desert. He motioned with his hand when we told him whither we were bound, and said it was close by. After leaving him we wandered on, and losing the tracks we were again very badly bushed. It seemed an hour or two before to our joy we saw a light ahead and prepared for a night's rest at the halfway house, which was our immediate destination. But when we reached the light what we saw was a florid bearded man sitting outside a small tent with a lamp upon a table. We had moved in a circle. Fresh explanations – and this time we really did keep to the track and reached a big deserted wooden hut, where we put up the horses, ate some cold food, and tumbled, very tired, into two of the bunks which lined it.

The morrow made amends for all. It broke cold and clear and I have seldom felt a greater sense of exhilaration than when I awoke and walking out before dressing saw the whole endless desert stretching away on every side of me, yellow sand and black rock, to the blue shimmering horizon. We harnessed up and within a few hours came on the Natron Lake, a great salt lake, with a few scattered houses at one end where the workers

dry out and prepare the salt. A couple of miles off was
the lonely monastery which we had come to see – less
lonely now, but before the salt works were established
one of the most inaccessible places one could imagine. It
consisted of a huge outer wall, which seemed to be made
of hardened clay. It had no doors or windows save one
little opening which could be easily defended against the
prowling Arabs, but I fear the garrison would not be very
stout-hearted, for it was said to be the fear of military
service which caused many of the monks to discover that
they had a vocation. On being admitted I was conscious
that we were not too welcome, though the military title
of my companion commanded respect. We were shown
round the inner courtyard, where there were palm
trees and a garden, and then round the scattered houses
within the wall. Near the latter there was, I remember,
a barrel full of some substance which seemed to me,
both by look and feel, to be rounded pieces of some
light stone, and I asked if it were to hurl down at the
Arabs if they attacked the door. It proved to be the store
of bread for the Monastery. We were treated to wine,
which was sweet tent wine, which is still used, I believe,
in the Holy Communion, showing how straight our
customs come from the East. The Abbot seemed to me
to be a decent man, but he complained of illness and was
gratified when I overhauled him thoroughly, percussed
his chest, and promised to send him out some medicine
from Cairo. I did so, but whether it ever reached my
remote patient I never learned. Some of the brothers,
however, looked debauched, and there was a general air
of nothing-to-do, which may have been deceptive but

which certainly impressed me that day. As I looked from
the walls and saw the desert on all sides, unbroken save
for one blue corner of the salt lake, it was strange to
consider that this was all which these men would ever
see of the world, and to contrast their fate with my own
busy and varied existence. There was a library, but the
books were scattered on the floor, all of them old and
some no doubt rare. Since the discovery of the 'Codex
Sinaiticus' I presume that all these old Coptic libraries
have been examined by scholars, but it certainly seemed
to me that there might be some valuable stuff in that
untidy heap ...

Memories and Adventures, London and New York, 1924

His contemporary articles for *The Westminster Gazette*
provide a first-hand account of his experiences.

Upper Egypt (Assouan, Korosko, Wadi Halfa and the Nile Valley)

Eight hard days of travel has brought us from Assouan
to Korosko – days which some of us at least will never
forget. For eight days the broad brown river has swirled
past us, and for eight days we have jogged along its
Arabian bank upon our camels, throwing ourselves
down at night under the nearest palm trees and
sleeping with the glorious blue velvet of a Nubian sky
for our bed hangings. How one did sleep after such a
day of heat and dust, and how murderous one felt when
with the rising of the moon there came the voice of
the Daily News, 'Reveille, gentlemen, Reveille, if you

please!' Then the shouts for Abbas, Mansour, Hussein, Mahomet, the sleepy 'Aiwas' in reply, the low murmur of a waking camp, the crackling of sticks and a single red spot of fire in the darkness, the roarings of the camels as their loads were once more fastened upon their backs, and then with our Bishareen Arab guide riding his white dromedary at our head, away went the long string of horses, asses, and camels for another day's march. Looking forward or back, the silent sponge-footed camels were like a row of flitting ghosts in the light of a waning moon. Dim palm trees fringed our path, and the river glinted behind them. In front the Southern Cross rose slowly above the skyline. For an hour at a time we would move without a word or a sound under the solemn loveliness of a tropical sky. Then from the van of the column would come a rich rolling voice:

Nut-brown maiden, you have a hazel, hazel eye,
Nut-brown maiden, you have a hazel eye,

A hazel eye is thine, love,
The image in it is mine, love,
Nut-brown maiden, you have a hazel eye.

And even as we broke into the chorus of our own English song there would rise a high quavering voice from behind us, pitched in the sad minor key which seems to have been the universal music of primitive man, and Hussein, Mahomet, Abbas, and the rest, would follow us under the starlight singing some plaintive Arabic love song of their own. But the moon would fade, the east would lighten, red feathers of cloud would drift in a colourless sky, and then, within a few minutes, night would have changed to full day, the golden edge of the sun would be showing over the orange desert, and all our vague night-begotten sentiment would turn to practical questions of how far we had come and where we were to halt.

He who travels with baggage camels – or 'baggles' as we came to call them – must be a man of patience. The baggle will go so far in a day, and at such a pace, but no other. His pace is two and a half miles an hour and he is the earliest and most consistent supporter of the eight-hours-a-day movement, for if he is forced to do more, he at once fines his employer fifteen pounds, by the simple expedient of lying down and dying. It follows then, that upon a journey one cannot hope to make more than a steady twenty miles a day. You may have the fleetest steed of Araby between your knees, but what use it is its fleetness, when the supercilious, slow-going baggle carries your food and your blankets upon his back? The riding camel can, in his curious jog trot, cover his fifty or sixty miles a day, and on a good Makloo's saddle the motion is not an unpleasant one; but you cannot carry both yourself and your needs upon your trotter. The ships of the desert, like those of the sea, have to regulate their pace by that of the lame duck of the squadron. Before leaving Assouan Colonel Lewis, the commandant, had warned us that we should need a guard, and had given us instructions to go up with 300 uploaded unloaded camels which were being escorted by some Egyptian cavalry. As luck would have it, however, the convoy passed us unseen, and as they were travelling light they rapidly increased their lead, so that they were soon two days ahead of us. The only traces which we ever saw of them were numerous footprints and two grotesquely swollen dead camels by the roadside. We had, I think, been a little inclined to underrate the necessity of the precautions which the commandant had enjoined upon us, in ordering us to remain near the convoy, and it is certain that we made no great effort to join it; but events showed us that he was perfectly right and we perfect perfectly wrong.

The Westminster Gazette, 27 April 1896

Our good friend the Commandant of Korosko – the walnut-faced Turk who struck us as being so much more virile than his Egyptian subordinates – kindly promised us to send us on by the first steamer to Halfa. A telegram from Assouan informed us, however, that no steamers were at present on their way, so beds were pitched on the verandah, and five weary men settled down to a comfortable night's rest. Hardly was the last lantern extinguished, however, before the hooting of a whistle from down the river informed us that the telegram was wrong, and that a steamer was close to the landing stage. We had five minutes in which to pack our beds and luggage, find our servants, dress, and reach the boat. Then might have been seen the sight of three great dailies and two penny evenings clawing madly for boots in the darkness, and shrieking for Hassan, Abdul and Mansour, while every fresh whistle of the steamer sounded near and louder until her yellow lights were seen rounding the point beneath us. The lighting of a lantern hastily improved the matter, for it served to reveal a very frisky little scorpion which was gambolling about among the stocking feet. However, the scorpion was killed, the luggage packed, the servants found, and at the critical moment our Turkish friends saved the situation by appearing in person with a fatigue party of stalwart soldiers who made short work of our luggage, and so within a few minutes of having settled comfortably down into our beds we were on board of a little buck-jumping sternwheeler upon our way to Halfa. The river was low, the boat heavily laden with fodder, and the soft thud and jar of the sandbank became a very familiar sensation; but with patience and luck we came through all right, and at daybreak yesterday we found ourselves lying opposite to the little scattered mud-coloured frontier.

The Westminster Gazette, 4 May 1896

He looked back on Egypt in his 1898 novel *The Tragedy of the Korosko*, which began as a serial in *The Strand Magazine* the previous year. This account of the kidnapping of a party of tourists by a band of Mahdist 'Dervishes' showed considerable respect for the physical feats of people of the desert, even if it was cast in a contemporary propagandist and Islamophobic framework. However, the appeal of vast arid spaces to Conan Doyle was abundantly clear.

Nubia

It is a singular country, this Nubia. Varying in breadth from a few miles to as many yards (for the name is

only applied to the narrow portion which is capable of
cultivation), it extends in a thin, green, palm-fringed
strip upon either side of the broad coffee-coloured
river. Beyond it there stretches on the Libyan bank
a savage and illimitable desert, extending to the
whole breadth of Africa. On the other side an equally
desolate wilderness is bounded only by the distant
Red Sea.

Between these two huge and barren expanses Nubia
writhes like a green sandworm along the course of
the river. Here and there it disappears altogether, and
the Nile runs between black and sun-cracked hills,
with the orange drift-sand lying like glaciers in their
valleys. Everywhere one sees traces of vanished races
and submerged civilisations. Grotesque graves dot the
hills or stand up against the sky-line: pyramidal graves,
tumulus graves, rock graves – everywhere, graves.
And, occasionally, as the boat rounds a rocky point,
one sees a deserted city up above – houses, walls,
battlements, with the sun shining through the empty
window squares. Sometimes you learn that it has been
Roman, sometimes Egyptian, sometimes all record
of its name or origin has been absolutely lost. You ask
yourself in amazement why any race should build in so
uncouth a solitude, and you find it difficult to accept
the theory that this has only been of value as a guard-
house to the richer country down below, and that
these frequent cities have been so many fortresses to
hold off the wild and predatory men of the south. But
whatever be their explanation, be it a fierce neighbour,
or be it a climatic change, there they stand, these grim

and silent cities, and up on the hills you can see the graves of their people, like the port-holes of a man-of-war. It is through this weird, dead country that the tourists smoke and gossip and flirt as they pass up to the Egyptian frontier ...

The little *Korosko* puffed and spluttered her way up the river, kicking up the white water behind her, and making more noise and fuss over her five knots an hour than an Atlantic liner on a record voyage. On deck, under the thick awning, sat her little family of passengers, and every few hours she eased down and sidled up to the bank to allow them to visit one more of that innumerable succession of temples. The remains, however, grow more modern as one ascends from Cairo, and travellers who have sated themselves at Gizeh and Sakara with the contemplation of the very oldest buildings which the hands of man have constructed, become impatient of temples which are hardly older than the Christian era. Ruins which would be gazed upon with wonder and veneration in any other country are hardly noticed in Egypt. The tourists viewed with languid interest the half-Greek art of the Nubian bas-reliefs; they climbed the hill of Korosko to see the sun rise over the savage Eastern desert; they were moved to wonder by the great shrine of Abou-Simbel, where some old race has hollowed out a mountain as if it were a cheese; and, finally, upon the evening of the fourth day of their travels they arrived at Wady Halfa, the frontier garrison town, some few hours after they were due, on account of a small mishap in the engine-room. The next morning was to be devoted to an expedition to the famous rock of Abousir, from which a great view may be obtained of the second cataract. At eight-thirty, as the passengers sat on deck after dinner, Mansoor, the dragoman, half Copt, half Syrian, came forward, according to the nightly custom, to announce the programme for the morrow.

'Ladies and gentlemen,' said he, plunging boldly into the rapid but broken stream of his English, 'to-morrow you will remember not to forget to rise when the gong strikes you for to compress the journey before twelve o'clock. Having arrived at the place where the donkeys expect us, we shall ride five miles over the desert, passing a temple of Ammon-ra, which dates itself from the eighteenth dynasty, upon the way, and so reach the celebrated pulpit rock of Abousir. The pulpit rock is supposed to have been called so, because it is a rock like a pulpit. When you have reached it, you will know that you are on the very edge of civilisation, and that very little more will take you into the country of the Dervishes, which will be obvious to you at the top. Having passed the summit, you will perceive the full extremity of the second cataract, embracing wild natural beauties of the most dreadful variety. Here all very famous people carve their names – and so you will carve your names also.' Mansoor waited expectantly for a titter, and bowed to it when it arrived. 'You will then return to Wady Halfa, and there remain two hours to suspect the Camel Corps, including the grooming of the beasts, and the bazaar before returning, so I wish you a very happy good-night.'

This fictional Nile cruise took on a different complexion when the passengers were captured by a band of Mahdists and forced to trek unwillingly through the desert. But the scenery and the ethnography had their compensations.

There was nothing to show them as they journeyed onwards that they were not on the very spot that they had passed at sunset upon the evening before. The region of fantastic black hills and orange sand which bordered the river had long been left behind, and everywhere now was the same brown, rolling, gravelly plain, the ground-swell with the shining rounded pebbles upon its surface, and the occasional little sprouts of sage-green camel-grass. Behind and before it extended, to where far away in front of them it sloped upwards towards a line of violet hills. The sun was not high enough yet to cause the tropical shimmer, and the wide landscape, brown with its violet edging, stood out with a hard clearness in that dry, pure air. The long caravan straggled along at the slow swing of the baggage-camels. Far out on the flanks rode the vedettes, halting at every rise, and peering backwards with their hands shading their eyes. In the distance their spears and rifles seemed to stick out of them, straight and thin, like needles in knitting.

... Across the brown of the hard, pebbly desert there had been visible for some time a single long, thin, yellow streak, extending north and south as far as they could see. It was a band of sand not more than a few hundred yards across, and rising at the highest to eight or ten feet. But the prisoners were astonished to observe that the Arabs pointed at this with an air of the utmost concern, and they halted when they came to the edge of it like men upon the brink of an unfordable river. It was very light, dusty sand, and every wandering breath of wind sent it dancing into the air like a whirl of midges. The Emir Abderrahman tried to force his camel into it, but the creature, after a step or two, stood still and shivered with terror. The two chiefs talked for a little, and then the whole caravan trailed off with their heads for the north, and the streak of sand upon their left.

'What is it?' asked Belmont, who found the dragoman riding at his elbow. 'Why are we going out of our course?'

'Drift sand,' Mansoor answered. 'Every sometimes the wind bring it all in one long place like that. To-morrow, if a wind comes, perhaps there will not be one grain left, but all will be carried up into the air again. An Arab will sometimes have to go fifty or a hundred miles to go round a drift. Suppose he tries to cross, his camel breaks its legs, and he himself is sucked in and swallowed.'

. . .

And now they came upon one of the most satisfying sights on which the human eye can ever rest. Here and there, in the depressions at either side of the road, there had been a thin scurf of green, which meant that water was not very far from the surface. And then, quite suddenly, the track dipped down into a bowl-shaped hollow, with a most dainty group of palm-trees, and a lovely green sward at the bottom of it. The sun gleaming upon that brilliant patch of clear, restful colour, with the dark glow of the bare desert around it, made it shine like the purest emerald in a setting of burnished copper. And then it was not its beauty only, but its promise for the future: water, shade, all that weary travellers could ask for. Even Sadie was revived by the cheery sight, and the spent camels snorted and stepped out more briskly, stretching their long necks and sniffing the air as they went. After the unhomely harshness of the desert, it seemed to all of them that they had never seen anything more beautiful than this. They looked below at the green sward with the dark, star-like shadows of the palm-crowns; then they looked up at those deep green leaves against the rich blue of the sky, and they forgot their impending death in the beauty of that Nature to whose bosom they were about to return.

The wells in the centre of the grove consisted of seven large and two small saucer-like cavities filled with peat-coloured water, enough to form a plentiful supply for any caravan. Camels and men drank it greedily, though it was tainted by the all-pervading natron. The camels were picketed, the Arabs threw their sleeping-mats down in the shade, and the prisoners, after receiving a ration of dates and of doora, were told that they might do what they would during the heat of the day, and that the Moolah would come to them before sunset. The ladies were given the thicker shade of an acacia tree, and the men lay down under the palms. The great green leaves swished slowly above them; they heard the low hum of the Arab talk, and the dull champing of the camels, and then in an instant, by that most mysterious and least understood of miracles, one was in a green Irish valley, and another saw the long straight line of Commonwealth Avenue, and a third was dining at a little round table opposite to the bust of Nelson in the Army and Navy Club, and for him the swishing of the palm branches had been transformed into the long-drawn hum of Pall Mall. So the spirits went their several ways, wandering back along the strange, un-traced tracks of the memory, while the weary, grimy bodies lay senseless under the palm-trees in the Oasis of the Libyan Desert.

The Tragedy of the Korosko
London and New York, 1898

In July 1906 the inevitable happened, and Louise Conan Doyle died of the tuberculosis which had caused such anguish to her and her family for over a decade. Little more than a year later in September 1907, her widower married Jean Leckie, a much younger woman whom he had met and fallen in love with in 1897. Their honeymoon took them to Germany and through the Mediterranean, as they visited Paris, Berlin, Venice, Rome, Constantinople, Dresden, Naples, Athens and Smyrna. Conan Doyle looked back on this trip in his memoirs:

Constantinople

Years of peaceful work followed my marriage, broken only by two journeys to the Mediterranean, in the course of which we explored some out-of-the-way

portions of Greece, and visited Egypt, where I found
hardly one single man left of all the good fellows
whom I had once known. In the course of our travels
we visited Constantinople, looking at the great guns
in the forts on the Dardanelles, with little thought
of all the British lives which were to be sacrificed
upon those low, dark, heather-clad hills which slope
down to the Northern shore. In Constantinople we
attended the weekly selamlik of Abdul Hamid, and
saw him with his dyed beard and the ladies of his
harem as they passed down to their devotions. It was
an incredible sight to Western eyes to see the crowd
of officers and officials, many of them fat and short
of wind, who ran like dogs behind his carriage in the
hope that they might catch the Imperial eye. It was
Ramadan, and the old Sultan sent me a message that he
had read my books and that he would gladly have seen
me had it not been the Holy month. He interviewed
me through his Chamberlain and presented me with
the Order of the Medjedie, and, what was more
pleasing to me, he gave the Order of the Chevekat
to my wife. As this is the Order of Compassion, and
as my wife ever since she set foot in Constantinople
had been endeavouring to feed the horde of starving
dogs who roamed the streets, no gift could have been
more appropriate.

We were admitted secretly and by very special
favour into the great Mosque of Sophia during the
sacred festival which is known as the Night of Power.
It was a most marvellous spectacle as from the upper
circle of pillared arches we looked down upon 60,000

lighted lamps and 12,000 worshippers, who made, as
they rose and fell in their devotions, a sound like the
wash of the sea. The priests in their high pulpits were
screaming like seagulls, and fanaticism was in the air.
It was at this moment that I saw a woman – I will not
call her a lady – young and flighty, seat herself jauntily
on the edge of the stone parapet, and look down at the
12,000 men who were facing us. No unbeliever should
be tolerated there, and a woman was the abomination
of abominations. I heard a low deep growl and saw
fierce bearded faces looking up. It only needed one
fiery spirit to head the rush and we should have been
massacred – with the poor consolation that some of
us at least had really asked for it. However, she was
pulled down, and we made our way as quickly and
as quietly as possible out of a side door. It was time,
I think.

Memories and Adventures,
London and New York, 1924

His experience of the Middle East continued after the
First World War when he passed through the Suez Canal,
en route to Australia.

Suez Canal

We tied up to the bank soon after entering the Canal,
and lay there most of the night while a procession of
great ships moving northwards swept silently past
us in the ring of vivid light cast by their searchlights
and our own. I stayed on deck most of the night to

watch them. The silence was impressive – those huge
structures sweeping past with only the slow beat of
their propellers and the wash of their bow wave on
either side. No sooner had one of these great shapes
slid past than, looking down the Canal, one saw the
brilliant head light of another in the distance. They are
only allowed to go at the slowest pace, so that their
wash may not wear away the banks. Finally, the last had
passed, and we were ourselves able to cast off our warps
and push southwards. I remained on deck seeing the
sun rise over the Eastern desert, and then a wonderful
slow-moving panorama of Egypt as the bank slid slowly
past us. First desert, then green oases, then the long
line of rude fortifications from Kantara downwards,
with the camp fires smoking, groups of early busy
Tommies and endless dumps of stores. Here and to the
south was the point where the Turks with their German
leaders attempted the invasion of Egypt, carrying flat-
bottomed boats to ford the Canal. How they were ever
allowed to get so far is barely comprehensible, but
how they were ever permitted to get back again across
one hundred miles of desert in the face of our cavalry
and camelry is altogether beyond me. Even their guns
got back untaken. They dropped a number of mines
in the Canal, but with true Turkish slovenliness they
left on the banks at each point the long bamboos on
which they had carried them across the desert, which
considerably lessened the work of those who had to
sweep them up. The sympathies of the Egyptians seem
to have been against us, and yet they have no desire to
pass again under the rule of the Turk. Our dominion

has had the effect of turning a very poor country into a very rich one, and of securing some sort of justice for the fellah or peasant, but since we get no gratitude and have no trade preference it is a little difficult to see how we are the better for all our labours. So long as the Canal is secure – and it is no one's interest to injure it – we should be better if the country governed itself. We have too many commitments, and if we have to take new ones, such as Mesopotamia, it would be well to get rid of some of the others where our task is reasonably complete. 'We never let the youngsters grow up,' said a friendly critic. There is, however, I admit, another side to the question, and the idea of permitting a healthy moral place like Port Said to relapse into the hotbed of gambling and syphilis which it used to be, is repugnant to the mind. Which is better – that a race be free, immoral and incompetent, or that it be forced into morality and prosperity? That question meets us at every turn.

The children have been delighted by the fish on the surface of the Canal. Their idea seems to be that the one aim and object of our excursion is to see sharks in the sea and snakes in Australia. We did actually see a shark half ashore upon a sandbank in one of the lower lakes near Suez. It was lashing about with a frantic tail, and so got itself off into deep water. To the west all day we see the very wild and barren country through which our ancestors used to drive upon the overland route when they travelled by land from Cairo to Suez. The smoke of a tiny mail-train marks the general line of that most desolate road. In the evening we were through the Canal and marked the rugged shore upon our left down which the Israelites pursued their way in the direction of Sinai. One wonders how much truth there is in the narrative. On the one hand it is impossible to doubt that something of the sort did occur. On the other, the impossibility of so huge a crowd living on the rare wells of the desert is manifest. But numbers are not the strong point of an Oriental historian. Perhaps a thousand or two may have followed their great leader upon that perilous journey. I have heard that Moses either on his own or through his wife was in touch with Babylonian habits. This would explain those tablets of stone, or of inscribed clay burned into brick, which we receive as the Ten Commandments, and which only differ from the moral precepts of other races in the strange limitations and omissions. At least ten new ones have long been needed to include drunkenness, gluttony, pride, envy, bigotry, lying and the rest.

At one point he docked at Aden:

Aden

Aden is remarkable only for the huge water tanks cut to catch rain, and carved out of solid rock. A whole captive people must have been set to work on so colossal a task, and one wonders where the poor wretches got water themselves the while. Their work is as fresh and efficient as when they left it. No doubt it was for the watering, not of the population, but of the Egyptian and other galleys on their way to Punt and King Solomon's mines. It must be a weary life for our garrison in such a place. There is strange fishing, sea snakes, parrot fish and the like. It is their only relaxation, for it is desert all round.

The Wanderings of a Spiritualist,
London and New York, 1921

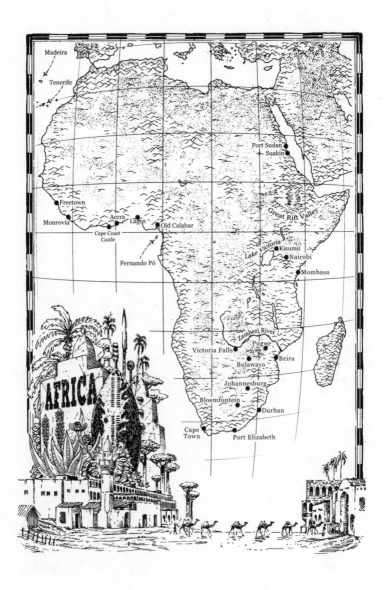

AFRICA

From Coast to Coast

West Africa – Old Calabar – Bloemfontein – Premier
Diamond Mine – Khami Ruins, Bulawayo – Pungwe
Marshes, Portuguese East Africa – Nairobi – Game
Reserve – Rift Valley and Kisumu – Port Sudan

Conan Doyle's involvement with the African continent
began immediately after university with his trip down the
west coast of the continent as the ship doctor on the SS
Mayumba. He wrote several accounts of this, including in
his memoirs. At the time he was particularly engrossed
with photography, so several of his most vivid recollections
are linked to this hobby.

West Africa

It was with a light heart that I packed up my boxes
about the middle of October, and set out for Liverpool
to join my vessel. There was a charm about the great list
of ports at which we were advertised to call – Madeira,
Tenerife, Canary, Sierra Leone, Monrovia, Cape Coast
Castle, Bonny, Lagos, Old Calabar, and a score of others,

whose very names had been hitherto unknown to me. I had a beatific vision of strange negatives. The luxuriant growth of the African forest; the haughty grace of the untamed savage as he trod his native wilderness, or yearned in his simple untutored way for a slice out of the calf of your leg; the mighty rivers and the cloud-capped mountains – all these should be transferred to the tell-tale paper and be a record among countless generations yet unborn of the adventurous spirit of their ancestors. Such were a few of my milder aspirations as I stowed away my chemicals in the old deal box, and got together all the other photographic apparatus necessary for a lengthy campaign.

The voyage was to extend over rather more than three months, and the important question now arose as to what was to be taken and how much of each. I knew that everything there was any possibility of my needing must go with me, as I was informed that there was no town on the coast where decent gunpowder, to say nothing of such refinements as photographic necessities, could he obtained. It may be of interest to some other unfortunate wanderer to know the conclusions at which I arrived, and how far they were justified by my subsequent experience ...

It was as well that we got it comfortably down among the lumber, for immediately after leaving the Mersey we found ourselves in the middle of a terrible hurricane. To quote an old Scotch song – 'It blew a most awfu' blow.' We passed down the Irish Sea and into the channel, steaming before the wind in a fog so thick that it was hardly possible to see a wave before it came crashing in a green wall over our bulwarks. Had we but known it, the ill-fated 'Clan Macduff' must at one time have been close beside us, but, even had we seen it, any attempt at a rescue would have been fruitless in such a sea. It was not until our third day out, when we were fairly in the Bay of Biscay, that the wind began to moderate, and that some appearance of order was restored among our goods and chattels. My own cabin had been flooded by a wave, but I was too busy attending to the prostrate ladies to have time to think about my own woes. As the sky cleared, however, and the angry sea changed into a long, greasy swell, there was a gradual divorce between our passengers and the basins. One of them even had the hardihood to appear upon deck with a sickly look of confidence upon his face, which, I regret to state, suddenly faded away, to give place to an earnest and all-absorbing interest in the appearance of the water alongside of the vessel.

...

After a week's pitching and tossing we made the rugged island of Porto Sancto inhabited by a few scattered fishermen and collectors of seaweed. Here, encouraged by the steadiness of the ship, my friend Tom and I began operations, and with very fair success. We had a most enjoyable little run ashore next morning at Funchal, the capital of Madeira, obtaining several excellent little 'bits' and characteristic groups. Our best result was a photograph of the town, done from the sea-side with a very wide-angle lens in the evening. We found that the soft light of the setting sun was better adapted for good work than the midday glare, as the whitewashed houses tend to produce a very chalky effect. This tendency to chalkiness caused me much mental perturbation in all the tropical views which included anything in the shape of a house. It was only by reducing the strength of the developer that I was enabled to obtain harmonious pictures, and even then some were sadly marred by the hard, white effects. We were unfortunate that day in other ways, as a misunderstanding as to who was to regulate the requisite exposure very nearly ruined one of our finest plates.

Leaving Madeira behind us, we got into the trade winds, and found ourselves within thirty-six hours lying abreast of Vera Cruz, the capital of Tenerife. I regret to say that, though we had a momentary glimpse of the Peak, it became clouded over with mist, and we were unable to add it to our little series. We got capital views of some of the lesser mountains, however, and of the quaint little town itself, with its cathedral and frowning batteries. It was these batteries which had the honour of inflicting upon our immortal Nelson the only defeat he ever sustained, and in the cathedral the ensign captured from him on that occasion used to be hung. A midshipman came ashore, however, some years ago from a British man-of-war, and managed to break into the cathedral and carry off the flag. What became of the young reefer I know not, though rumour says dismissal from the service was the reward of his ill-judged patriotism.

After touching at Canary we pursued our way to Sierra Leone. This was the most pleasant part of our voyage, steaming steadily for seven days through a lonely and unruffled sea ...

Sierra Leone — cheerfully designated 'The White Man's Grave' — is situated on the bed of a river about five miles from the sea. As we lay in front of the town a whole fleet of canoes passed us having aboard some negro chieftain of eminence, as was indicated by the shouts of the rowers and the beating of the drums. The appearance of this flotilla induced me to fix to my camera the rapid lens and shutter. Under the combined influence of current and paddles they were passing very rapidly. They were so far away that the lens, having been focussed for the 'distance', did not require to be altered. In such cases I never use the focussing glass, but trusted to my eye to inform me when the nearest canoe was crossing the axis of the lens. Let me here once again lay stress upon having the aperture in the shutter several times the diameter of the lens in the direction in which the shutter moves, otherwise the amount of light which reaches the plate is practically reduced, without the advantages resulting from the same reduction of light if caused by a smaller diaphragm. In this particular instance one plate was a failure, but three others were all fairly successful.

It would probably weary my readers to hear of our uneventful cruise down that fever-haunted coast. Many of our men were struck down by the miasma, and for some weeks the quinine bottle was more familiar to me than the developing tray. Passing the model colony of Liberia — pompously called 'The New States' — and flying the American flag with one star in the corner, we rounded Cape Palmas and steamed down what may be fairly called 'The Cannibal Coast,' if we may believe the accounts of the natives given by those who know them best and have had most opportunities of studying their customs. A great deal has been said about the regeneration of our black brothers and the latent virtues of the swarthy races. My own experience is that you abhor them on first meeting them, and gradually learn to dislike them a very great deal more as you become better acquainted with them. In spite of the epidemic of sickness which broke out among us, I succeeded in getting photographs of many of the men of light and leading among these interesting and primitive races. The majority of them are depicted as, to quote Mark Twain, wearing a smile and nothing more. I have one, however, resplendent in all the glory of a plug hat and umbrella. The rest of his clothing, however, he had apparently left behind in the family wardrobe!

A rather amusing incident occurred at Accra, which was our first important port after leaving Cape Coast Castle. A large canoe full of negroes happened to be engaged fishing within twenty yards of the ship, as she lay at her anchorage. I thought the opportunity of getting a characteristic and lifelike group too good to be neglected. I therefore got up my camera and was engaged focussing them, when, to my astonishment they gave a united yell and sprang overboard. The effect of the row of woolly heads glaring at me from the other side of the boat was so ludicrous that I attempted to make good use of the opportunity and expended a plate upon the group. I am sorry to say, however, that the results exhibited little better than a chaotic mass of white foam, distorted faces, and waving paddles, hardly distinguishable from each other. I then hailed them and asked what was the matter. 'Me know dem thing,' shouted one of them. 'Me serve in man-o'-war. Dem thing gatling gun – all same Queen's ship have in tops. What you want point him at poor nigger for?' It was only when I had carried off the obnoxious instrument that the unfortunate fishermen could be persuaded to creep into their boat once more.

At Lagos I was myself knocked over with the fever, and was for several days in a semi-delirious condition. I am blessed, however, with a strong constitution, and before reaching Bonny, at the mouth of the Niger, I was able to crawl upon deck – very weak, it is true, but otherwise none the worse for what was undoubtedly a dangerous attack.

I had an opportunity, while at Bonny, of photographing one of the great war-chiefs, Wawirra by name – a sort of African Duke of Cambridge. He informed us that in his last campaign he had taken five hundred men. I remarked that I could 'take' as many as that in a single moment. This small joke had to be explained to him at great length, until it gradually lost what little fun there was originally in it, and struck me as being about the most dismal piece of pleasantry that had ever been perpetrated. In spite of my frantic efforts I am convinced that that African left the ship with the deeply-rooted impression that I was a blood-curdling warrior, and was consumed by a chronic thirst for human gore! I afterwards learned that, in spite of his high position and ferocious exterior, he was a poor fighter himself – 'too full of pluck to stand up,' as my informant expressed it, so he lies at the bottom of the canoe and does the heavy work and the shouting ...

Fernando Po was our next port, and here again I was enabled to secure something which I flatter myself was a photographic novelty, namely, the picture of a large shark as it cruised about close to the surface of the water. These tigers of the sea are as numerous as flies on some parts of the African coast. If you drop anything with a splash into the water you will see far down on the confines of the realms of eternal darkness a horrible shadow appear, and this will come flickering up, developing a fin here and a patch of colour there; then you will see a cruel green eye looking up at you out of the water, and you will know that you have seen the Devil, or as near an approach to him as is to be found in this world. After photographing my friend I had the ingratitude to put a bullet through his dorsal fin, which seemed to astonish him considerably; for, after a wobble to express his opinion of the unwarrantable liberty I taken with him, he dived under the ship and disappeared.

Another interesting picture which I secured was that of the interior of one of the old slave barracoons, with the iron rings and fetters still riveted to the walls. In these horrible caves, dug out of the rock, hundreds of unfortunate negroes – men, women, and children – used to be packed pending the arrival of the slaver. From what I saw of them I should think that, when full of their struggling, thirsty occupants, the Black Hole of Calcutta would be a sanatorium by comparison.

Leaving Fernando Po we arrived at Old Calabar – a British colony situated sixty miles up the Calabar

River. This was the turning point in our voyage, and we lay in the river for nearly a week, getting cargo aboard ...

There were few incidents worth recording upon our homeward journey, until after we left Madeira. The Peak of Tenerife was once again shrouded in vapour, and avoided our ever-watchful lenses.

After leaving Madeira we had a little temporary excitement, owing to the ship taking fire. The cause of it was unknown, but the mischief lay at the bottom of one of the great coal bunkers. It seemed a serious matter, as the greater part of our cargo consisted of palm oil. We hoped at first that it would smoulder until our arrival in Liverpool, but by the third morning matters looked so threatening that energetic measures had to be taken. All hands were called, and as many men as would fit sent below to move the coal, while the rest hoisted up the buckets from below. I took a photograph of the deck at this time, but such was the coolness and discipline aboard that no one looking casually at the picture would guess that anything was amiss. Four ominous streams of smoke, however, from the bunker-ventilators, disclose to a nautical eye the great danger in which the vessel lay. After twenty-four hours' anxiety, however, we were able to get the fire under, and the weary and exhausted crew were permitted to take a much-needed rest. The remainder of our voyage was devoid of interest, and the 14th of January found us once again in the docks of Liverpool ...

'On the Slave Coast with a Camera', *British Journal of Photography,* 31 March, 7 April 1882

He wrote more fully elsewhere about his experiences at Old Calabar, a trading station in the Efik city-state of that name, now a city in Cross River State in south-eastern modern Nigeria.

Old Calabar

The great ship is lying at her anchor in the Calabar River, and the groaning of her chains and the whizzing of her steam-winches as she hoists the hogsheads of palm-oil on board show that her loading is not yet done. What can the idlers and passengers do, then? Why not explore, a little higher up, the mysterious pea soup-coloured stream, and, since a camera is to be had, take a few plates, which may be of interest in days to come?

It needs but a word to the amiable captain, and the thing is done. Down goes the gig with a splash into the water. Her crew of red-capped, copper-faced Kroomen clamber like monkeys down the falls, and then sit like swarthy Apollos with the long oars in their dark sinewy hands. The camera is handed into the stern; its owner and his companions follow, and push off from the high black hull; four blades dip simultaneously into the water; and the long, thin boat speeds swiftly on its way.

The popular notion of a West African river is not usually associated with beauty. The fever and the miasma have given an evil reputation to those deadly streams, and their very name calls up visions of decaying vegetation and of malarious swamps. Yet in the coolness of the early morning there was much that was beautiful in the luxuriant foliage which skirted the banks and the tangle of palm trees which formed a background in every direction.

Opposite us in the town of Old Calabar, a confused assemblage of brown thatched native huts, and just along the water's edge a row of whitewashed factories in which the European agents do their business. Hills, all clad in feathery foliage, rise up behind the town. It is worth a plate now, for at this early hour there is some hope of a soft effect. A little later and the glaring sun will admit only those of chalky and hard effects which mar so many tropical pictures.

As we row lazily upstream there is much on either bank which would furnish a pretty and interesting picture. Here is a great mangrove tree with its hundred sinuous roots – a vegetable patriarch which has flourished there for generations. There on that muddy bank is a great crocodile basking in the morning sun. We turn our camera on him and are about to perpetuate his charms, but he looks up, sees what he no doubt considers to be the latest invention in fire-arms turned in his direction, and at once shuffles off into the yellow stream. Birds of the most beautiful colours, and butterflies almost as large as the birds, dart above and across our course, like flashes of coloured lightning. No doubt when the photographic millennium has come we shall be able to take these too, and to reproduce all their native brilliancy. At present we could but watch and wish.

Here is an island in mid-stream; a fluffy, feathery, palmtree-bearing island, on which some fever-proof Paul and Virginia might have taken up their abode. It is as pretty a 'bit' as could be desired and we take it *en passant*. Even as we take the cap from the lens a solemn old pelican emerges from the bushes, like some quaint genius loci, and includes himself in the picture.

We have another characteristic group now in a dozen or more canoes coming down the stream with merchandise for Calabar. Their occupants with their dark childish smiling faces make an excellent study. Behind them comes the larger canoe of some chief. A priest in the bows waves a miniature broom from side to side, by means of which the evil spirits are supposed to be swept out of the great man's way. His lordship sits very complacently under an awning in the sheets of the boat, and the canoemen under his august eye bend sturdily to their strokes.

And now our appetite reminds us that, interesting as all this may he, the sight of our breakfasts would be more so still. The tide and stream aid our homeward journey and within an hour we are seated round the hospitable board of the *Mayumba*. Perhaps, some day in England, looking over our portfolio we may acknowledge that that morning was spent to advantage.

'With a Camera on an African River',
British Journal of Photography, 30 October 1885

Once again Conan Doyle offered a fictional account of these events, this time in his story 'J. Habakuk Jephson's Statement'.

November 13. A most extraordinary event has happened, so extraordinary as to be almost inexplicable. Either Hyson has blundered wonderfully, or some magnetic influence has disturbed our instruments. Just about daybreak the watch on the fo'csle-head shouted out that

Conan Doyle (third from left) with colleagues aboard SS Hope en route to the
Arctic, 1872.

" HOLMES GAVE ME A SKETCH OF THE EVENTS."

The great detective on the move. Sherlock Holmes with Dr Watson en route to Herefordshire (illustration by Sidney Paget, *The Boscombe Valley Mystery, Strand Magazine*, 1891, above). Holmes and his arch enemy Professor Moriarty battle on the Reichenbach Falls, Meiringen, Switzerland (illustration by Sidney Paget, *The Adventure of the Final Problem, Strand Magazine*, 1893, right).

Skiing in Switzerland. With friends and family Davos, 1894 (above); with guide in Alps, 1894 (below).

Conan Doyle in Egypt, 1896 (above); his photo of Bishareen Arabs at Aswan, 1896 (below).

Travel by hot air balloon. Conan Doyle (on right) preparing to fly in 'City of York' at Hendon, 1901.

Conan Doyle and gondolier Venice, 1908.

Conan Doyle and his new wife Jean on honeymoon Parthenon Athens, 1908.

Conan Doyle by melon stall Tangiers, 1909 (above); playing cricket on RMS Dunottar Castle en route to Portugal, Spain and Morocco, 1909 (below).

On a horse, Algeria, 1911.

Golf in Le Touquet, 1912 (above); Conan Doyle at the French front, 1916 (below).

Astride the Alberta/British Columbia border, 1914 (above left); tepee in the Rockies, 1914 (above right); baseball in Jasper, 1914 (below).

Conan Doyle (with two of his children) in Colombo Sri Lanka, 1920 (above); Conan Doyle and his children at the Blue Mountains, New South Wales, Australia, 1921 (below).

Conan Doyle and family with Harry Houdini and wife, Atlantic Beach, 1923; Conan Doyle and his wife visiting a Hollywood Studio; Conan Doyle at Catalina Island California, 1923.

Overlooking the River Zambezi, 1929 (above); outside offices of Trans-Zambezia Railway, Beira, Portuguese East Africa (Mozambique), 1929 (below).

The Conan Doyles' ship, the Karoa, being met by local boats at Dar es Salaam, 1929
(above); Conan Doyle's photo of a Kenyan welcome in Nairobi, 1929 (below).

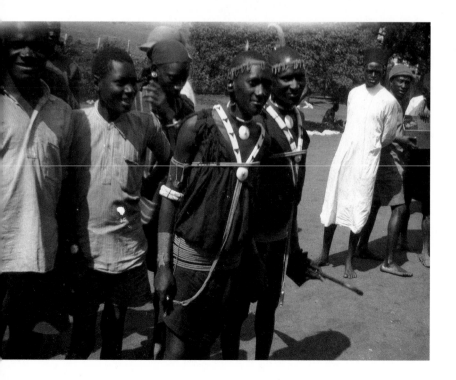

Conan Doyle and wife arriving in Stockholm, 1929 (above); Life's Journey (below).

he heard the sound of surf ahead, and Hyson thought he saw the loom of land. The ship was put about, and, though no lights were seen, none of us doubted that we had struck the Portuguese coast a little sooner than we had expected. What was our surprise to see the scene which was revealed to us at break of day! As far as we could look on either side was one long line of surf, great, green billows rolling in and breaking into a cloud of foam. But behind the surf what was there! Not the green banks nor the high cliffs of the shores of Portugal, but a great sandy waste which stretched away and away until it blended with the skyline. To right and left, look where you would, there was nothing but yellow sand, heaped in some places into fantastic mounds, some of them several hundred feet high, while in other parts were long stretches as level apparently as a billiard board. Harton and I, who had come on deck together, looked at each other in astonishment, and Harton burst out laughing. Hyson is exceedingly mortified at the occurrence, and protests that the instruments have been tampered with. There is no doubt that this is the mainland of Africa, and that it was really the Peak of Teneriffe which we saw some days ago upon the northern horizon. At the time when we saw the land birds we must have been passing some of the Canary Islands. If we continued on the same course, we are now to the north of Cape Blanco, near the unexplored country which skirts the great Sahara. All we can do is to rectify our instruments as far as possible and start afresh for our destination.

'J. Habakuk Jephson's Statement',
The Cornhill Magazine, January 1884

Despite being a best-selling author, Conan Doyle wanted to sign up as a soldier in the Boer War, which began in South Africa in 1899. As he was deemed too old for service, he worked in a military hospital in Bloemfontein. He wrote up his experiences in several places, including his history of the conflict, *The Great Boer War* (1900). This is from his memoirs:

Bloemfontein

> We had been waiting for orders and now we suddenly left Capetown on March 26, reaching East London on the 28th. There we disembarked, and I was surprised to find Leo Trevor, of amateur theatrical fame, acting as transport officer. In spite of his efforts (I hope it was not through them) our hospital stuff was divided between two trains, and when we reached Bloemfontein after days of travel we found that the other half had wandered off and was engulfed in the general chaos. There were nights of that journey which I shall never forget – the great train roaring through the darkness, the fires beside the line, the dark groups silhouetted against the flames, the shouts of 'Who are you?' and the crash of voices as our mates cried back, 'The Camerons', for this famous regiment was our companion. Wonderful is the atmosphere of war. When the millennium comes the world will gain much, but it will lose its greatest thrill.
>
> It is a strange wild place, the veldt, with its vast green plains and peculiar flat-topped hills, relics of some extraordinary geological episode. It is poor pasture – a sheep to two acres – so it must always be sparsely

inhabited. Little white farms, each with its eucalyptus grove and its dam, were scattered over it. When we crossed the Free State border by a makeshift bridge, beside the ruins of the old one, we noticed that many of these little houses were flying the white flag. Everyone seemed very good-humoured, burghers and soldiers alike, but the guerilla war afterwards altered all that.

It was April 2, and 5 a.m. when we at last reached the capital of the Free State, and were dumped down outside the town in a great green expanse covered with all sorts of encampments and animals. There was said to be a large force of Boers close to the town, and they had cut up one of our columns a few days before at Sanna's Post. Some troops were moving out, so I, with Gwynne whom I had known in Egypt, and that great sportsman Claude de Crespigny, set forth to see what we could, an artilleryman lending me his led horse. There was nothing doing, however, for it was Brother Boer's way never to come when you wanted him and always when you didn't. Save for good company, I got nothing out of a long hot day.

Memories and Adventures, London and New York, 1924

Conan Doyle returned to Africa towards the end of his life, a full decade after the First World War, when he undertook a lengthy journey with his family to South and East Africa from November 1928 to April 1929. His main aim was to advance the cause of spiritualism, which dominated his life after the First World War. As a result, his accounts of South African towns on this trip are often clouded by his religious beliefs, and therefore bland, but he had interesting observations on the wider countryside, and, later, when he continued north, on parts of Rhodesia and Kenya. Here he recounted a visit to the Premier Diamond Mine at Cullinan, 25 miles east of Pretoria, where in 1905 the Cullinan Diamond, the largest ever rough diamond of gem quality, was found.

Premier Diamond Mine

One more excursion was undertaken before we left Johannesburg. It was to the Premier Diamond Mine, which involved a trip of 130 miles or so, much of it over very rough roads. It was a tiring excursion, but well worth doing in spite of its unfortunate sequel to myself. The mine is the biggest hole in the ground ever yet dug by man, and it literally made one gasp when one looked down into it and saw men like ants crawling about at the bottom, against a background of bluish soil. It is in this soil, hardened to rock, that the diamonds are found, though why it should be so is still a puzzle. The procedure is to blast a whole long line of the rock, to put the broken-off chunks into little trucks, to run the trucks down to the machines, and there to smash them up until they are mere gravel, at which stage the diamonds are extracted. As we looked down into the abyss the blasting began – several tons of dynamite being exploded in many different shots. First we saw the smoke of the fuses, then we saw the little figures all running for shelter, and then a dead silence until the first crash, followed by volleys of them, more like a barrage in the Great War than anything I have seen. The instant the silence was resumed out rushed the little figures, and were tugging and hauling to get the debris into the trucks, for they are paid by results, and a Kaffir can earn as much as 12s. or 15s. a day, which is an enormous wage in his eyes. It was a very animated scene. A wire cage runs on a steel rope down into the pit, and we all went down in this so as to get a closer view and finally returned in it to the surface. The place where the great Cullinan diamond was excavated was shown to us, but even moderate stones seem to be rare, and though we saw quite a large handful which had been cleared up that day, there was none which could not have been set in an ordinary ring.

Our African Winter, London, 1929

On his way north he passed through Bechuanaland (now Botswana) and visited the Khami Ruins near Bulawayo in Rhodesia, now Zimbabwe.

Khami Ruins, Bulawayo

It is a wearisome journey of two nights and a day – nearly 600 miles – from Jo'burg to Bulawayo, but we found it less trying than we had expected. The train was slow but comfortable, and the line was so good that one could write without extreme difficulty. The first morning found us at historical Mafeking. Then for a long day we traversed Bechuanaland, with the legendary Kalahari Desert upon our left, in which some of our scientific men think that life originated. It is a huge waste now, in which a few Bushmen lead a mysterious existence. I hope the time will come when the artesian well will change all that and the wilderness may blossom. At present it is rather the other way, and the area of desert seems inclined to come east and south so as to involve the Karoo. Everyone agrees that the country grows drier and droughts more common.

We stopped at many little wayside stations where the Bechuanas brought down rude wooden figures of animals for sale. I amused them by doing some conjuring tricks with them from the open carriage window, and they stared open-eyed when they saw a little wooden crocodile scamper up my arm. I expect I have introduced a new occupation into Bechuanaland, and that many will try to acquire the art ...

It has an attraction of its own, that vast Kalahari Desert, to which I have alluded so casually. The huge tract is inhabited only by a few tribes of wandering Bushmen, the survivors of a race which once stretched from the caves of Northern Spain to those of Rhodesia, or even farther south. They are peaceable enough, these poor people, most miserable of the human race; but the land has to be policed, and patrols are sent out upon camels. This Bechuanaland police are a curious body, comprising some 30 Europeans and 250 natives. It is a deadly land. Once in 1879 a well-equipped body of Boers trekked across it, but they left their oxen and their wagons upon the face of the desert and they hardly escaped with their lives. The police, however, are used to its conditions, and they with their camels perform extraordinary journeys. The camels only need watering every fifth day, and the record is held by a policeman and camel who traversed without water, the man for three and the camel for twelve days. Both were laid up by overindulgence when they came to the wells. A party recently with motors

went right across the Kalahari, covering 500 miles. To
their amazement they found in the centre a large tract
of land, the Mecca of the Bushmen, as fertile as the best
land in Africa. I hope it will be long before the poor little
people are driven out of their last refuge.

The second morning found us at Bulawayo, which has
now some 30,000 inhabitants, 7,000 of which are white.
We were amazed to find what a young giant it was, with
its broad streets and fine shops, which would do credit
to any English provincial town. The Grand Hotel presents
every reasonable comfort to the traveller. As our time
was limited and we wanted to see the Victoria Falls, we
started sightseeing at once, and set off that very afternoon
in the care of Mr. Vincent, the theatre representative, who
showed us great courtesy and attention. The Khami Ruins,
some 14 miles from the town, were our destination.

These are of the same class as the great Zimbabwe
Ruins and present the same mystery. There are remains
of a considerable city and the walls are built of squared
stone without mortar. There are no signs or inscriptions
of any kind. I have examined a great many implements
found on this or similar sites, and none of them present
any signs of civilisation. They vary from stone neolithic
weapons to copper and finally to iron spear-heads and
axes, but at no time would it seem that a cultured race
occupied the ground.

At the same time curious signs of trade intercourse
with distant regions crop up. I observed a broken
Nankin Chinese plate and some chips of undoubted
Venetian glass. Malcolm got a huge scorpion from
under a stone and cunningly enticed it into his killing

bottle. It was the one living inhabitant which we saw in what was once a great city.

...

The reason for these walled towns, which are found in all parts of Rhodesia, is plainly that they should be centres for the ancient gold-miners, and possibly forts for protection against the natives. The old gold diggings are usually found not far off, though strangely enough in the case of the chief town, Zimbabwe, there are none in the immediate neighbourhood. It was probably a central depot or collecting station, and there are traces of a line of block-houses which protect an old road from there to the point of shipment at Sofala. Thence the gold is usually supposed to have gone to Ophir in Southern Arabia, and then on to Phoenicia and the world at large. It is reckoned that not less than 100 million pounds worth of gold have been taken out, so that it probably formed a considerable proportion of the old-world supply.

The portion mined has been very thoroughly gutted, but luckily for modern investors and for Rhodesia itself the ancients had no pumps; and when on the 100-foot level they struck water, as they usually did, they abandoned the mine.

The most successful mines in the country now are continuations of these abandoned workings. There was one curious point which was confirmed to me by two separate observers, namely that some of the stopes or rock cuttings are only 18 inches wide and yet have been worked. No ordinary man could find room to wield a pick there, so the inference is that the workers of old were enslaved Bushmen, who were small enough to fit into such a crevice. It is a curious problem why the whole place with its flourishing industry should have been suddenly and utterly abandoned. The probable reason, I think, is that the first wave of the fierce virile Bantu, the ancestors of Zulus, Matabeles, and all fighting negroid tribes, came down from the North and cleared the country. This would probably be in the early Middle Ages, and then wave after wave followed, who exterminated the aborigines, and would have utterly conquered the whole of Africa had they not at last met the Dutch and the British coming up from the South. The assagai then, though it beat the bow, was no use against the musket.

Our African Winter, London, 1929

His most challenging experiences came when he journeyed by train through the Pungwe Marshes from Salisbury, now Harare, to Beira in Portuguese East Africa, now Mozambique.

Pungwe Marshes, Portuguese East Africa

We have bad news as we hear that a section of the line connecting us with Beira has been washed away by the heavy rains. It is very serious, as our tickets are taken for the boat at Beira next Friday, which is to carry us to Mombasa. To catch it we have to start on Wednesday. I write on Tuesday morning, and we have no assurance of getting through. The break is in the Pungwe Marshes, in Portuguese territory and it would be no joke for us to be stranded in that mosquito-infested swamp. However, these floods go down as quickly as they rise, and we will hope for the best.

In the end the matter proved to be as dangerous as we had expected. Since it was a case of getting through or missing our boat, we took the chance. This bad washaway was confirmed as being at an unholy place, 40 miles from Beira, and we were told that no single train could possibly pass, though perhaps another train might pick us up at the farther side of the danger-point. We were compelled to sign an indemnity form to say that we took the risk and that in case of accident we would make no claim. Thus in the morning we steamed out of Salisbury, a knot of friends, including Judge McIlwaine and his wife, waving adieux in spite of the early hour.

It is an amazing stretch of country, the 200 miles which stretch from Salisbury to the Portuguese frontier. There are long tracts which are covered by such extraordinary collections of rocks, piled upon each other, that my wife remarked that it might have been the playground of some race of giants in ancient days who left these fantastic building bricks behind them. Occasionally one came upon splendid stretches of veld, of every shade of green, ringed round with hills of the deepest, most exquisite blue. I have never seen such blue in a landscape. Above all are the heavy clouds of the rainy season, great bulging grey udders, swelling with moisture and ready at any moment to burst and to descend, not in a sprinkle but in a solid rush of water. Such a cloud-burst was a contributary cause to the troubles which now faced us, though two great rivers, the Pungwe and the Zambesi, are both said to have overflowed their banks.

Everything now depended upon the weather keeping fine, but my heart sank rather when I rose in the middle of the night, stood on the rear platform of the train and found that it was pouring and that 3 inches had been registered in two hours. About seven o'clock in the morning the sky cleared and we entered the terrible Pungwe Marshes, a place which Dante might have made one of his Circles in hell. For hundreds of square miles, when the waters are out, there is a horrible morass, a primitive chaos of slime, weeds and oozing dark brown water in which every vile creature which crawls or flies and can shoot venom into man finds its home. Mosquitoes buzzed round us and poisonous flies and hornets shot through the windows, while if we closed them the humid heat became more than one could stand. It was a nightmare place, reeking with putrescence. Along a very narrow sandy bank the train gingerly crept, and it was clear, as one looked at the fissured sides, that they had been badly shaken by the floods and might give way under the weight. As we were in the first train to pass it was purely experimental, and no one could tell what would happen. One side slip and the carriage would have reeled down into that awful marsh, giving us a peculiarly slow and unpleasant exit, which would have furnished a text no doubt for some of our more bitter clerical opponents. However, by crawling along we made our way onwards until we came to a place which was too dangerous to pass. Here we were all turned out, and as we tramped along the line to meet the rescue train which we could see in the far distance we met the long drove of the passengers from Beira three days over-due who were making their way to the train which we had just quitted. Four snakes were accounted for by our party in that short walk. The only redeeming feature of this hellish place, where there is death in the very air, is the bird life, which is very full and varied. There are great cranes everywhere. We saw pelicans in the distance. Coloured kingfishers flitted about, and there was one little red bird, no larger than a wren, which was like a flying flame. No doubt in dry weather the Pungwe Flats may have attractions, but the Lord save us from ever again sampling it in the rains.

Our African Winter, London, 1929

In early February he reached the British East African colony of Kenya and proceeded by rail from Mombasa to Nairobi.

Nairobi

At half-past four we started our journey upon the famous Uganda Railway, which combines the attractions of a Zoo to the usual amenities of travel. We gathered that it was not till morning that we would see the sights, and indeed there was no need for us to rise early, for it is not until the journey is three-quarters completed that one really gets in touch with the wild fauna. There is a huge plain, an immense savannah, with distant blue hills, and at one point far and dim a distant bulk with a white summit. This is Kilimanjaro, the highest peak in Africa, but nearly 100 miles away. Over the great plain one sees on both sides of the line very large herds of buck, of antelopes, and of gnu, with occasional little groups of ostriches. The spacious days are past when rhino horns were picked out of the boilers, and the favourite stamping ground of the Baboo station-master

was the top of the water tank, but none the less it would
be an unreasonable tourist who did not admit that a trip
up this line of railway was a very unique experience.

The first view of Nairobi is not dignified, as it
comprises the native quarters, but the town itself gives
that young giant-on-the-make impression which classes
it with Salisbury and Bulawayo. Considerable stone buildings alternate with primitive wooden shacks. We were
met by several kind friends, one of whom, Mr. Mayer,
the proprietor of the *East African Standard*, took us off at
once to our hotel, the Norfolk, a comfortable but rather
old-fashioned hostel, which proved eventually to be one
of the most restful spots which we had found in all our
travels. A large modern hotel has been built in the town,
but never once did we feel inclined to change our repose
for the dust and noise of the main street.

Our African Winter, London, 1929

He took time off to visit a local game reserve.

Game Reserve

We had a wonderful experience upon February 14th,
when Mr. Henry Tarlton took us out to his game
preserve, where no shooting is allowed, save the many
shots which I took with my camera. Though it is only 6
miles from the town this estate, which covers 10,000
acres of broken and varied country, is swarming with
all sorts of wild creatures. My wife, Billy and I made
up the party, and with Tarlton driving us we careered
wildly over the vast plain, flying down declivities and
up slopes in a way which should have qualified us as

dirt-track experts. The whole savannah was studded with groups of animals, and in many cases they allowed us to come quite close before they took alarm. There were great droves of the beautiful little Thompson's gazelles, tawny brown striped with white. Then there were the larger kongonis, many of them finely antlered and the size of small cows. A drove of wild boars and warthogs scuttled past us, and then we saw the finest sight of all, a herd of zebras, a hundred or more strong, who galloped past, their hoofs drumming, their manes streaming, their heads tossing, the very embodiment of glorious and tumultuous life. A number of large elands were embedded among them and joined in their frantic stampede. One water-buck, a big grey sad-eyed creature, allowed me to approach within 20 yards of him. Ostriches abounded. Some poacher has been putting in his murderous work, for in four separate places we found vultures scrabbling over the carcases of buffaloes, which had bullet marks upon their hides. [This proved to be a mistake. They had died of disease.] Tarlton is a small man, but he has a grim face and is dangerous when angered. He loves his animals, and I should have pitied the poachers if they had fallen into his hands. Once we thought we saw the movement of a lion among some bushes, but we were unable to put him up, though his little pal the jackal was much in evidence. Altogether it was an unforgettable day, and as we came back, heading towards a strange blood-red sun which shone through a cloud bank, we marvelled over the beauty and wonder of Nature.

Our African Winter, London, 1929

He also travelled to the Rift Valley and on to Kisumu on the shores of Lake Victoria.

Rift Valley and Kisumu

Today, February 26th, we start upon our great adventure, which is to go round Lake Victoria Nyanza in one of the small steamers which ply along the coasts. There are two ways of getting to the Lake, by train or by motor-car. The former is cheap and comfortable. The latter is very dear and entails a most trying journey of over 230 miles of elementary roads. With the perversity of Britons we all voted for the latter.

This involved our spending the night at the half-way town of Nakuru. The journey from Nairobi to Nakuru is monotonous in its early stages, though it is pleasant to see the many good, well-cared-for farms. Then one runs into the native reserve of the Kikuyu, and for 30 miles or so the country is wild. Once a large baboon crossed our road, and once a little herd of impala buck; but otherwise it was uneventful until we came to the escarpment of the Rift Valley, and looked down at that wonderful scene. The valley, which was explored and named by Professor Gregory, is part of a great scar or weal which lies across the face of the world, starting up in the Dead Sea and reaching across Africa to the latitude of Madagascar. It is over 50 miles across, a monstrous groove, with many volcanic traces to point to its origin. As it rises in the place of the dead cities, where the rumour of great destruction still prevails, one wonders whether the whole cataclysm which produced it may not have been the same the legend of which is found in our Scriptures.

It was certainly some tremendous cause which produced such a result. Looking down from the eastern lip an enormous furrow is apparent, held in by mountains, with a vast plain studded with trees at the bottom. One descends by a Class Z road for some 2,000 feet, and then continues one's journey up the plain, passing signs of volcanic activity upon every side. There is one sinister hill, Longanot, with a 3-mile crater, upon the left, which is viewed with horror by the natives, who will not approach its gnarled and channelled sides after dark. They say that the game avoid it too. This also may be a reminiscence of some terrible disaster. One passes several considerable lakes much impregnated with natron, in spite of which the boys were able to distinguish two distant dark spots, the heads of hippopotami, appearing above the surface. If pickle is a preservative, they should live for ever. A rock stands by the wayside where a white trader was killed by the Masai many years ago. Every Masai who passed used to put a pebble on the rock, and the heap of them was plainly visible, though whether this meant approbation of the deed, or whether it was an offering to the spirit of the dead man, was more than we could discover. Some zebras in the distance, and a dignified secretary bird which strutted along the road, completed the sights of interest. To-night we sleep in a snug little bungalow attached to the Nakuru Hotel, where every comfort can be found for the weary traveller. It is strange how often one finds, in such places, all that is wanting in the pretentious city hotel.

In the morning we surveyed – from a distance – the Nakuru Lake, which is one of many which lie in the gut of the Rift Valley. All these lakes are impregnated with salt, which links them up with the Dead Sea, and the legend of the pillar of salt, all concerned with this great slash in the world's face. The seismic cause of it is accentuated by the fact that one of the largest craters in the world, Menangai, is to be found behind the Nakuru Hotel.

Our drive of 120 miles upon the second day was not all easy going. We took a short cut which runs over the mountains and saves 70 miles as compared with the main road which goes through Eldoret. Few people hazard themselves or their cars in such a journey, but our time was limited, so we chanced it. In parts the road was fair, but there was one long mountain stretch, the best of which was a cart-track and the worst not far off the bed of a river. Our driver was an experienced man, and the boys took turn about to drive the luggage car, relieving the capable young mechanic. There were places on the mountain where a skid would have sent us down the side, and many places where another car, coming the other way, would have presented an impossible problem, for there was no room to pass, and to back on a narrow rocky path for half a mile or so on a steep slope would have tried any driver. Much of the land over which we passed was native reserve, and we were conscious occasionally of a by no means friendly atmosphere. Women grimaced at us and men once or twice glared. Several were carrying spears. On the whole, however, they seemed a harmless and good-humoured crowd.

The land which was open to Europeans seemed to me to be well cultivated. Indeed, I was more impressed by the evidences of permanent settlement in Kenya than I was in Rhodesia, where the great veld seems so unbroken. Here, apart from the game preserves and the native districts, one sees an endless succession of coffee, sizal, sugar and tea plantations, with many houses each in its grove of trees. The scenery during the day was magnificent and on the most mighty scale. I cannot remember anything finer. We saw little, however, of the wild life of the country. A Duiker deer, not larger than an Airedale terrier, ran before us. Among birds I noticed the coraan or lesser bustard, the big black red-beaked bustard, and many varieties of stork and of hawk. In the Vegetable Kingdom the most striking objects were the weird euphorbia, out of which the natives distil poison, and the cork tree with no leaves, and flowers of sealing-wax red shaped like bottle cleaners. The sausage tree, with a whole larder of vegetable sausages hanging down, was also new to me. It was evening before we came quite suddenly upon Kisumu, which lies in an inlet of the lake and is the starting-point for our voyage. There is no hotel and nowhere to sleep except a Dak bungalow, and there in the mosquito-netted verandah I sit while I make these notes. To-morrow early we go aboard.

Our African Winter, London, 1929

Returning to Europe, via the east coast of Africa, he halted at Port Soudan (modern Port Sudan) in the Red Sea.

Port Sudan

To-day, March 23rd, we are past the Twelve Apostle rocks and we expect to-morrow to halt at Port Soudan.

This place was a great surprise to me. There is no doubt in my mind that it is destined to be a considerable city, though it was only founded in our own time. When the idea first took root of sending a short-cut railway from the Red Sea to tap the Soudan, the old port of Suakin was made the terminus. Presently, however, it became apparent that navigation there was very difficult, and that another bay some 40 miles to the north was very much more convenient. Therefore this town was established, and as it is the only direct outlet, and as the output of the Soudan continually increases, it will soon be a city. Already the harbour is crowded with shipping; it is fitted up with modern loading and unloading tackle, and it has huge warehouses and all the other appurtenances of a well-run port. We found 2,000 tons of cargo – mostly cotton-seeds to be converted into oil waiting for us, and the quays were piled with other cargoes. It is a great centre of industry.

The disadvantage – or the advantage, according to how it suits one – in travelling by ships which are mainly cargo vessels is that you can never tell where you may be hung up and all your dates become uncertain. We shall not touch Marseilles with the majestic right-to-the-tick precision with which the great Cape liners come booming round Robin's [Robben] Island. In this particular case it was clear that at least a day would pass before our stuff was aboard, and a ship is no pleasant residence when three winches are clattering and thumping all day. The boys and Billy were content to have a swim in the coral-enclosed bathing-place, and afterwards to fish for sharks; but my wife and I thought that we would go by train to Suakin and see that quaint old town, which was only 42 miles away. The line runs across a parched desert all the way with camel scrub and low mimosa bushes here and there. We passed the field of Handoub, where the Egyptian column was massacred, and we must have been near El Teb, where the British avenged their death. The train drew up some distance from the town, and we had a very tiring walk in the heat of the day before we got back to the welcome shade of our carriage. One passes through the so-called Gordon Gate which pierces the old brown wall of coral rock which surrounds the city. Inside we came upon an outer town which was fairly populous, and then crossing a bridge, we entered the old city, which covers the end of the peninsula and has the sea all round it. It is a nightmare place – a city of the dead. It is composed of huge ancient white houses with much decorative woodwork, the houses once of rich merchants or noblemen, but the whole place is as dead as Pompeii. We saw no single living soul in all the streets save two Arabs upon the quay who were gutting a great pile of silvery fish which looked like bream. It was like some impossible place seen in a dream. The wonderful blue water, turning to emerald green in the shallows – and broken by gleaming golden sandbanks, lapped right up to the huge white tomb-like houses. Finally we made our way back to the waiting train.

Our African Winter, London, 1929

NORTH AMERICA

Cities, Rockies and Prairies

New York – Montreal – Canadian Pacific Railway – The Great Lakes and beyond – West of Winnipeg – The Rockies – Algonquin Park – Athabasca Trail – New York – Boston – Washington – Niagara Falls – Chicago – Atlantic City – Pueblo – Salt Lake City – Catalina Island – San Francisco

Conan Doyle first went to the United States in 1894 on a whirlwind lecture tour arranged by the enterprising New York agent, Major J. B. Pond. He was accompanied by his younger brother Innes. On a stopover in Vermont they visited the author Rudyard Kipling, who was living there with his American wife. The highlight of their stay was a game of golf on the rolling fields outside Kipling's house.

Conan Doyle returned to North America in 1914, shortly before the First World War, when he extended his travels to Canada. This time his travelling companion was his second wife, Jean. As well as recording his impressions of various cities, he was inspired by signs of economic and social progress in the Canadian mid-West. However his observations tended to be rather more political than topographical, revealing his paternalism.

New York

Twenty years ago this was an ill-paved, noisy city. The surfaces now are excellent and the noises abated. Twenty years ago the police force consisted of stout, elderly, coarse-looking men, who seemed, so far as traffic management was concerned, to be very inefficient. Now the men are young, vigorous, and exceedingly capable at their job. The traffic handling is remarkably good, and reflects equal credit upon the police organisation and upon the discipline of the drivers. A certain air of truculence has also departed from the men. In all ways – so far as superficial outward inspection goes – they seem to me worthy to compare with our own admirable force.

But the people in the streets – they make the finest spectacle in America. I write on a Sunday morning, with the New York church bells chiming. This afternoon my wife and I will go down to Coney Island to see the crowds of pleasure-seekers. I know already what our experience will be. We shall meet many thousands of cheerful, good-humoured men, and as many smiling, happy women; we shall find a very high average of physical beauty in each sex; we shall see great swarms of people in innocent enjoyment, and among them all we shall not encounter one ragged person, one wicked, drink-blotched face; not one of those half sad, half comic, shambling, cringing, broken-down figures who are delightful in Dickens, but surely loathsome in life. They tell me it is a period of stagnation here. I can only answer that I have never seen such evidences of prosperity anywhere. By what magic of American energy or natural resources or tariff juggling they do it I know not, but only a blind man could go down Broadway and watch the crowds and doubt that this civilisation is more evenly distributed and has a higher average than our own.

They say that the chief industry of New York is knocking itself down and building itself up again. It is amazing to see the immense changes which twenty years have brought about. How surprised a Londoner would be if after such an absence, he found that Regent Street, Oxford Street, and Bond Street had been entirely rebuilt, with not one of the famous shops or houses left standing! That would just about describe what has happened here. It is another city. I lived here in 1894, and now I hunt about to show my wife the place and I am unable to find it. The houses, of course, are sprouting for ever higher. We have not yet quite reached the point foretold by a friend of mine, when the journey from the street to his office above would be the same as to his suburban home, the one horizontal and the other perpendicular. But when you have been fired up the fifty-nine storeys of the Woolworth pile, and when in the rapid ascent you feel the throb in your ears and incipient headache which comes from the change of atmospheric pressure, you realise the size of this greatest of inhabited buildings. Eighteen thousand persons are, as I am told, under its roof, and if it were to fall it would cut a swath of nearly one-sixth of a mile amid the smaller houses around it.

We stood on the summit and looked down on the wonderful panorama, the long thin city, the two great rivers, the island-studded bay, the swarming streets, with the thousands of hurrying straw-hatted pigmies. What a lot of humanity there is, and how very small is each unit! ...

There are few very few old buildings left in New York. I think Americans will some day bitterly regret that they have not been more reverent in this matter. I could not hear of any actual buildings of the Dutch period. The Battery no doubt stands upon the site of the old fort, but I do not think any of the original stonework is left. The only Dutch relic that I have seen is a gnarled branch of Peter Stuyvesant's pear-tree which he brought from Holland in 1665. This is piously preserved in the City Hall, which is itself of the very earliest nineteenth century, and contains a good deal of eighteenth-century furniture. There is the table on which Washington wrote his first message to Congress. There too and there again looking down from each wall is the strong face, with the tight lips and slightly underhung jaw, of the great father of his country. He has heavy, brooding, steadfast eyes. He was a worthy leader in so great a cause. The pitiable part of it is that independence must have come in another generation or two, without any bloodshed or ill-feeling, from the natural growth of the American people. It would have been an evil thing for Great Britain had it not been so, as in that case, with our 45 millions, we should now be a mere appendix to our 100 million consort, and be planning perhaps a patriotic rising and declaration of independence upon our own account ...

The Cornhill Magazine, January to April 1915.
Collected in *Western Wanderings*, New York, 1915

Montreal

Things are not well with Montreal. It pains a Briton to have to say so when it is the first British city to which he comes. But things are not well with it. The visitor has realised that before he has got from the station to his hotel. It is rich and should be prosperous, the busy port of a great country. But the streets are in a bad state, and everywhere one sees signs of neglect. One important street has been up, as I am credibly informed, for four years. Is it incompetence, or is it the old enemy 'graft'? It is not for a stranger to say. No one admires the French-Canadian race more than I do, and I was grieved to hear that the guilty town council are nearly all of that race. I wish some high-nosed old Governor of their own breed could come back to deal with them – de Frontenac for choice. It would not be long before the City Fathers would be testing one of their own institutions. My only day in the town was a cheerless one, with rain above, mud below, fog over all, and an after-luncheon speech to deliver, so perhaps the gloom has reached my thoughts, and things may seem other when I visit the town on my return.

The Cornhill Magazine, January to April 1915.
Collected in *Western Wanderings*, New York, 1915

He was impressed by the railway's potential as a nation builder. Here he waxed lyrical about the Canadian Pacific Railway:

Canadian Pacific Railway

Canada within recent memory was, outside the old provinces, a land of wild animals and their trappers, with a single thin belt of humanity across it. This loosely-connected community was clamped together by the steel of the Canadian Pacific. But the country was still length without breadth. Now the map has been rolled back. The Grand Trunk Pacific Railway has put a fresh girdle round the country, and the Canadian Northern promises yet a third. In England we have come to understand what an enormously important Imperial asset the Canadian Pacific has been. But I do not think that we have realised yet what the Grand Trunk Pacific stands for. Crossing the prairie a good deal to the north of the line of the Canadian Pacific, it has opened up a vast stretch of country which was useless before. The recent joining up of the lines from East to West marked the triumphant end of a campaign against nature quite as important to the Empire as many a military campaign. Never, until you follow such a railway in its early days, do you realise how civilisation and even life itself spring from that Aaron's rod of steel.

Five years ago there was hardly a townlet, save Edmonton, in the thousand-mile stretch between Winnipeg and the Rockies. Only five years ago. Now there are fifty, only villages as yet, but with the seeds of growth in all, and of greatness in some. They toe the

line – the iron line – like a string of runners starting
upon a race. Already you can see which is making a
good start and which a bad. Each is the centre for a
circumference of farm land, and on this depends the
advance of the town. Biggar and Scott and Wainwright
and Watrous catch the eye for the moment, but there
are plenty of likely outsiders, and it's the riding that
does it. A big man can at any time make a big town.
At present they are very much alike the little wooden
church, the raw hotel, a couple of stores, a red-painted
livery stable, and a dozen houses. On the horizon here
and there one sees far-off farm buildings, but beyond
them and away fifty miles over the horizon there are
others, and others, and yet others, for whom this
townlet and the railway line mean life and the world.

The Cornhill Magazine, January to April 1915.
Collected in *Western Wanderings*, New York, 1915

The Great Lakes and beyond

I seem to have passed with one giant stride from
Montreal to the Prairie, but, as a matter of fact, it is not
until one has reached the Prairie that the traveller meets
with new conditions and new problems. He traverses
Ontario with its prosperous mixed farms and its fruit-
growing villages, but the general effect is the same as in
Eastern America. Then comes the enormous stretch of
the Great Lakes, that wonderful inland sea, with great
ocean-going steamers. We saw the newly built *Noronic*,
destined altogether for passenger traffic, and worthy
to compare, both in internal fittings and outward

appearance, with many an Atlantic liner. The Indians
looked in amazement at La Salle's little vessel. I wonder
what La Salle and his men would think of the *Noronic*!
For two days in great comfort we voyaged over the
inland waters. They lay peaceful for our passage, but we
heard grim stories of winter gusts and of ships which
were never heard of more. It is not surprising that
there should be accidents, for the number of vessels is
extraordinary, and being constructed with the one idea
of carrying the maximum of cargo, they appear to be
not very stable. I am speaking now of the whale-back
freight carriers and not of the fine passenger service,
which could not be beaten.

I have said that the number of vessels is extraordinary.
I have been told that the tonnage passing through Sault
Ste. Marie, where the lakes join, is greater than that of
any port in the world. All the supplies and manufactures
for the West move one way, while the corn of the
great prairie, and the ores from the Lake Superior
copper and iron mines move the other. In the Fall
there comes the triumphant procession of the harvest.
Surely in more poetic days banners might have waved
and cymbals clashed, and priests of Ceres sung their
hymns in the vanguard, as this flotilla of mercy moved
majestically over the face of the waters to the aid of
hungry Europe. However, we have cut out the frills,
to use the vernacular, though life would be none the
worse could we tinge it a little with the iridescence of
romance. Suffice it now to say, that an average railway
truck contains 1,000 bushels of wheat, that there are
forty trucks in a corn train, the whole lift being 40,000

bushels, and that there exists at least one freighter which is capable of carrying 400,000 bushels, or ten train loads. The sinking of such a ship would seem to be a world's calamity.

We stopped at Sault Ste. Marie, the neck of the hour-glass between the two great lakes of Huron and Superior. There were several things there which are worthy of record. The lakes are of a different level, and the lock which avoids the dangerous rapids is on an enormous scale; but, beside it, unnoticed save by those who know where to look and what to look for, there is a little stone-lined cutting no larger than an uncovered drain – it is the detour by which for centuries the voyageurs, trappers, and explorers moved their canoes round the Sault or fall on their journey to the great solitudes beyond. Close by it is one of the old Hudson Bay log forts, with its fireproof roof, its loop-holed walls, and every other device for Indian fighting. Very small and mean these things look by the side of the great locks and the huge steamers within them. But where would locks and steamers have been had these others not taken their lives in their hands to clear the way?

...

The Twin Cities of Fort William and Port Arthur, at the head of Lake Superior, form, I think, the most growing community of Canada. They call them Twin Cities, but I expect, like their Siamese predecessors, they will grow into one. Already the suburbs join each other, though proximity does not always lead to amalgamation or even to cordiality, as in the adjacent towns of St. Paul and Minneapolis. When the little

American boy was asked in Sunday school who persecuted Saint Paul, he 'guessed it was Minneapolis'. But in the case of Fort William and Port Arthur they are so evidently interdependent that it is difficult to believe that they will fail to coalesce; when they do, I am of opinion that they may grow to be a Canadian Chicago, and possibly become the greatest city in the country. All lines converge there, as does all the lake traffic, and everything from East and West must pass through it. If I were a rich man and wished to become richer, I should assuredly buy land in the Twin Cities. Though they lie in the very centre of the broadest portion of the Continent, the water communications are so wonderful that an ocean-going steamer from Liverpool or Glasgow can now unload at their quays.

The grain elevators of Fort William are really majestic erections, and with a little change of their construction might be aesthetic as well. Even now the huge cylinders into which they are divided look at a little distance not unlike the columns of Luxor. This branch of human ingenuity has been pushed at Fort William to its extreme. The last word has been said there upon every question covering the handling of grain. By some process, which is far beyond my unmechanical brain, the stuff is even divided automatically according to its quality, and there are special hospital elevators where damaged grain can be worked up into a more perfect article.

By the way, it was here, while lying at a steamship wharf on the very edge of the city, that I first made the acquaintance of one of the original inhabitants of Canada. A cleared plain stretched from the ship to a wood some hundreds of yards off. As I stood upon deck I saw what I imagined to be a horse wander out of the wood and begin to graze in the clearing. The creature seemed ewe-necked beyond all possibility, and looking closer I saw to my surprise that it was a wild moose. Could anything be more characteristic of the present condition of Canada – the great mechanical developments of Fort William within gun-shot of me on one side, and this shy wanderer of the wilderness upon the other? In a few years the dweller in the great city will read of my experience with the same mixture of incredulity and surprise with which we read the letter of the occasional correspondent whose grandfather shot a woodcock in Maida Vale. Talking of moose, an extraordinary adventure befell the train in which we travelled, some few hours before we boarded it. In the middle of the night the engine, rounding a curve, crashed into a bull moose which was standing between the metals. I daresay the glaring headlights petrified the poor creature with terror. The body passed under the engine and uncoupled it from the tender, so that it ran on by itself, leaving the train behind. It was only when the engine returned and the cause of the incident was searched for that the dead body of the creature was discovered at the rear of the train, jammed under the dining-car.

Beside the growing modern town I saw some rude mouldering shacks which are, as I learn, the wooden houses of the old original Jesuit mission of Thunder Bay, the farthest point reached in the old days by these brave priests, who reckoned that it took them always a full year in canoes up the Ottawa and along the chain of lakes before they could reach their parish. I am intensely conscious of how valuable every link with the past will be in the days to come, and I implored some leading citizens to remove one of these huts to their town park, to furnish it in the old fashion, and to piously preserve it for all time. I should be proud to feel that I had helped to rescue such a national possession.

The true division between the East and West of Canada is not the Great Lakes, which are so valuable as a waterway, but lies in the five hundred miles of country between the Lakes and Winnipeg. It is barren, but beautiful, covered with forest which is not large enough to be of value as lumber. It is a country of rolling plains covered with low trees with rivers in the valleys. The soil is poor. It is really a problem what to do with this belt, which is small according to Canadian distances, but is none the less broader than the distance between London and Edinburgh. Unless minerals are found in it, I should think that it will be to Canada what the Highlands of Scotland are to Britain: a region set apart for sport because it has no other economic use. The singular thing about this barren tree land is that it quite suddenly changes to the fertile prairie at a point to the east of Winnipeg. I presume that there is some geological reason, but it was strange to see the fertile plain run up to the barren woods with as clear a division as between the sea and the shore.

The Cornhill Magazine, January to April 1915.
Collected in *Western Wanderings*, New York, 1915

West of Winnipeg

And now at last I am to the west of Winnipeg and on that prairie which means so much both to Canada and to the world. It is wonderfully impressive to travel swiftly all day from the early summer dawn to the latest evening light, and to see always the same little clusters of houses, always the same distant farms, always the same huge expanse stretching to the sky-line, mottled with cattle, or green with the half-grown crops. You think these people are lonely. What about the people beyond them and beyond them again, each family in its rude barracks in the midst of the 160 acres which form the minimum farm? No doubt they are lonely, and yet there are alleviations. When a man or woman is working on their own property and seeing their fortune growing, they have pleasant thoughts to bear them company. It is the women, I am told, who feel it most, and who go prairie-mad. Now they have rigged up telephone circles which connect up small groups of farms and enable the women to relieve their lives by a little friendly gossip, when the whole district thrills to the news that Mrs Jones has been in the cars to Winnipeg and bought a new bonnet. At the worst the loneliness of the prairie can never, one would think, have the soul-killing effect of loneliness in a town. 'There is always the wind on the heath, brother.'

Land is not so easily picked up now by the emigrant as in the old days, when 160 acres beside the railroad were given away free. There is still free land to be had, but it is in the back country. However, this back

country of to-day is always liable to be opened up by
the branch railway lines to-morrow. On the whole,
however, it seems to be more economical, if the
emigrant has the money, to buy a partially developed
well-situated farm, than to take up a virgin homestead.
That is what the American emigrants usually do who
have been pouring into the country, and they know
best the value of such farms, having usually come from
exactly similar ones just across the border, the only
difference being that they can get ten acres in Canada
for the price of one in Minnesota or Iowa. They hasten
to take out their papers of naturalisation and make, it
is said, most excellent and contented citizens. Their
energy and industry are remarkable. A body of them
had reached the land which they proposed to buy about
the time that I was in the West; they had come over
the border with their wagons, their horses, and their
ploughs. Being taken to the spot by the land agent, the
leader of the party tested the soil, cast a rapid glance
over the general prairie, and then cried, 'I guess this
will do, boys. Get off the ploughs.' The agent who was
present told me that they had broken an acre of the
prairie before they slept that night.

These men were German Lutherans from
Minnesota and they settled in the neighbourhood of
Scott. It may be hard for the British farmer, unused
to the conditions, to compete against such men; but
at least it must be clear to him that there is no use his
emigrating with a view to agriculture in the Western
States of America, when the Americans are themselves
flocking into Canada. The gains upon the farms are

very considerable. It is not unusual for a man to pay every expense which he has incurred, including the price of the land, within the first two years. After that, with decent luck, he should be a prosperous man, able to bring up a family in ease and comfort. If he be British and desires to return to the Old Country, it should not be difficult for him to save enough in ten or twelve years to make him, after selling his farm, more or less independent for life. That is, as it seems to me, an important consideration for many people who hesitate to break all the old ties and feel that they are leaving their motherland for ever. Everyone agrees that the emigrant farmer should have a hundred pounds as a minimum for his actual start, apart from whatever he may have to give for the land. The man who has not the money must earn it before he can take over even a free homestead. But it is not difficult for him to earn it if he is saving and industrious. Two or three years' working for others, or, better still, learning his trade in some mixed farm in Ontario, would give him the pounds. It is to be noted that even in the corn-growing West the mixed farms are those which seem to give the best and most secure results. Hog-raising, horse-breeding, dairy produce — these are lucrative insurances against a bad crop. There is no end to the agricultural possibilities of the West and North-West of Canada. There is only an end to the railway development, but that is being pushed forward as fast as the necessary capital can be supplied. Up in the Peace River district, far to the north of the present grainlands, there is an enormous area where the soil is so luxuriantly prolific that fifty bushels can be taken from the acre, and the wheat which has been sown in June can be gathered within ten weeks. There is room for a million large farms in this quarter. Considering how rich these farmers may become, and how long is the winter at that high latitude, I should not be surprised to see the development of a large migratory population, who would come with the early spring, and in the late fall would descend to the warm, pleasant places of the British Columbian coast, there to amuse themselves until work time came round once more.

So much about farms and farming. I cannot see how one can write about this western part and avoid the subject which is written in green and gold from sky to sky. Here is nothing else. Nowhere is there any sign of yesterday – not a cairn, not a monument. Life has passed here, but has left no footstep behind. But stay, the one thing which the old life still leaves is just this one thing – footsteps. Look at them in the little narrow black paths which converge to the water – little dark ruts which wind and twist. Those are the buffalo runs of old. Gone are the Cree and Blackfoot hunters who shot them down. Gone, too, the fur traders who bought the skins – Chief Factor MacTavish, who entered into the great Company's service as a boy, spent his life in slow promotion from Fort This to Fort That, made a decent Presbyterian Woman of some Indian squaw, and finally saw with horror in his old age that the world was crowding his wild beasts out of their pastures. Gone are the great herds upon which both Indian hunter and fur trader were parasitical. Indian, trader, and buffalo all have passed, and here on the great plains are these narrow runways as the last remaining sign of a vanished world.

The Cornhill Magazine, January to April 1915.
Collected in *Western Wanderings*, New York, 1915

The Rockies

A line of low distant hills breaks the interminable plain which has extended with hardly a rising for fifteen hundred miles. Above them is here and there a peak of snow. Shades of Mayne Reid, they are the Rockies – my old familiar Rockies! Have I been here before? What an absurd question, when I lived there for about ten years of my life in all the hours of dreamland. What deeds have I not done among redskins and trappers and grizzlies within their wilds! And here they are at last glimmering bright in the rising morning sun. At least, I have seen my dream mountains. Most boys never do.

It is a marvellous line, this Grand Trunk Pacific, and destined to a mighty future, for it crosses these great mountains so deftly that it never has a grade above two per cent, or needs any help for an ordinary engine with a standard train. When in the immediate future the wheat of the west and north-west comes pouring out to the western ports to find the Panama Canal, the easy haulage should place this line above all its compeers as a commercial success. And here, by its very side as we enter the mountains, I see to my surprise the shafts of coal mines rising in the wilderness. Just beyond them we reach the edges of the new National Park, which is our destination; but as it is about half the size of Belgium, it is still an hour or two before we pull up at Jasper, where the superintendent, Colonel Maynard Rogers, and his charming wife, whose guests we are, have their headquarters. Colonel Rogers is a soldier of Empire whom I first met with his Canadians in South Africa and who now, as I correct these proofs, is encamped on Salisbury Plain – a development we little thought of in those peaceful days of June.

Jasper Park is one of the great national playgrounds and health resorts which the Canadian Government with great wisdom has laid out for the benefit of the citizens. When Canada has filled up and carries a large population, she will bless the foresight of the administrators who took possession of broad tracts of the most picturesque land and put them forever out of the power of the speculative dealer. The National Park at Banff has for twenty years been a Mecca for tourists. That at Algonquin gives a great pleasure ground to those who cannot extend their travels beyond Eastern Canada. But this new Jasper Park, which only awaits the forthcoming hotel to be a glorious place for the lover of nature, is the latest and the wildest of all these reserves. Two years ago it was absolute wilderness, and much of it impenetrable. Now, through the energy of Colonel Rogers, trails have been cut through it in various directions, and a great number of adventurous trips into Country which is practically unknown can be carried out with ease and comfort. The packer plays the part of a dragoman in the east, arranging the whole expedition, food, cooking, and everything else on inclusive terms;

and once in the hands of a first-class Rocky Mountain packer, a man of the standing of Fred Stephens or the Otto Brothers, the traveller can rely upon a square deal and the companionship of one whom he will find to be a most excellent comrade. There is no shooting in the park – it is a preserve for all wild animals – but there is excellent fishing, and everywhere there are the most wonderful excursions, where you sleep at night under the stars upon the balsamic fir branches which the packer gathers for your couch. I could not imagine an experience which would be more likely to give a freshet of vitality when the stream runs thin. For a week we lived the life of simplicity and nature.

The park is not yet as full of wild creatures as it will be after a few years of preservation. The Indians who lived in this part rounded up everything that they could before moving to their reservation. But even now, the bear lumbers through the brushwood, the eagle soars above the lake, the timber wolf still skulks in the night, and the deer graze in the valleys. Above, near the snow-line, the wild goat are not uncommon, while at a lower altitude are found the mountain sheep. On the last day of our visit the rare cinnamon bear exposed his yellow coat upon a clearing within a few hundred yards of the village. I saw his clumsy good-humoured head looking at me from over a dead trunk, and I thanked the kindly Canadian law which has given him a place of sanctuary. What a bloodthirsty baboon man must appear to the lower animals! If any superhuman demon treated us exactly as we treat the pheasants, we should begin to reconsider our views as to what is sport.

The porcupine is another creature which abounds in the woods. I did not see any, but a friend described the encounter between one and his dog. The creature's quills are detachable when he wishes to be nasty, and at the end of the fight it was not easy to say which was the dog and which the porcupine! Life in Jasper interested me as an experience of the first stage of a raw Canadian town. It will certainly grow into a considerable place, but now, bar Colonel Rogers' house and the station, there are only log-huts and small wooden dwellings. Christianity is apostolic in its simplicity and in its freedom from strife – though one has to go back remarkably early in apostolic times to find those characteristics. Two churches were being built, the pastor in each case acting also as head mason and carpenter. One, the corner-stone of which I had the honour of laying, was to be used alternately by several nonconformist bodies. To the ceremony came the Anglican parson, grimy from his labours on the opposition building, and prayed for the well-being of his rival. The whole function, with its simplicity and earnestness, carried out by a group of ill-clad men standing bare-headed in a drizzle of rain, seemed to me to have in it the essence of religion. As I ventured to remark to them, Kikuyu and Jasper can give some lessons to London.

We made a day's excursion by rail to the Tête Jaune Cache, which is across the British Columbian border and marks the watershed between east and west. Here we saw the Fraser, already a formidable river, rushing down to the Pacific. At the head of the pass stands the village of the railway workers, exactly like one of the

mining townships of Bret Harte, save that the bad man
is never allowed to be too bad. There is a worse man
in a red serge coat and a Stetson hat, who is told off by
the State to look after him, and does his duty in such
fashion that the most fire-eating desperado from across
the border falls into the line of law. But apart from the
gunman, this village presented exactly the same queer
cabins, strange signs, and gambling rooms which the
great American master has made so familiar to us.

The actual workers upon the railroad construction
who are at the present moment the most indispensable
citizens in Canada are for the most part Ruthenians,
Galicians, Croats, and other weird people. The Italians
come in for the higher work. The Irishman has worked
up and disappeared from among the navvies. On the
other hand, he makes a spirited contractor, and many an
Irishman becomes rich in construction work. Blasting
operations are a field which offers great chances to a
smart man. They are a huge gamble and may ruin a
contractor or make him wealthy in a very short time.
The work is leased out by the railroad, who engage to
pay so much for the removal of so many cubic yards of
rock. The contractor finds the men and the explosives
and arranges the mines. No one ever knows what their
exact effect is going to be. Sometimes the whole rock
is cleared at one blast and the result is a huge profit to
the agent. At other times it may all settle down into the
same place again and he may be a ruined man before he
gets it off. Perhaps it is this element of chance which
makes an appeal to the adventurous Irish nature. Apart
from liquor saloons, journalism, and the police, which

were supposed to be their specialities, the American fish have done remarkably well in many different forms of business, so that those who imagine that a self-governed Ireland would necessarily be an ill-administered Ireland might find themselves very mistaken. Again and again I found that the leading man in a rising Canadian city was a Celtic Irishman of humble origin, a lumberman or transport-man, who had worked his way up by his energy and his tact. As to political graft, it is the curse of America, and the native American or the German is as much involved in it as the Irishman.

The Cornhill Magazine, January to April 1915.
Collected in *Western Wanderings*, New York, 1915

Algonquin Park

... And how we are homeward bound! Back through Edmonton, back through Winnipeg, back through that young giant, Fort William, but not back across the Great Lakes. Instead of that transit we took train, by the courtesy of the Canadian Pacific, round the northern shore of Superior, a beautiful wooded desolate country, which, without minerals, offers little prospect for the future. Some two hundred miles north of it, the Grand Trunk, that enterprising pioneer of empire, has opened up another line which extends for a thousand miles, and should develop a new corn and lumber district. Canada is like an expanding flower: wherever you look you see some fresh petal unrolling.

We spent three days at Algonquin Park. This place is within easy distance of Montreal or Ottawa, and should become a resort of British fishermen and lovers of nature. After all, it is little more than a week from London, and many a river in Finland takes nearly as long to reach. There is good hotel accommodation, and out of the thousand odd lakes in this enormous natural preserve one can find all sorts of fishing, though the best is naturally the most remote. I had no particular luck myself, but my wife caught an eight-pound trout, which Mr. Bartlett, the courteous superintendent of the park, is now engaged in mounting, so as to confound all doubters. Deer abound in the park, and the black bear is not uncommon, while wolves can often be heard howling in the night-time. I'm afraid I said something harsh of Montreal the last time I was here. It still holds good as to the paving of the streets. But no one could go up to the Upper Park and look down at that wonderful view and then go away with an evil word for the city. It is magnificent. No wonder that old Jacques Cartier, the rude Breton sailor, when first he looked upon it 350 years ago, called it the Royal Mount and saw that France could plant its city here. I have seen many of the great panoramas of the world, but none, I think, so fine as this. There is a huge stretch of the St. Lawrence winding beneath you, shimmering away into the heat haze in the remotest distance. Down there to the south, behind the distant mountains, lies the American frontier, with that vast iron bridge connecting the rails up which lead to it. The river is broken with islands, St. Helen's Island, Nun's Island, and there, far to the right, a white streak marks the rapids of La Chine. There it was that on that dreadful night the bale-fires blazed while the frightened burghers of Montreal, staring helplessly from their palisade, saw the shooting flames in which their fellow-countrymen were being tortured by the Indians. But between the river and the hill on which you stand, lies the real wonder, the vast outspread city, much larger than I had thought, though I was aware that its inhabitants were considerably more than half a million. The spires and domes give it an aspect of great solidity, and this impression is increased when you descend into its streets, for I have seen no American city which exceeds it in this respect. There is one street of banks and insurance offices which recalls the old world in the grey stone monotony of its cyclopean buildings. In Notre Dame they have also one of the finest Roman Catholic churches that I have entered, where the decorator has succeeded for once in being rich without being cheap or meretricious ...

The Cornhill Magazine, January to April 1915.
Collected in *Western Wanderings*, New York, 1915

En route he visited the Athabasca Trail, a 100 mile-long former portage route that linked Edmonton and Athabasca, both in Alberta. This occasioned one of his poems.

Athabasca Trail

My life is gliding downwards; it speeds swifter to the day
    When it shoots the last dark Canyon to the Plains of Far-away,
    But while its stream is running through the years that are to be,
    The mighty voice of Canada will ever call to me.

I shall hear her mighty rivers where the waters foam
and tear;

I shall smell her virgin uplands with their balsam-
laden air;

And in dreams I shall be riding down the winding
wooded vale

With the packer and the pack-horse on the Athabasca
Trail.

I have passed the warden cities by the eastern water-gate

Where the hero and the martyr laid the corner-stone
of state;

The habitant, courier-du-bois, and hardy voyageur,

Where dwells the breed more strong at need to
venture and endure.

I have passed the gorge of Erie, where the foaming
waters run;

I have crossed the inland ocean lying golden in the sun;

But the last and best and sweetest is the ride by hill
and dale

With the packer and the pack-horse on the Athabasca
Trail.

I will dream again of fields of grain that stretch from
sky to sky,

And little prairie hamlets where the cars go roaring
by;

Wooden hamlets as I saw them, mighty cities yet to
be,

To girdle stately Canada with gems from sea to sea.

Mother of a mighty manhood, land of promise and of
hope,

From your eastern sea-swept islands to your sunny
western slope,

Evermore my heart is with you, evermore till life
shall fail,

I'll be out with pack and packer on the Athabasca
Trail.

The Cornhill Magazine, April 1915.
Collected in *The Guards Came Through
and Other Poems*, London and New York, 1919

From April to June 1922 he was back in the United States,
this time mainly on a spiritualist mission, but also with
time to observe and comment on his surroundings.

New York

We have all been up the Woolworth Building – shot up
in something which was a cross between a lift and a Fat
Bertha – so that you were not quite sure if you were
merely elevated or projected into the air. One moment
we were on the ground, and a few moments later, with
one change on the way, at the 57th or topmost floor. It
reminded me of a saying by my friend the late Kendrick
Bangs, that he hesitated whether to live in the suburbs
of New York or at the top flat which he had rented.
The journey was the same in either case, but one was
horizontal, the other perpendicular.

The children, of course, were delighted. An old
traveller told me once that his great maxim was always to

go to the highest point of every city he visited, be it hill, steeple, or tower, and get a general idea before descending to detail. I have often found the idea a good one. On this occasion we saw that wonderful map laid out beneath us — the two rivers, the great harbours, the long, thin, tapering city, with the curved coast of Long Island, and the fields and houses of New Jersey stretching away to the southern horizon. It was a great introduction to the new world.

New York at the time of our arrival was in the throes of a crime wave. In the first ninety days of the year there had been ninety homicides in the city, an average of one per day, and there was no sign of abatement. Hold-ups were also common, and had extended from taxi-cabs to larger game, for a Broadway motor-bus was attacked shortly after our arrival. This remarkable wave of crime was not confined to New York, but was even greater in Chicago, and greater still, as I am informed, in St. Louis. It is very unfortunate for the advocates of Prohibition that this should have occurred at such a time, and that Sing-Sing, the State prison, should have been forced for the first time to confess that it could hold no more. I have been over it, and I know it to be a very commodious institution — very different to the Tombs in New York City, which is much more select.

Our American Adventure,
London and New York, 1923

Boston

Here I was in Boston again after twenty-eight years. Save for the gilded dome of the State house I should hardly have known the place. Gone or thrust into a corner and dwarfed are the dear old crooked streets of faded brick in which a European felt at home. It is now rich and broad and spacious. It seems to have gained the whole world and lost some of its own soul. Miles of motor-factories and saleshops line the busy thoroughfare. Commerce has triumphed. But where now are the Parkmans, the Emersons, the Lowells, the Longfellows, all the wonderful circle which for a time put New England above old England in culture? Boston then was a world-force. No doubt it will be so again. But much of the good old stock has moved to the Middle West, and no one can wonder at it who sees the barren and boulder-studded farms from which they have gone. Has culture gone with them? A young friend of mine at Harvard assures me that it is not so, and that a great school, mainly of poetry, is springing up there, the fame of which has not yet reached us in Europe. Well, maybe so. Anyhow, somewhere in America the old literary blood must linger and must from time to time ferment into immortal production. At present, however, it seems very quiescent.

Our American Adventure,
London and New York, 1923

Washington

It seems absurd to be always speaking in superlatives, and yet it is difficult to avoid it when one mentions some of the sights of Washington. The Capitol is superlative, so is the Obelisk, so is the Lincoln Memorial, and finally,

what could be more superlative than the inside of the
Congressional Library? It really is the most perfect
interior of a building which I have ever seen.

An architect might have something to say about a
mixture of styles, but I can only say that our eyes
and senses were absolutely satisfied with its grace
and beauty. The inside of the Capitol and the Senate
House, which we visited, were commonplace in
comparison. The Senate was in session and we looked
down on a scattered assembly who were carrying
on a languid debate. If brain size is really an index
of mental power, I should say the American Senate
was the most intellectual of all assemblies, for I am
convinced that the average size of hat would be the
largest that I have ever known in any body of men.
And yet when I think of Joseph Chamberlain and
many others I realise that quality of brain may be
more important than quantity.

The Americans are certainly adorning Washington
as lovingly as a man might his beloved. Besides the
wonderful Lincoln Memorial they have just put a fine
bronze statue of Grant at the side of the Capitol, which
was only uncovered on the day before our arrival. The
statue itself, equestrian, is conventional. The battle
groups on either side of it are, in my opinion, among
the finest bronzes of action in the world. There is one
of a gun under fire, the horses down, a dead gunner
seated on the limber and his companion staring wide-
eyed before him, which could not be beaten for spirit
and realism. We have no such work of art in the streets
of London.

The one thing we had to hope from the German air-raids was that some of our statues might vanish into powder.

Our American Adventure,
London and New York, 1923

Niagara Falls

We were greatly interested at Niagara by the new electric-power developments upon the Canadian side. It represents far the greatest thing in this line that has ever been done, and is an example of practical Socialism, as it is financed by a number of municipalities with public money. As it is costing a good deal more than the estimate, the ratepayers are looking blue, but I expect they will resume their normal colour when the results begin to show, for they expect to get 600,000 horse-power and to run huge factories of all sorts. It should be a national asset.

The idea was to tap the river above the falls, to make a canal 13 miles long, and then to throw this canal down a tube 300 feet deep, until the 20-foot rush of water hits the turbine at the bottom and so converts itself into electric force. They have had smaller plants running both on the American and on the Canadian sides, so there is no question as to the feasibility. Our whole party put on waterproofs and made its way down the dark and slippery duck-boarded passage which suddenly emerges right under the fall, which roars and spouts in front and on either side of you. Niagara, its colossal strength and impression of might, never has been described and never will be.

Down at the base as much water seems to be ascending from the shock as descending from above, and wild, mad turmoil is the result, which is intensified by the terrible din.

To look upwards from the platform and see the sun shine dimly through the great arch of yellow water above you, as through alabaster, is one of the most wonderful impressions in the world.

Certainly the children will never forget it. We take a great responsibility in breaking their education, but surely there are bigger things and more vital than Euclid or Algebra. Few adults have travelled so much as they, and yet we flatter ourselves that they have retained all their freshness. Mother-love is the best of all headmasters.

It is curious that Niagara, which is probably the chief tourist resort in the world, is singularly weak in hotels. If it were in Switzerland there would be a dozen. As it is, there are only one or two on either bank which can be called decent. The result is that visitors are birds of passage, with no temptation to stay, as they might well do, in that wonderful atmosphere.

They have stretched a wire rope, or several, over the broad expanse of the Whirlpool, and they run a small car across it with passengers. It was an alarming sight for us to see our whole family in this small box suspended hundreds of feet above that dreadful place. However, they made the double transit in all comfort.

Our American Adventure,
London and New York, 1923

Chicago

Chicago is the very noisiest city I have ever known. It is a serious drawback to its amenity. All the pavements seem to rumble, all the trains whistle, the taxis hoot, the brakes grind, and the wheels scream. It has other disadvantages in that the Blackstone Hotel at which we stayed is the most expensive and least accommodating that we had met. It is meant for millionaires and we were out of the picture. Our rooms alone cost a good ten pounds a day, and the service of a meal cost as much as a meal itself would have done in England. On the other hand, the great lake is splendid, and I see it sparkling in the sun even as I write. The drives and parks are beautiful, and the people among the kindest and best that we have met. The level of prices is far higher than in New York, and if I may encroach upon mysteries, the general level of ladies' dresses, etc., at Marshall Field's, and the whole attraction of the establishment, are far inferior to such rivals as Macy's in New York or Shoolbred's in London.

Our American Adventure,
London and New York, 1923

Atlantic City

The weather was getting very hot in New York, with that peculiar brew of damp heat for which the island city is notorious, so we were glad to change our quarters, now that the work was done, to Atlantic

City, the celebrated New Jersey watering-place. Our Ambassador Hotel had a daughter there, even larger and more wonderful than her mother, so that my only fear was that our party would become enervated from the luxury we were enjoying. It is difficult to describe Atlantic City, for we have nothing in England which is at all like it. The whole town is built upon a great sandbank with the Atlantic in front and the swamps of the Delaware River behind. It is so little above sea-level that it would be no surprise to me if a tidal wave some day were to wash it clean. Meanwhile, it is quite the liveliest place which we have found in our extended travels, and can only be compared to Manly near Sydney, for the excellence of the surf-bathing. The Atlantic roller has not the glorious slow heave and roar of its Pacific brother, but it is big enough to give you a merry romp if you care to go out to play. The sea has always been a nurse to me, and I have spent two full years of my life actually on her bosom, so I was glad to be in her arms once again. To lie floating on a blue ocean and look up to a blue sky is the nearest approach to detachment from earth that normal life can give.

Though so pleasant, it is not a very safe beach, for there is a queer tricky goblin of a current which comes and goes, suddenly catching at your legs and sweeping you seaward. Several were drowned while we were there, and Houdini, who is one of the finest swimmers in the world, told me that he had to fight for his life on one occasion. They keep a patrol, however, of very competent men upon the

beach, who are stripped and ready from morning
to night ...

Our American Adventure,
London and New York, 1923

Conan Doyle returned to North America from March
to August 1923, venturing for the first time beyond
his much-loved Rockies to the Pacific coast where he
particularly admired the city of San Francisco. He visited
a number of cities which, while not without interest, did
not result in any memorable travel writing. They included
Rochester, Cleveland, Cincinnati, Chicago, St Louis and
Denver. It wasn't until he reached Pueblo, on the Arkansas
River south of Denver, that he began to get excited by his
environment, and that was because of the proximity of the
vast Rocky mountain range.

Pueblo

From Pueblo the line turns right into the mountains
running up the gorge formed by the Arkansas River.
It is surely one of the finest routes in the world, and
the skill of the engineers is amazing. There are several
places where there is just room for the river and the
railway through gorges where the granite cliffs rise for
2,000 feet on either side. Here and there a dark band
of iron is visible, slashed across the ruddy face of the
cliff. How did it get there? We have not, as it seems
to me, begun to understand the real formation of our
globe, and, as usual, disguise our ignorance with long
names. This journey through the gorge of the Arkansas

is a wonderful experience and it is made more pleasant by the fixing of an open observation-car to the rear of the train, though you have to buy a pair of tinted protective glasses before you dare use it, as the smoke comes back upon you. Sometimes you may see wild mountain sheep on the crags, but none appeared to us, though we did see several large birds of prey which were probably buzzards, though we should like to call them eagles.

It is an amazing line, for it climbs over the 10,000-foot level without any cogs – the highest normal railroad, I am told, in the world. When near the top we saw Leadville in the distance, which is surely the most lofty of towns. It has 5,000 inhabitants, turns out over a million pounds worth of gold every year, and is nearly 10,000 feet in the air. It would be interesting to have the health statistics of such a community.

When you have climbed to this summit you are at the great Divide. A marsh of melted snow lies all around you, from which the Arkansas gets its springs, and flows down to the Gulf of Mexico. Pass on a few miles and the slope is westward and every stream discharges into the Californian Sea.

The breadth of the Rockies is a surprise to me. You cannot look at a map without appreciating their length, but to travel for days and see the ranges running from east to west parallel with your train is a surprise. An enormous tuck seems to have been taken in the earth's outer garment at this spot. Why, here more than elsewhere, there are unsolved mysteries at every turn.

When you are clear of the Arkansas Pass and down on the farther side you get your first view of the American Desert. It is much like that of Egypt. I saw it in early morning, with subdued and delicate tints of lemon, of melon, and of cinnamon lying over it, yellow deepening to brown or warming to pink, with low, distant hills of sandstone. It is a place of death — a terrible place. Once I saw a man striding across it. He walked past the train but never glanced up. He was tall and thin, walking swiftly, as one who knows he has to cover certain ground in a certain time lest a worse thing befall him. Some poor hobo or tramp, I suppose, who had no railroad fare and took his life in his hands in order to get across. There are bones and skulls scattered about from animals which have died upon the trail.

Our Second American Adventure,
London and New York, 1924

From there he passed to Salt Lake City in Utah, scene of important scenes in his first novel, *A Study in Scarlet*, and on to Los Angeles.

Salt Lake City

Everything about Salt Lake City seemed to me wonderful and unusual, even the railway-station. Fancy an English railway-station of a city which is not larger than Coventry with two magnificent frescoes spanning each end of the waiting-room. One is of the pioneer band coming through the end of the pass with their wagons, while the leaders look down on the Land of Promise. The other is the joining-up of the transcontinental line in 1869. Each is a really splendid work of art. That is one of the things which our railways must learn from the Americans. They are not there merely as a money-making means of transport. They must adorn cities as well as serve them. If they take the public money, they must give beauty as well as services. When one looks at the great marble station at Washington and then compares it with Waterloo or Victoria, one understands what a gulf separates our ideas and how much we have to learn.

In the journey from Salt Lake City one passes rapidly out of the irrigated cultivated region and finds oneself in a stretch of desert which is sometimes a mere flat plain covered with tufts of sagebrush and greasewood, and at other times breaks into rocky canyons with weather-worn limestone cliffs. The sagebrush and greasewood form little olive-green bushes, very much alike to the eye, but with this important difference, that sagebrush grows on ground which may be reclaimed, while greasewood is a sign that the land is hopeless. Apparently a great part of this plain is the bed of a huge salt-water lake, cut off from the ocean and elevated 5,000 feet in the air by some gigantic push from below. The salt water evaporated, save for such residual lakes as still remain, and the salt or alkali has impregnated the soil so that the only cure is to soak it in fresh water and so gradually get it clear. When this can be done it will make an enormous difference in the United

States, for no one can realise unless they have passed
over it how great is the surface which is now barren
and useless – a mere impediment to communication.
The snows of Canada have perhaps saved her from a
similar misfortune. This journey was rather a trial to
us, for we varied from over 5,000 feet on the crest
of the pass down to some hundreds of feet below the
sea-level when we passed the terrible Death Valley
which skirts California. We were a very weary group
when at last we ran from desert into irrigation and
from irrigation into natural verdure, with oranges
glowing on the trees, and cactus-palms and strange
semi-tropical growths on every side. Just a day after
leaving the Land of the Saints we were in what some
have called the Land of the Sinners – the famous
home of the cinema industry.

Our Second American Adventure,
London and New York, 1924

From Los Angeles he visited Catalina Island, off the
Californian coast.

Catalina Island

Catalina Island lies twenty-five miles from the mainland.
It was a fine though cloudy day, the ocean was smooth,
and the passage very pleasant as we were allowed the
privilege of the captain's bridge. The children were
delighted to see the fins of numerous 'sharks', so called.
Personally, I thought they were really large dogfish,
which are the jackals of the ocean. A number of pelicans

flew near the ship and a few flying fish skimmed over
the gentle Pacific heave.

There is a good hotel, the St. Catherine, at Avalon,
which is the little town at which one lands. The whole
place belongs to Mr. Wrigley, the Chewing-gum King,
who is said to have given a million pounds to buy out
all other interests. He has a fine house upon one of the
hills. His enormous wealth is a sign of the prevalence
of this horrible habit of chewing which does much to
disfigure American life in the eyes of the traveller, and
to discount the appearance of the fine men and pretty
women who make up the nation. Venus would look
vulgar if she chewed, and Shakespeare a lout. There was
never so hopelessly undignified a custom. A man may
drink and look a king among men, he may smoke and
look a fine fellow and a sportsman, but the man, or,
worse still, the woman, who chews becomes all animal
at once. And yet the habit is incredibly prevalent. I have
seen seven out of ten people, young and old, ruminating
like cows, in the single line of a tram-car. Therefore,
as I love both the Americans and their country, I have
no love for Mr. Wrigley, who has demoralised the
one by his products and disfigured the other by his
advertisements. But surely it is a passing habit, like the
expectoration of the last generation, or the snuff-taking
of our ancestors, and it will remain only as an ugly and
ludicrous memory.

Catalina Island has a general resemblance to Capri,
though less precipitous. It rises at its highest to 2,000
feet, and it is the home of thousands of wild goats
which are rounded up from time to time. The length

of the island is 15 miles, and the breadth about 8. It has been cleverly exploited as a pleasure-resort, and its glass-bottomed boats are famous the world over. They are good-sized steamers and the people sit in rows, their backs to the ocean, staring down into the glass tanks, consuming Mr. Wrigley's products while they admire, through the crystal water, the wonders of the deep. It is certainly very beautiful – the huge fronds in slow rhythmical motion, the deep blues and greens where the vegetation opens out, the unconscious fish who go about their lawful occasions, with no regard at all to the boat above them. It is a huge natural aquarium and I have seen nothing like it. None of the fish were large – nothing over five or six pounds – but some were very brilliant, especially the golden perch, of a beautiful orange-red. The striped rock-bass were the most numerous, and we caught glimpses far below us of strange sea-slugs and sea cucumbers crawling on a sandy bottom.

Our Second American Adventure,
London and New York, 1924

He loved driving up to the west coast and stopping in San Francisco.

San Francisco

The journey from Los Angeles to San Francisco is about as far as from London to Dundee, and includes a climb over a considerable range of hills, so it took us from eight in the morning till nearly eleven at night. I retain

a panoramic view of the long journey, as seen between
snatches of sleep – a hundred miles of barren hills with
oil-derricks dotted over them, a hundred miles of
wonderful ocean breaking into spray just under the train,
the great loops which carried us over the Santa Lucia
Mountains, the famous Lick Observatory, the beautiful
fruit district, and then finally salt water on both sides of
the train as we drew up to the City of the Golden Gate.
If I come to be bedridden I shall always have memory
pictures on which to ponder. We were all very weary
when we arrived at eleven at night, but none the less the
relentless Press-gang was there. It was very late before
we were safe in our rooms of the famous Clift Hotel.

It was wonderful for me to wake in San Francisco. It
has always been one of my dream-cities, for it has the
glamour of literature, without which matter is a dead
thing. It was here that Bret Harte's heroes swaggered
and drank and gambled and pistolled each other in
the early gold-days. Jack Oakhurst's gambling saloon
was in one of these streets, and Colonel Starbottle,
one of the creations of American literature, posed
upon those sidewalks. Here, too, one comes within
touch of another of the Immortals. Here was the
bay down which Jack London worked in an oyster-
pirate – most envied of all boys. Here, too, was the
Golden Gate, the opening of many a sea-story, with
the Farallones on the far skyline. There it was that
the master-pirate in Jack London's narrative went
down with his schooner, and there also Frank Norris
steered his bark in his splendid *Shanghaied*. Was it not
from here also that Stevenson set sail in *The Wrecker*?

The glamour of Romance is all over the waterfront and the bay.

It is a nice question whether San Francisco does not stand first in natural beauty of all cities in the world. I speak of natural advantages only and not of historical glamour, which would make many European cities pre-eminent. But taking Nature alone, here is a harbour which is second only to that of Sydney; here is beautiful hill-scenery in the very city itself; and finally there is Tamalpais, the one and only Tamalpais, which should be ascended by the traveller if he has only a single clear day in the city of the Golden Gate. Our whole party went up it on the day after our arrival, and we were agreed that in all our wanderings we had never had a more glorious experience.

You cross the harbour in a ferry, the trip taking you twenty minutes, and find yourself in a small town called Sausalito – there is a welcome dignity in these Spanish names. There the railroad begins, and after a short journey you change into a mountain-train and begin your ascent. The line is curved so skilfully that at no place is the rise more than one in seven, and no cogs are needed. It would charm a botanist – would that I were one! – to note how you start from subtropical palms and cacti and yuccas, mounting up through the various flora, the tanbark oaks, the bay trees with their delicious scents, the eucalypti of various orders, and the maples, until you emerge into rhododendrons and firs and heaths and ferns with wild lupin and kingcups, and much to remind us of the dear uplands of Sussex. One is faced here with the eternal problem as to how on earth this high altitude vegetation ever got there, whether blown by the winds or brought by the birds, or how. In isolated mountains in the heart of Africa you will find, as I understand, all our upland English shrubs and flowers. It is one more mystery of Nature.

Finally, after an hour of slow clanking progress, we were at the inn on the top of the mountain, 2,600 feet above the Bay, which lay in its glory, with many convolutions and gulfs and extensions, more like some motionless model of the world than the world itself. There were wonderful gradations of colour there, the deep blue of the sea, the olive-green of the dried-up plains and foothills, the deep green of the fir groves on the mountainside, and the drabs and yellows of the sands. Seven counties were visible, and a mountain a hundred miles away stood up as a white cone upon a clear day. The great city lay below us on its promontory, and we saw Oakland across the bay, and all the outlying towns in which the business men have their homes. It was a truly majestic sight, the powers of Nature and of man, each admirable in its own domain.

We walked round the crest of the mountain, and then descended in a car which ran by its own gravity, a delightful mode of progression when it continues for nearly an hour. The end of this wonderful toboggan course was the Muir Woods, where in a cleft of the hill the great Sequoias lie. All words are futile to describe the tremendous majesty of the great redwoods, and mere figures such as 300 feet as their height, or the fact that a hollow trunk can contain thirty-six people, leaves the imagination cold. One has to be alone or with some single very intimate companion to get the true impression, the deep silence of the grove, the shadowy religious light, the tremendous majesty of the red columns, the vistas between them, the solemn subconscious effect produced by their two thousand years of age. There are no insects in their bark, and nothing, not even fire, can destroy them. We saw scars of old brush fires upon their flanks, and noted that considerable oaks nearby had no such scar, which gave an idea of how many years had elapsed since that mark was branded on them. We wandered for two hours along the borders of the clear trout-stream which runs through the Redwood Grove.

The whole mountain has been most reverently and excellently developed by a private company, the representative of which, Mr. Whitmore, acted as our guide. It could not have been better done, for it has been made accessible and yet tenderly guarded from all vulgarity. One is not allowed to pick a flower in the Redwood Grove. The latter place has been taken over by the Government, and one feels that it should all be national property. The only place which I can recall resembling Tamalpais is the famous Tibidabo Hill above Barcelona; but the Californian effect is on a far grander scale.

Our Second American Adventure,
London and New York, 1924

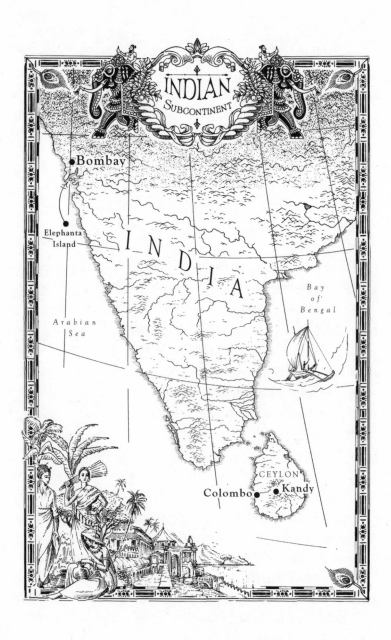

INDIAN SUBCONTINENT

Dignity and Reverence

India – Elephanta Island – Sri Lanka (Ceylon) – Kandy (Candy)

Conan Doyle did not spend much time in Asia. He only set foot on the continent en route to Australia. He didn't have much to say about India, though his recollections of visiting Elephanta Island off Mumbai (then Bombay) are illuminating. He was rather more charmed by Sri Lanka (then Ceylon). His account of his journey to the ancient capital of Candy (Kandy) is a fine example of his later travel writing.

India

> One cannot spend even a single long day in India without carrying away a wonderful impression of the gentle dignity of the Indian people. Our motor drivers were extraordinarily intelligent and polite, and all we met gave the same impression.
>
> India may be held by the sword, but it is certainly kept very carefully in the scabbard, for we hardly saw a

soldier in the streets of this, its greatest city. I observed some splendid types of manhood, however, among the native police. We lunched at the Taj Mahal Hotel, and got back tired and full of mixed impressions.

The Wanderings of a Spiritualist,
London and New York, 1921

Elephanta Island

We have seen the Island of Elephanta, and may the curse of Ernulphus, which comprises all other curses, be upon that old Portuguese Governor who desecrated it, and turned his guns upon the wonderful stone carvings. It reminds me of Abou Simbel in Nubia, and the whole place has an Egyptian flavour. In a vast hollow in the hill, a series of very elaborate bas reliefs have been carved, showing Brahma, Vishnu and Siva, the old Hindoo trinity, with all those strange satellites, the bulls, the kites, the dwarfs, the elephant-headed giants with which Hindoo mythology has so grotesquely endowed them. Surely a visitor from some wiser planet, examining our traces, would judge that the human race, though sane in all else, was mad the moment that it touched religion, whether he judged it by such examples as these, or by the wearisome iteration of expressionless Buddhas, the sacred crocodiles and hawk-headed gods of Egypt, the monstrosities of Central America, or the lambs and doves which adorn our own churches. It is only in the Mohammedan faith that such an observer would find nothing which could offend, since all mortal symbolism is there forbidden. And yet if these strange conceptions did indeed help these poor people through their journey of life – and even now they come from far with their offerings – then we should morally be as the Portuguese governor, if we were to say or do that which might leave them prostrate and mutilated in their minds ...

The Wanderings of a Spiritualist,
London and New York, 1921

Sri Lanka (Ceylon)

In Colombo harbour lay H. M. S. 'Highflyer', which we looked upon with the reverence which everybody and everything which did well in the war deserve from us – a saucy, rakish, speedy craft. Several other steamers were flying the yellow quarantine flag, but our captain confided to me that it was a recognised way of saying 'no visitors', and did not necessarily bear any pathological meaning. As we had nearly two days before we resumed our voyage I was able to give all our party a long stretch on shore, finally staying with my wife for the night at the Galle Face Hotel, a place where the preposterous charges are partly compensated for by the glorious rollers which break upon the beach outside. I was interested in the afternoon by a native conjurer giving us what was practically a private performance of the mango-tree trick. He did it so admirably that I can well understand those who think that it is an occult process. I watched the man narrowly, and believe that I solved the little mystery, though even now I cannot be sure. In doing it he began by laying several objects out in a casual way while hunting in his bag for his mango seed. These were small odds and ends including a little rag doll, very rudely fashioned, about six or eight inches long. One got accustomed to the presence of these things and ceased to remark them. He showed the seed and passed it for examination, a sort of large Brazil nut. He then laid it among some loose earth, poured some water on it, covered it with a handkerchief, and crooned over it. In about a minute he exhibited the same, or another seed, the capsule burst, and a light green leaf protruding. I took it in my hands, and it was certainly a real bursting mango seed, but clearly it had been palmed and substituted for the other. He then buried it again and kept raising the handkerchief upon his own side, and scrabbling about with his long brown fingers underneath its cover. Then he suddenly whisked off the handkerchief and there was the plant, a foot or so high, with thick foliage and blossoms, its root well planted in the earth. It was certainly very startling.

My explanation is that by a miracle of packing the whole of the plant had been compressed into the rag doll, or little cloth cylinder already mentioned. The scrabbling of the hands under the cloth was to smooth out the leaves after it was freed from this covering. I observed that the leaves were still rather crumpled, and that there were dark specks of fungi which would not be there if the plant were straight from nature's manufactory. But it was wonderfully done when you consider that the man was squatting in our midst, we standing in a semi-circle around him, with no adventitious aid whatever. I do not believe that the famous Mr. Maskeleyne or any of those other wise conjurors who are good enough occasionally to put Lodge, Crookes and Lombroso in their places, could have wrought a better illusion.

The fellow had a cobra with him which he challenged me to pick up. I did so and gazed into its strange eyes, which some devilry of man's had turned to a lapis lazuli blue. The juggler said it was the result of its skin-sloughing, but I have my doubts. The poison bag had, I suppose, been extracted, but the man seemed nervous and slipped his brown hand between my own and the swaying venomous head with its peculiar flattened hood. It is a fearsome beast, and I can realise what was told me by a lover of animals that the snake was the one creature from which he could get no return of affection. I remember that I once had three in my employ when the 'Speckled Band' was produced in London, fine, lively rock pythons, and yet in spite of this profusion of realism I had the experience of reading a review which, after duly slating the play, wound up with the scathing sentence, 'The performance ended with the production of a palpably artificial serpent.' Such is the reward of virtue. Afterwards when the necessities of several travelling companies compelled us to use dummy snakes we produced a much more realistic effect. The real article either hung down like a pudgy yellow bell rope, or else when his tail was pinched, endeavoured to squirm back and get level with the stage carpenter, who pinched him, which was not in the plot. The latter individual had no doubts at all as to the dummy being an improvement upon the real.

Never, save on the west coast of Africa, have I seen 'the league-long roller thundering on the shore' as here, where the Indian Ocean with its thousand leagues of momentum hits the western coast of Ceylon. It looks smooth out at sea, and then you are surprised to observe that a good-sized boat has suddenly vanished. Then it scoops upwards once more on the smooth arch of the billow, disappearing on the further slope.

The native catamarans are almost invisible, so that you see a row of standing figures from time to time on the crest of the waves. I cannot think that any craft in the world would come through rough water as these catamarans with their long outriggers can do. Man has made few more simple and more effective inventions, and if I were a younger man I would endeavour to introduce them to Brighton beach, as once I introduced ski to Switzerland, or auto-wheels to the British roads. I have other work to do now, but why does not some sportsman take the model, have it made in England, and then give an exhibition in a gale of wind on the south coast. It would teach our fishermen some possibilities of which they are ignorant.

As I stood in a sandy cove one of them came flying in, a group of natives rushing out and pulling it up on the beach. The craft consists only of two planks edgewise and lengthwise. In the nine-inch slit between them lay a number of great twelve-pound fish, like cod, and tied to the side of the boat was a ten-foot sword fish. To catch that creature while standing on a couple of floating planks must have been sport indeed, and yet the craft is so ingenious that to a man who can at a pinch swim for it, there is very small element of danger. The really great men of our race, the inventor of the wheel, the inventor of the lever, the inventor of the catamaran, are all lost in the mists of the past, but ethnologists have found that the cubic capacity of the neolithic brain is as great as our own.

There are two robbers' castles, as the unhappy visitor calls them, facing the glorious sea, the one the Galle Face, the other the Mount Lavinia Hotel. They are connected by an eight-mile road, which has all the colour and life and variety of the East for every inch of the way. In that glorious sun, under the blue arch of such a sky, and with the tropical trees and flowers around, the poverty of these people is very different from the poverty of a London slum. Is there in all God's world such a life as that, and can it really be God's world while we suffer it to exist! Surely, it is a palpable truth that no one has a right to luxuries until everyone has been provided with necessities, and among such necessities a decent environment is the first. If we had spent money to fight slumland as we spent it to fight Germany, what a different England it would be. The world moves all the same, and we have eternity before us. But some folk need it.

The Wanderings of a Spiritualist,
London and New York, 1921

Kandy (Candy)

We have just returned from a dream journey to Candy. The old capital is in the very centre of the island, and

seventy-two miles from Colombo, but, finding that
we had one clear night, we all crammed ourselves (my
wife, the children and self) into a motor car, and made
for it, while Major Wood and Jakeman did the same
by train. It was a wonderful experience, a hundred
and forty miles of the most lovely-coloured cinema
reel that God ever released. I carry away the confused
but beautiful impression of a good broad red-tinted
road, winding amid all shades of green, from the dark
foliage of overhanging trees, to the light stretches of the
half-grown rice fields. Tea groves, rubber plantations,
banana gardens, and everywhere the coconut palms,
with their graceful, drooping fronds. Along this great
road streamed the people, and their houses lined the
way, so that it was seldom that one was out of sight of
human life. They were of all types and colours, from the
light brown of the real Singalese to the negroid black of
the Tamils, but all shared the love of bright tints, and we
were delighted by the succession of mauves, purples,
crimsons, ambers and greens. Water buffaloes, with
the resigned and half-comic air of the London landlady
who has seen better days, looked up at us from their
mud-holes, and jackal-like dogs lay thick on the path,
hardly moving to let our motor pass. Once, my lord
the elephant came round a corner, with his soft, easy-
going stride, and surveyed us with inscrutable little
eyes. It was the unchanged East, even as it had always
been, save for the neat little police stations and their
smart occupants, who represented the gentle, but very
efficient, British Raj. It may have been the merit of
that Raj, or it may have been the inherent virtue of the

people, but in all that journey we were never conscious of an unhappy or of a wicked face. They were very sensitive, speaking faces, too, and it was not hard to read the thoughts within.

As we approached Candy, our road ran through the wonderful Botanical Gardens, unmatched for beauty in the world, though I still give Melbourne pride of place for charm. As we sped down one avenue an elderly keeper in front of us raised his gun and fired into the thick foliage of a high tree. An instant later something fell heavily to the ground. A swarm of crows had risen, so that we had imagined it was one of these, but when we stopped the car a boy came running up with the victim, which was a great bat, or flying fox, with a two-foot span of leathery wing. It had the appealing face of a mouse, and two black, round eyes, as bright as polished shoe buttons. It was wounded, so the boy struck it hard upon the ground, and held it up once more, the dark eyes glazed, and the graceful head bubbling blood from either nostril ...

This intrusion of tragedy into that paradise of a garden reminded us of the shadows of life. There is something very intimately moving in the evil fate of the animals. I have seen a man's hand blown off in warfare, and have not been conscious of the same haunting horror which the pains of animals have caused me.

And here I may give another incident from our Candy excursion. The boys are wild over snakes, and I, since I sat in the front of the motor, was implored to keep a look-out. We were passing through a village, where a large lump of concrete, or stone, was lying by the road. A stick, about five feet long, was resting against it. As we flew past, I saw, to my amazement, the top of the stick bend back a little. I shouted to the driver, and we first halted, and then ran back to the spot. Sure enough, it was a long, yellow snake, basking in this peculiar position. The village was alarmed, and peasants came running, while the boys, wildly excited, tumbled out of the motor. 'Kill it!' they cried. 'No, no!' cried the chauffeur. 'There is the voice of the Buddhist,' I thought, so I cried, 'No! no!' also. The snake, meanwhile, squirmed over the stone, and we saw it lashing about among the bushes. Perhaps we were wrong to spare it, for I fear it was full of venom. However, the villagers remained round the spot, and they had sticks, so perhaps the story was not ended.

Candy, the old capital, is indeed a dream city, and we spent a long, wonderful evening beside the lovely lake, where the lazy tortoises paddled about, and the fireflies gleamed upon the margin. We visited also the old Buddhist temple, where, as in all those places, the atmosphere is ruined by the perpetual demand for small coins. The few mosques which I have visited were not desecrated in this fashion, and it seems to be an unenviable peculiarity of the Buddhists, whose yellow-robed shaven priests have a keen eye for money. Beside the temple, but in ruins, lay the old palace of the native kings.

I wish we could have seen the temple under better conditions, for it is really the chief shrine of the most numerous religion upon earth, serving the Buddhist as the Kaaba serves the Moslem, or St. Peter's the

Catholic. It is strange how the mind of man drags high things down to its own wretched level, the priests in each creed being the chief culprits. Buddha under his Boh tree was a beautiful example of sweet, unselfish benevolence and spirituality. And the upshot, after two thousand years, is that his followers come to adore a horse's tooth (proclaimed to be Buddha's, and three inches long), at Candy, and to crawl up Adam's Peak, in order to worship at a hole in the ground which is supposed to be his yard-long footstep. It is not more senseless than some Christian observances, but that does not make it less deplorable.

I was very anxious to visit one of the buried cities further inland, and especially to see the ancient Boh tree, which must surely be the doyen of the whole vegetable kingdom, since it is undoubtedly a slip taken from Buddha's original Boh tree, transplanted into Ceylon about two hundred years before Christ. Its history is certain and unbroken. Now, I understand, it is a very doddering old trunk, with withered limbs which are supported by crutches, but may yet hang on for some centuries to come. On the whole, we employed our time very well, but Ceylon will always remain to each of us as an earthly paradise, and I could imagine no greater pleasure than to have a clear month to wander over its beauties.

The Wanderings of a Spiritualist,
London and New York, 1921

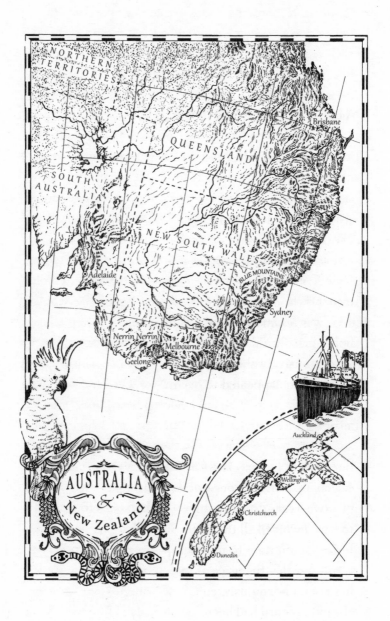

AUSTRALIA AND NEW ZEALAND

Wine, Sheep and Development

Adelaide – Melbourne – Geelong – Nerrin-Nerrin
(Western Victoria) – Sydney – Blue Mountains
(New South Wales) – Queensland – Auckland – Maoris

Conan Doyle only visited Australasia once, in 1920–21.
But he was fascinated by the country and its potential for
mainly agricultural and agro-industrial development. He
wrote extensively about its major cities and also about the
outback which appealed to his love of wide open spaces.

Adelaide

In Adelaide I appreciated, for the first time, the crisis
which Australia has been passing through in the shape
of a two-years drought, only recently broken. It seems
to have involved all the States and to have caused great
losses, amounting to millions of sheep and cattle. The
result was that the price of those cattle which survived
has risen enormously, and at the time of our visit an
absolute record had been established, a bullock having
been sold for £41. The normal price would be about

£13. Sheep were about £3 each, the normal being fifteen shillings. This had, of course, sent the price of meat soaring with the usual popular unrest and agitation as a result. It was clear, however, that with the heavy rains the prices would fall. These Australian droughts are really terrible things, especially when they come upon newly-opened country and in the hotter regions of Queensland and the North. One lady told us that she had endured a drought in Queensland which lasted so long that children of five had never seen a drop of rain. You could travel a hundred miles and find the brown earth the whole way, with no sign of green anywhere, the sheep eating twigs or gnawing bark until they died. Her brother sold his surviving sheep for one shilling each, and when the drought broke had to restock at 50s. a head. This is a common experience, and all but the man with savings have to take to some subordinate work, ruined men. No doubt, with afforestation, artesian wells, irrigation and water storage things may be modified, but all these things need capital, and capital in these days is hard to seek, nor can it be expected that capitalists will pour their money into States which have wild politicians who talk lightly of past obligations. You cannot tell the investor that he is a bloated incubus one moment, and go hat in hand for further incubation the next. I fear that this grand country as a whole may suffer from the wild ideas of some of its representatives. But under it all lies the solid self-respecting British stuff, which will never repudiate a just debt, however heavily it may press. Australians may groan under the burden, but they should remember that for every pound of taxation they carry the home Briton carries nearly three.

But to return for a moment to the droughts; has any writer of fiction invented or described a more long-drawn agony than that of the man, his nerves the more tired and sensitive from the constant unbroken heat, waiting day after day for the cloud that never comes, while under the glaring sun from the unchanging blue above him, his sheep, which represent all his life's work and his hopes, perish before his eyes? A revolver shot has often ended the long vigil and the pioneer has joined his vanished flocks. I have just come in contact with a case where two young returned soldiers, demobilised from the war and planted on the land had forty-two cattle given them by the State to stock their little farm. Not a drop of water fell for over a year, the feed failed, and these two warriors of Palestine and Flanders wept at their own helplessness while their little herd died before their eyes. Such are the trials which the Australian farmer has to bear.

While waiting for my first lecture I do what I can to understand the country and its problems. To this end I visited the vineyards and wine plant of a local firm which possesses every factor for success, save the capacity to answer letters. The originator started grape culture as a private hobby about 60 years ago, and now such an industry has risen that this firm alone has £700,000 sunk in the business, and yet it is only one of several. The product can be most excellent, but little or any ever reaches Europe, for it cannot overtake

the local demand. The quality was good and purer than
the corresponding wines in Europe – especially the
champagnes, which seem to be devoid of that poison,
whatever it may be, which has for a symptom a dry
tongue with internal acidity, driving elderly gentlemen
to whisky and soda. The Australian product, taken in
moderate doses, seems to have no poisonous quality,
and is without that lime-like dryness which appears to
be the cause of it …

We went over the vineyards, ourselves mildly
interested in the vines, and the children wildly excited
over the possibility of concealed snakes. Then we did
the vats and the cellars with their countless bottles.
We were taught the secrets of fermentation, how the
wonderful Pasteur had discovered that the best and
quickest was produced not by the grape itself, as of
old, but by the scraped bloom of the grape inserted in
the bottle. After viewing the number of times a bottle
must be turned, a hundred at least, and the complex
processes which lead up to the finished article, I will
pay my wine bills in future with a better grace. The
place was all polished wood and shining brass, like
the fittings of a man-of-war, and a great impression of
cleanliness and efficiency was left upon our minds. We
only know the Australian wines at present by the rough
article sold in flasks, but when the supply has increased
the world will learn that this country has some very
different stuff in its cellars, and will try to transport it
to their tables.

The Wanderings of a Spiritualist,
London and New York, 1921

Melbourne

Melbourne is a remarkable city, far more solid and old-established than the European visitor would expect. We spent some days in exploring it. There are few cities which have the same natural advantages, for it is near the sea, with many charming watering places close at hand, while inland it has some beautiful hills for the week-end villas of the citizens. Edinburgh is the nearest analogy which I can recall. Parks and gardens are beautiful, but, as in most British cities, the public statues are more solid than impressive. The best of them, that to Burke and Wills, the heroic explorers, has no name upon it to signify who the two figures are, so that they mean nothing at all to the casual observer, in spite of some excellent bas-reliefs, round the base, which show the triumphant start and the terrible end of that tragic but successful journey, which first penetrated the Continent from south to north.

. . .

In some ways the Australians are more English than the English. We have been imperceptibly Americanised, while our brethren over the sea have kept the old type. The Australian is less ready to show emotion, cooler in his bearing, more restrained in applause, more devoted to personal liberty, keener on sport, and quieter in expression (as witness the absence of scare lines in the papers) than our people are. Indeed, they remind me more of the Scotch than the English, and Melbourne on a Sunday, without posts, or Sunday papers, or any amenity whatever, is like the Edinburgh of my boyhood. Sydney is more advanced. There are curious anomalies in both towns. Their telephone systems are so bad that they can only be balanced against each other, for they are in a class by themselves. One smiles when one recollects that one used to grumble at the London lines. On the other hand the tramway services in both towns are wonderful, and so continuous that one never hastens one's step to catch a tram since another comes within a minute. The Melbourne trams have open bogey cars in front, which make a drive a real pleasure.

The Wanderings of a Spiritualist,
London and New York, 1921

Geelong

I had little time to inspect Geelong, which is a prosperous port with 35,000 inhabitants. What interested me more was the huge plain of lava which stretches around it and connects it with Melbourne. This plain is a good hundred miles across, and as it is of great depth one can only imagine that there must be monstrous cavities inside the earth to correspond with the huge amount extruded. Here and there one sees stunted green cones which are the remains of the volcanoes which spewed up all this stuff. The lava has disintegrated on the surface to the extent of making good arable soil, but the harder bits remain unbroken, so that the surface is covered with rocks, which are used to build up walls for the fields after the Irish fashion. Every here and there a peak of granite has remained as an island amid the lava, to show what was there before the great outflow. Eruptions appear to be caused by water pouring in through some crack and reaching the heated inside of the earth where the water is turned to steam, expands, and so gains the force to spread destruction. If this process went on it is clear that the whole sea might continue to pour down the crack until the heat had been all absorbed by the water. I have wondered whether the lava may not be a clever healing process of nature, by which this soft plastic material is sent oozing out in every direction with the idea that it may find the crack and then set hard and stop it up. Wild speculation no doubt, but the guess must always precede the proof.

The Wanderings of a Spiritualist,
London and New York, 1921

Nerrin-Nerrin (Western Victoria)

It was interesting to us to find ourselves upon an old-established station, typical of the real life of Australia, for cities are much the same the world over. Nerrin had been a sheep station for eighty years, but the comfortable verandahed bungalow house, with every convenience within it, was comparatively modern. What charmed us most, apart from the kindness of our hosts, was a huge marsh or lagoon which extended for many miles immediately behind the house, and which was a bird sanctuary, so that it was crowded with ibises, wild black swans, geese, ducks, herons and all sorts of fowl. We crept out of our bedroom in the dead of the night and stood under the cloud-swept moon listening to the chorus of screams, hoots, croaks and whistles coming out of the vast expanse of reeds. It would make a most wonderful hunting ground for a naturalist who was content to observe and not to slay. The great morass of Nerrin will ever stand out in our memories.

Next day we were driven round the borders of this wonderful marsh, Mr. Wynne, after the Australian fashion, taking no note of roads, and going right across country with alarming results to anyone not used to it. Finally, the swaying and rolling became so terrific that he was himself thrown off the box seat and fell down between the buggy and the front wheel, narrowly escaping a very serious accident. He was able to show us the nests and eggs which filled the reed-beds, and even offered to drive us out into the morass to inspect them, a proposal which was rejected by the unanimous vote of a full buggy. I never knew an answer more decidedly in the negative. As we drove home we passed a great gum tree, and halfway up the trunk was a deep incision where the bark had been stripped in an oval shape some four foot by two. It was where some savage in days of old had cut his shield. Such a mark outside a modern house with every amenity of cultured life is an object lesson of how two systems have overlapped, and how short a time it is since this great continent was washed by a receding wave, ere the great Anglo-Saxon tide came creeping forward.

Apart from the constant charm of the wild life of the marsh there did not seem to be much for the naturalist around Nerrin. Opossums bounded upon

the roof at night and snakes were not uncommon. A
dangerous tiger-snake was killed on the day of our
arrival. I was amazed also at the size of the Australian
eels. A returned soldier had taken up fishing as a
trade, renting a water for a certain time and putting
the contents, so far as he could realise them, upon
the market. It struck me that after this wily digger
had passed that way there would not be much for
the sportsman who followed him. But the eels were
enormous. He took a dozen at a time from his cunning
eel-pots, and not one under six pounds. I should have
said that they were certainly congers had I seen them
in England.

I wonder whether all this part of the country has not
been swept by a tidal wave at some not very remote
period. It is a low coastline with this great lava plain as
a hinterland, and I can see nothing to prevent a big wave
even now from sweeping the civilisation of Victoria off
the planet, should there be any really great disturbance
under the Pacific. At any rate, it is my impression that
it has actually occurred once already, for I cannot
otherwise understand the existence of great shallow
lakes of salt water in these inland parts. Are they not
the pools left behind by that terrible tide? There are
great banks of sand, too, here and there on the top of
the lava which I can in no way account for unless they
were swept here in some tremendous world-shaking
catastrophe which took the beach from St. Kilda and
threw it up at Nerrin. God save Australia from such a
night as that must have been if my reading of the signs
be correct.

One of the sights of Nerrin is the shearing of the sheep by electric machinery. These sheep are merinos, which have been bred as wool-producers to such an extent that they can hardly see, and the wool grows thick right down to their hoofs. The large stately creature is a poor little shadow when his wonderful fleece has been taken from him. The electric clips with which the operation is performed, are, I am told, the invention of a brother of Garnet Wolseley, who worked away at the idea, earning the name of being a half-crazy crank, until at last the invention materialised and did away with the whole slow and clumsy process of the hand-shearer. It is not, however, a pleasant process to watch even for a man, far less a sensitive woman, for the poor creatures get cut about a good deal in the process. The shearer seizes a sheep, fixes him head up between his knees, and then plunges the swiftly-moving clippers into the thick wool which covers the stomach. With wonderful speed he runs it along and the creature is turned out of its covering, and left as bare as a turkey in a poulterer's window, but, alas, its white and tender skin is too often gashed and ripped with vivid lines of crimson by the haste and clumsiness of the shearer. I am bound to say, however, that the creature makes no fuss about it, remains perfectly still, and does not appear to suffer any pain. Nature is often kinder than we know, even to her most humble children, and some soothing and healing process seems to be at work.

The shearers appear to be a rough set of men, and spend their whole time moving in gangs from station to station, beginning up in the far north and winding up on the plains of South Australia. They are complete masters of the situation, having a powerful union at their back. They not only demand and receive some two pounds a day in wages, but they work or not by vote, the majority being able to grant a complete holiday.

The Wanderings of a Spiritualist,
London and New York, 1921

Sydney

I had no idea that Sydney was so great a place. The population is now very nearly a million, which represents more than one-sixth of the whole vast Continent. It seems a weak point of the Australian system that 41 percent, of the whole population dwell in the six capital cities. The vital statistics of Sydney are extraordinarily good, for the death rate is now only twelve per thousand per annum. Our standard in such matters is continually rising, for I can remember the days when twenty per thousand was reckoned to be a very good result. In every civic amenity Sydney stands very high. Her Botanical Gardens are not so supremely good as those of Melbourne, but her Zoo is among the very best in the world. The animals seem to be confined by trenches rather than by bars, so that they have the appearance of being at large. It was only after Jakeman had done a level hundred with a child under each arm that she realised that a bear, which she saw approaching, was not really in a state of freedom.

As to the natural situation of Sydney, especially its harbour, it is so world-renowned that it is hardly necessary to allude to it. I can well imagine that a

Sydney man would grow homesick elsewhere, for he could never find the same surroundings. The splendid landlocked bay with its numerous side estuaries and its narrow entrance is a grand playground for a sea-loving race. On a Saturday it is covered with every kind of craft, from canoe to hundred-tonner. The fact that the water swarms with sharks seems to present no fears to these strong-nerved people, and I have found myself horrified as I watched little craft, manned by boys, heeling over in a fresh breeze until the water was up to their gunwales. At very long intervals someone gets eaten, but the fun goes on all the same.

The people of Sydney have their residences (bungalows with verandahs) all round this beautiful bay, forming dozens of little townlets. The system of ferry steamers becomes as important as the trams, and is extraordinarily cheap and convenient. To Manly, for example, which lies some eight miles out, and is a favourite watering place, the fare is five pence for adults and twopence for children. So frequent are the boats that you never worry about catching them, for if one is gone another will presently start. Thus, the whole life of Sydney seems to converge into the Circular Quay, from which as many as half a dozen of these busy little steamers may be seen casting off simultaneously for one or another of the oversea suburbs. Now and then, in a real cyclone, the service gets suspended, but it is a rare event, and there is a supplementary, but roundabout, service of trams.

The Wanderings of a Spiritualist,
London and New York, 1921

Blue Mountains (New South Wales)

One finds in the Blue Mountains that opportunity of getting alone with real Nature, which is so healing and soothing a thing. The wild scrub flows up the hillsides to the very grounds of the hotels, and in a very few minutes one may find oneself in the wilderness of ferns and gum trees unchanged from immemorial ages. It is a very real danger to the young or to those who have no sense of direction, for many people have wandered off and never come back alive – in fact, there is a specially enrolled body of searchers who hunt for the missing visitor. I have never in all my travels seen anything more spacious and wonderful than the view from the different sandstone bluffs, looking down into the huge gullies beneath, a thousand feet deep, where the great gum trees look like rows of cabbages. I suppose that in water lies the force which, in the course of ages, has worn down the soft, sandy rock and formed these colossal clefts, but the effects are so enormous that one is inclined to think some great earth convulsion must also have been concerned in their production. Some of the cliffs have a sheer drop of over one thousand feet, which is said to be unequalled in the world.

These mountains are so precipitous and tortuous, presenting such a maze to the explorer, that for many years they were a formidable barrier to the extension of the young Colony. There were only about forty miles of arable land from the coast to the great Hawkesbury River, which winds round the base of the mountains. Then came this rocky labyrinth. At last, in 1812, four brave and persevering men – Blaxland, Evans, Wentworth and Lawson – took the matter in hand, and after many adventures, blazed a trail across, by which all the splendid hinterland was opened up, including the gold fields, which found their centre in the new town of Bathurst. When one reflects that all the gold had to be brought across this wilderness, with unexplored woodlands fringing the road, it is no wonder that a race of bushrangers sprang into existence, and the marvel is that the police should ever have been able to hunt them down. So fresh is all this very vital history in the development of a nation, that one can still see upon the trees the marks of the explorers' axes, as they endeavoured to find a straight trail among the countless winding gullies. At Mount York, the highest view-point, a monument has been erected to them, at the place from which they got the first glimpse of the promised land beyond.

The Wanderings of a Spiritualist,
London and New York, 1921

Queensland

The country north of Sydney is exactly like the Blue Mountains, on a lesser scale – riven ranges of sandstone covered with gum trees. I cannot understand those who say there is nothing worth seeing in Australia, for I know no big city which has glorious scenery so near it as Sydney. After crossing the Queensland border, one comes to the Darling Downs, unsurpassed for cattle and wheat. Our first impressions of the new State were that it was the most naturally rich of any Australian Colony, and the longer we were in it, the more did we realise that this was indeed so. It is so enormous, however, that it is certain, sooner or later, to be divided into a South, Middle, and North, each of which will be a large and flourishing community. We observed from the railway all sorts of new vegetable life, and I was especially interested to notice that our English Yellow Mullein was lining the track, making its way gradually up country.

Even Sydney did not provide a warmer and more personal welcome than that which we both received when we at last reached Brisbane.

. . .

We recuperated after our Brisbane tour by spending the next week at Medlow Bath, that little earthly paradise, which is the most restful spot we have found in our wanderings. It was built originally by Mr. Mark Foy, a successful draper of Sydney, and he is certainly a man of taste, for he has adorned it with a collection of prints and of paintings – hundreds of each – which would attract attention in any city, but which on a mountain top amid the wildest scenery give one the idea of an Arabian Nights palace. There was a passage some hundreds of yards long, which one has to traverse on the way to each meal, and there was a certain series of French prints, representing events of Byzantine history, which I found it difficult to pass, so that I was often a late comer. A very fair library is among the other attractions of this remarkable place.

Before leaving we spent one long day at the famous Jenolan Caves, which are distant about forty-five miles. As the said miles are very up-and-down, and as the cave exploration involves several hours of climbing, it makes a fairly hard day's work. We started all seven in a motor, as depicted by the wayside photographers, but Baby got sick and had to be left with Jakeman at the half-way house, where we picked her up, quite recovered, on our return.

It was as well, for the walk would have been quite beyond her, and yet having once started there is no return, so we should have ended by carrying her through all the subterranean labyrinths. The road is a remarkably good one, and represents a considerable engineering feat. It passes at last through an enormous archway of rock which marks the entrance to the cave formations. These caves are hollowed out of what was once a coral reef in a tropical sea, but is now sixty miles inland with a mountain upon the top of it – such changes this old world has seen. If the world were formed only that man might play his drama upon it, then mankind must be in the very earliest days of his history, for who would build so elaborate a stage if the play were to be so short and insignificant?

The caves are truly prodigious. They were discovered first in the pursuit of some poor devil of a bushranger who must have been hard put to it before he took up his residence in this damp and dreary retreat. A brave man, Wilson, did most of the actual exploring, lowering himself by a thin rope into noisome abysses of unknown depth and charting out the whole of this devil's warren. It is so vast that many weeks would be needed to go through it, and it is usual at one visit to take only a single sample. On this occasion it was the River Cave, so named because after many wanderings you come on a river about twenty feet across and forty-five feet deep which has to be navigated for some distance in a punt. The stalactite effects, though very wonderful, are not, I think, superior to those which I have seen in Derbyshire, and the caves have none of that historical glamour which is needed in order to link some large natural object to our own comprehension. I can remember in Derbyshire how my imagination and sympathy were stirred by a Roman lady's brooch which had been found among the rubble. Either a wild beast or a bandit knew best how it got there. Jenolan has few visible links with the past, but one of them is a tremendous one. It is the complete, though fractured, skeleton of a very large man – seven foot four said the guide, but he may have put it on a little – who was found partly imbedded in the lime. Many ages ago he seems to have fallen through the roof of the cavern, and the bones of a wallaby hard by give some indication that he was hunting at the time, and that his quarry shared his fate ...

We all emerged rather exhausted from the bowels of the earth, dazed with the endless succession of strange gypsum formations which we had seen, minarets, thrones, shawls, coronets, some of them so made that one could imagine that the old kobolds had employed their leisure hours in fashioning their freakish outlines. It was a memorable drive home in the evening. Once as a bird flew above my head, the slanting ray of the declining sun struck it and turned it suddenly to a vivid scarlet and green. It was the first of many parrots. Once also a couple of kangaroos bounded across the road, amid wild cries of delight from the children. Once, too, a long snake writhed across and was caught by one of the wheels of the motor. Rabbits, I am sorry to say, abounded. If they would confine themselves to these primeval woods, Australia would be content.

The Wanderings of a Spiritualist,
London and New York, 1921

He also ventured across the Tasman Sea to New Zealand, where he was initially impressed by Auckland.

Auckland

Auckland is the port of call of the American steamers, and had some of that air of activity and progress which America brings with her. The spirit of enterprise, however, took curious shapes, as in the case of one man who was a local miller, and pushed his trade by long advertisements at the head of the newspapers, which began with abuse of me and my ways, and ended by a recommendation to eat dessicated corn, or whatever his particular commodity may have been.

The result was a comic jumble which was too funny to be offensive, though Auckland should discourage such pleasantries, as they naturally mar the beautiful impression which her fair city and surroundings make upon the visitor. I hope I was the only victim, and that every stranger within her gates is not held up to ridicule for the purpose of calling attention to Mr. Blank's dessicated corn.

...

This town is very wonderfully situated, and I have never seen a more magnificent view than that from Mount Eden, an extinct volcano about 900 feet high, at the back of it. The only one which I could class with it is that from Arthur's Seat, also an extinct volcano about 900 feet high, as one looks on Edinburgh and its environs. Edinburgh, however, is for ever shrouded in smoke, while here the air is crystal clear, and I could clearly see Great Barrier Island, which is a good eighty miles to the north. Below lay the most marvelous medley of light blue water and light green land mottled with darker foliage. We could see not only the whole vista of the wonderful winding harbour, and the seas upon the east of the island, but we could look across and see the firths which connected with the seas of the west. Only a seven-mile canal is needed to link the two up, and to save at least two hundred miles of dangerous navigation amid those rock-strewn waters from which we had so happily emerged. Of course it will be done, and when it is done it should easily pay its way, for what ship coming from Australia – or going to it – but would gladly pay the fees? The real difficulty lies not in cutting the canal, but in dredging the western opening, where shifting sandbanks and ocean currents combine to make a dangerous approach. I see in my mind's eye two great breakwaters, stretching like nippers into the Pacific at that point, while, between the points of the nippers, the dredgers will for ever be at work. It will be difficult, but it is needed and it will be done.

Maoris

If you look at the wonderful ornaments of their old war canoes, which carry a hundred men, and can traverse the whole Pacific, it seems almost incredible that human patience and ingenuity could construct the whole fabric with instruments of stone. They valued them greatly when once they were made, and the actual names of the twenty-two original invading canoes are still recorded.

In the public gallery of Auckland they have a duplicate of one of these enormous canoes. It is 87 feet in length and the thwarts are broad enough to hold three or four men. When it was filled with its hundred warriors, with the chief standing in the centre to give time to the rowers, it must, as it dashed through the waves, have been a truly terrific object. I should think that it represented the supreme achievement of neolithic man ...

Reference has been made to the patient industry of the Maori race. A supreme example of this is that every man had his tikki, or image of a little idol made of greenstone, which was hung round his neck. Now, this New Zealand greenstone is one of the hardest objects in nature, and yet it is worn down without metals into these quaint figures. On an average it took ten years to make one, and it was rubbed down from a chunk of stone into an image by the constant friction of a woman's foot ...

The Wanderings of a Spiritualist,
London and New York, 1921

South America

Mount Roraima

Brazil

Galapagos

Huanchaca
Plateau

State of
Mato Grosso

SOUTH PACIFIC OCEAN

SOUTH ATLANTIC OCEAN

SOUTH AMERICA

Rivers and Mountains

Conan Doyle never visited South America himself, but
he discussed it with many people, including Sir Roger
Casement, the Irish-born British diplomat whom he had
befriended in their campaign against Belgian atrocities
in the Congo and with whom he maintained contact
when he took up consular duties in Brazil. Casement
was one of several travellers who provided Conan Doyle
with background material for his 'wild boy's book',
The Lost World (1912), featuring Professor Challenger.
Another was the ill-fated explorer Percy Fawcett who
supplied information on the Mato Grosso. The terrain
was so powerfully described in Conan Doyle's novel that
it is difficult to imagine that he never set foot on the
continent.

Mato Grosso

Lord John Roxton has chartered a large steam launch,
the *Esmeralda*, which was to carry us up the river. So far
as climate goes, it was immaterial what time we chose
for our expedition, as the temperature ranges from

seventy-five to ninety degrees both summer and winter, with no appreciable difference in heat. In moisture, however, it is otherwise; from December to May is the period of the rains, and during this time the river slowly rises until it attains a height of nearly forty feet above its low-water mark. It floods the banks, extends in great lagoons over a monstrous waste of country, and forms a huge district, called locally the Gapo, which is for the most part too marshy for foot-travel and too shallow for boating. About June the waters begin to fall, and are at their lowest at October or November. Thus our expedition was at the time of the dry season, when the great river and its tributaries were more or less in a normal condition.

The current of the river is a slight one, the drop being not greater than eight inches in a mile. No stream could be more convenient for navigation, since the prevailing wind is south-east, and sailing boats may make a continuous progress to the Peruvian frontier, dropping down again with the current. In our own case the excellent engines of the *Esmeralda* could disregard the sluggish flow of the stream, and we made as rapid progress as if we were navigating a stagnant lake. For three days we steamed north-westwards up a stream which even here, a thousand miles from its mouth, was still so enormous that from its centre the two banks were mere shadows upon the distant skyline. On the fourth day after leaving Manaos we turned into a tributary which at its mouth was little smaller than the main stream. It narrowed rapidly, however, and after two more days' steaming we reached an Indian village, where the Professor insisted that we should land, and that the *Esmeralda* should be sent back to Manaos. We should soon come upon rapids, he explained, which would make its further use impossible. He added privately that we were now approaching the door of the unknown country, and that the fewer whom we took into our confidence the better it would be. To this end also he made each of us give our word of honour that we would publish or say nothing which would give any exact clue as to the whereabouts of our travels, while the servants were all solemnly sworn to the same effect. It is for this reason that I am compelled to be vague in my narrative, and I would warn my readers that in any map or diagram which I may give the relation of places to each other may be correct, but the points of the compass are carefully confused, so that in no way can it be taken as an actual guide to the country. Professor Challenger's reasons for secrecy may be valid or not, but we had no choice but to adopt them, for he was prepared to abandon the whole expedition rather than modify the conditions upon which he would guide us.

. . .

It was indeed a wonderful place. Having reached the spot marked by a line of light-green rushes, we poled out two canoes through them for some hundreds of yards, and eventually emerged into a placid and shallow stream, running clear and transparent over a sandy bottom. It may have been twenty yards across, and was banked in on each side by most luxuriant vegetation. No one who had not observed that for a short distance reeds had taken the place of shrubs, could possibly have guessed the existence of such a stream or dreamed of the fairyland beyond.

For a fairyland it was — the most wonderful that the imagination of man could conceive. The thick vegetation met overhead, interlacing into a natural pergola, and through this tunnel of verdure in a golden twilight flowed the green, pellucid river, beautiful in itself, but marvelous from the strange tints thrown by the vivid light from above filtered and tempered in its fall. Clear as crystal, motionless as a sheet of glass, green as the edge of an iceberg, it stretched in front of us under its leafy archway, every stroke of our paddles sending a thousand ripples across its shining surface. It was a fitting avenue to a land of wonders. All sign of the Indians had passed away, but animal life was more frequent, and the tameness of the creatures showed that they knew nothing of the hunter. Fuzzy little black-velvet monkeys, with snow-white teeth and gleaming, mocking eyes, chattered at us as we passed. With a dull, heavy splash an occasional cayman plunged in from the bank. Once a dark, clumsy tapir stared at us from a gap in the bushes, and then lumbered away through the forest; once, too, the yellow, sinuous form of a great puma whisked amid the brushwood, and its green, baleful eyes glared hatred at us over its tawny shoulder. Bird life was abundant, especially the wading birds, stork, heron, and ibis gathering in little groups, blue, scarlet, and white, upon every log which jutted from the bank, while beneath us the crystal water was alive with fish of every shape and colour.

For three days we made our way up this tunnel of hazy green sunshine. On the longer stretches one could hardly tell as one looked ahead where the distant green water ended and the distant green archway began. The deep peace of this strange waterway was unbroken by any sign of man.

'No Indian here. Too much afraid. Curupuri,' said Gomez.

'Curupuri is the spirit of the woods,' Lord John explained. 'It's a name for any kind of devil. The poor beggars think that there is something fearsome in this direction, and therefore they avoid it.'

On the third day it became evident that our journey in the canoes could not last much longer, for the stream was rapidly growing more shallow. Twice in as many hours we stuck upon the bottom. Finally we pulled the boats up among the brushwood and spent the night on the bank of the river. In the morning Lord John and I made our way for a couple of miles through the forest, keeping parallel with the stream; but as it grew ever shallower we returned and reported, what Professor Challenger had already suspected, that we had reached the highest point to which the canoes could be brought. We drew them up, therefore, and concealed them among the bushes, blazing a tree with our axes, so that we should find them again. Then we distributed the various burdens among us – guns, ammunition, food, a tent, blankets, and the rest – and, shouldering our packages, we set forth upon the more laborious stage of our journey.

...

Advancing in single file along the bank of the stream, we soon found that it narrowed down to a mere brook, and finally that it lost itself in a great green morass of sponge-like mosses, into which we sank up to our knees. The place was horribly haunted by clouds of mosquitoes and every form of flying pest, so we were glad to find solid ground again and to make a circuit among the trees, which enabled us to outflank this pestilent morass, which droned like an organ in the distance, so loud was it with insect life.

On the second day after leaving our canoes we found that the whole character of the country changed. Our road was persistently upwards, and as we ascended the woods became thinner and lost their tropical luxuriance. The huge trees of the alluvial Amazonian plain gave place to the Phoenix and coco palms, growing in scattered clumps, with thick brushwood between. In the damper hollows the Mauritia palms threw out their graceful drooping fronds. We travelled entirely by compass, and once or twice there were differences of opinion between Challenger and the two Indians, when, to quote the Professor's indignant words, the whole party agreed to 'trust the fallacious instincts of undeveloped savages rather than the highest product of modern European culture.' That we were justified in doing so was shown upon the third day, when Challenger admitted that he recognised several landmarks of his former journey, and in one spot we actually came upon four fire-blackened stones, which must have marked a camping-place.

The road still ascended, and we crossed a rock-studded slope which took two days to traverse. The vegetation had again changed, and only the vegetable ivory tree remained, with a great profusion of wonderful orchids, among which I learned to recognise the rare Nuttonia Vexillaria and the glorious pink and scarlet blossoms of Cattleya and odontoglossum. Occasional brooks with pebbly bottoms and fern-draped banks gurgled down the shallow gorges in the hill, and offered good camping-grounds every evening on the banks of some rock-studded pool, where swarms of little blue-backed fish, about the size and shape of English trout, gave us a delicious supper.

On the ninth day after leaving the canoes, having done, as I reckon, about a hundred and twenty miles, we began to emerge from the trees, which had grown smaller until they were mere shrubs. Their place was taken by an immense wilderness of bamboo, which grew so thickly that we could only penetrate it by cutting a pathway with the machetes and billhooks of the Indians. It took us a long day, traveling from seven in the morning till eight at night, with only two breaks of one hour each, to get through this obstacle. Anything more monotonous and wearying could not be imagined, for, even at the most open places, I could not see more than ten or twelve yards, while usually my vision was limited to the back of Lord John's cotton jacket in front of me, and to the yellow wall within a foot of me on either side. From above came one thin knife-edge of sunshine, and fifteen feet over our heads one saw the tops of the reeds swaying against the deep blue sky. I do not know what kind of creatures inhabit such a thicket, but several times we heard the plunging of large, heavy animals quite close to us. From their sounds Lord John judged them to be some form of wild cattle. Just as night fell we cleared the belt of bamboos, and at once formed our camp, exhausted by the interminable day.

Early next morning we were again afoot, and found that the character of the country had changed once again. Behind us was the wall of bamboo, as definite as if it marked the course of a river. In front was an open plain, sloping slightly upwards and dotted with clumps of tree-ferns, the whole curving before us until it ended in a long, whale-backed ridge. This we reached about midday, only to find a shallow valley beyond, rising once again into a gentle incline which led to a low, rounded sky-line. It was here, while we crossed the first of these hills, that an incident occurred which may or may not have been important.

. . .

After a long pause, therefore, to recover my breath and my courage, I continued my ascent. Once I put my weight upon a rotten branch and swung for a few seconds by my hands, but in the main it was all easy climbing. Gradually the leaves thinned around me, and I was aware, from the wind upon my face, that I had topped all the trees of the forest. I was determined, however, not to look about me before I had reached the very highest point, so I scrambled on until I had got so far that the topmost branch was bending beneath my weight. There I settled into a convenient fork, and, balancing myself securely, I found myself looking down at a most wonderful panorama of this strange country in which we found ourselves.

The sun was just above the western sky-line, and the evening was a particularly bright and clear one, so that the whole extent of the plateau was visible beneath me. It was, as seen from this height, of an oval contour, with a breadth of about thirty miles and a width of twenty. Its general shape was that of a shallow funnel, all the sides sloping down to a considerable lake in the centre. This lake may have been ten miles in circumference, and lay very green and beautiful in the evening light, with a thick fringe of reeds at its edges, and with its surface broken by several yellow sandbanks, which gleamed golden in the mellow sunshine. A number of long dark objects, which were too large for alligators and too long for canoes, lay upon the edges of these patches of sand. With my glass I could clearly see that they were alive, but what their nature might be I could not imagine.

From the side of the plateau on which we were, slopes of woodland, with occasional glades, stretched down for five or six miles to the central lake. I could see at my very feet the glade of the iguanodons, and farther off was a round opening in the trees which marked the swamp of the pterodactyls. On the side facing me, however, the plateau presented a very different aspect. There the basalt cliffs of the outside were reproduced upon the inside, forming an escarpment about two hundred feet high, with a woody slope beneath it. Along the base of these red cliffs, some distance above the ground, I could see a number of dark holes through the glass, which I conjectured to be the mouths of caves. At the opening of one of these something white was shimmering, but I was unable to make out what it was. I sat charting the country until the sun had set and it was so dark that I could no longer distinguish details. Then I climbed down to my companions waiting for me so eagerly at the bottom of the great tree. For once I was the hero of the expedition. Alone I had thought of it, and alone I had done it; and here was the chart which would save us a month's blind groping among unknown dangers. Each of them shook me solemnly by the hand.

. . .

I had not gone a hundred yards before I deeply repented my rashness. I may have said somewhere in this chronicle that I am too imaginative to be a really courageous man, but that I have an overpowering fear of seeming afraid. This was the power which now carried me onwards. I simply could not slink back with nothing done. Even if my comrades should not have missed me, and should never know of my weakness, there would still remain some intolerable self-shame in my own soul. And yet I shuddered at the position in which I found myself, and would have given all I possessed at that moment to have been honorably free of the whole business.

It was dreadful in the forest. The trees grew so thickly and their foliage spread so widely that I could see nothing of the moonlight save that here and there the high branches made a tangled filigree against the starry sky. As the eyes became more used to the obscurity one learned that there were different degrees of darkness among the trees – that some were dimly visible, while between and among them there were coal-black shadowed patches, like the mouths of caves, from which I shrank in horror as I passed. I thought of the despairing yell of the tortured iguanodon – that dreadful cry which had echoed through the woods. I thought, too, of the glimpse I had in the light of Lord John's torch of that bloated, warty, blood-slavering muzzle. Even now I was on its hunting-ground. At any instant it might spring upon me from the shadows – this nameless and horrible monster. I stopped, and, picking a cartridge from my pocket, I opened the breech of my gun. As I touched the lever my heart leaped within me. It was the shot-gun, not the rifle, which I had taken!

Again the impulse to return swept over me. Here, surely, was a most excellent reason for my failure – one for which no one would think the less of me. But again the foolish pride fought against that very word. I could not – must not – fail. After all, my rifle would probably have been as useless as a shot-gun against such dangers as I might meet. If I were to go back to camp to change my weapon I could hardly expect to enter and to leave again without being seen. In that case there would be explanations, and my attempt would no longer be all my own. After a little hesitation, then, I screwed up my courage and continued upon my way, my useless gun under my arm.

The darkness of the forest had been alarming, but even worse was the white, still flood of moonlight in the open glade of the iguanodons. Hid among the bushes, I looked out at it. None of the great brutes were in sight. Perhaps the tragedy which had befallen one of them had driven them from their feeding-ground. In the misty, silvery night I could see no sign of any living thing. Taking courage, therefore, I slipped rapidly across it, and among the jungle on the farther side I picked up once again the brook which was my guide. It was a cheery companion, gurgling and chuckling as it ran, like the dear old trout-stream in the West Country where I have fished at night in my boyhood. So long as I followed it down I must come to the lake, and so long as I followed it back I must come to the camp. Often I had to lose sight of it on account of the tangled brush-wood, but I was always within earshot of its tinkle and splash.

As one descended the slope the woods became thinner, and bushes, with occasional high trees, took the place of the forest. I could make good progress, therefore, and I could see without being seen. I passed close to the pterodactyl swamp, and as I did so, with a dry, crisp, leathery rattle of wings, one of these great creatures – it was twenty feet at least from tip to tip – rose up from somewhere near me and soared into the air. As it passed across the face of the moon the light shone clearly through the membranous wings, and it looked like a flying skeleton against the white, tropical radiance. I crouched low among the bushes, for I knew from past experience that with a single cry the creature could bring a hundred of its loathsome mates about my ears. It was not until it had settled again that I dared to steal onwards upon my journey.

The night had been exceedingly still, but as I advanced I became conscious of a low, rumbling sound, a continuous murmur, somewhere in front of me. This grew louder as I proceeded, until at last it was clearly quite close to me. When I stood still the sound was constant, so that it seemed to come from some stationary cause. It was like a boiling kettle or the bubbling of some great pot. Soon I came upon the source of it, for in the centre of a small clearing I found a lake – or a pool, rather, for it was not larger than the basin of the Trafalgar Square fountain – of some black, pitch-like stuff, the surface of which rose and fell in great blisters of bursting gas. The air above it was shimmering with heat, and the ground round was so hot that I could hardly bear to lay my hand on it. It was clear that the great volcanic outburst which had raised this strange plateau so many years ago had not yet entirely spent its forces. Blackened rocks and mounds of lava I had already seen everywhere peeping out from amid the luxuriant vegetation which draped them, but this asphalt pool in the jungle was the first sign that we had of actual existing activity on the slopes of the ancient crater. I had no time to examine it further for I had need to hurry if I were to be back in camp in the morning.

It was a fearsome walk, and one which will be with me so long as memory holds. In the great moonlight clearings I slunk along among the shadows on the margin. In the jungle I crept forward, stopping with a beating heart whenever I heard, as I often did, the crash of breaking branches as some wild beast went past.

Now and then great shadows loomed up for an instant and were gone – great, silent shadows which seemed to prowl upon padded feet. How often I stopped with the intention of returning, and yet every time my pride conquered my fear, and sent me on again until my object should be attained.

At last (my watch showed that it was one in the morning) I saw the gleam of water amid the openings of the jungle, and ten minutes later I was among the reeds upon the borders of the central lake. I was exceedingly dry, so I lay down and took a long draught of its waters, which were fresh and cold. There was a broad pathway with many tracks upon it at the spot which I had found, so that it was clearly one of the drinking-places of the animals. Close to the water's edge there was a huge isolated block of lava. Up this I climbed, and, lying on the top, I had an excellent view in every direction.

The first thing which I saw filled me with amazement. When I described the view from the summit of the great tree, I said that on the farther cliff I could see a number of dark spots, which appeared to be the mouths of caves. Now, as I looked up at the same cliffs, I saw discs of light in every direction, ruddy, clearly-defined patches, like the port-holes of a liner in the darkness. For a moment I thought it was the lava-glow from some volcanic action; but this could not be so. Any volcanic action would surely be down in the hollow and not high among the rocks. What, then, was the alternative? It was wonderful, and yet it must surely be. These ruddy spots must be the reflection of fires within the caves – fires which could only be lit by the hand of man. There were human beings, then, upon the plateau. How gloriously my expedition was justified! Here was news indeed for us to bear back with us to London!

For a long time I lay and watched these red, quivering blotches of light. I suppose they were ten miles off from me, yet even at that distance one could observe how, from time to time, they twinkled or were obscured as someone passed before them. What would I not have given to be able to crawl up to them, to peep in, and to take back some word to my comrades as to the appearance and character of the race who lived in so strange a place! It was out of the question for the moment, and yet surely we could not leave the plateau until we had some definite knowledge upon the point.

Lake Gladys – my own lake – lay like a sheet of quicksilver before me, with a reflected moon shining brightly in the centre of it. It was shallow, for in many places I saw low sandbanks protruding above the water. Everywhere upon the still surface I could see signs of life, sometimes mere rings and ripples in the water, sometimes the gleam of a great silver-sided fish in the air, sometimes the arched, slate-colored back of some passing monster. Once upon a yellow sandbank I saw a creature like a huge swan, with a clumsy body and a high, flexible neck, shuffling about upon the margin. Presently it plunged in, and for some time I could see the arched neck and darting head undulating over the water. Then it dived, and I saw it no more.

My attention was soon drawn away from these distant sights and brought back to what was going on at my very feet. Two creatures like large armadillos had

come down to the drinking-place, and were squatting
at the edge of the water, their long, flexible tongues
like red ribbons shooting in and out as they lapped.
A huge deer, with branching horns, a magnificent
creature which carried itself like a king, came down
with its doe and two fawns and drank beside the
armadillos. No such deer exist anywhere else upon
earth, for the moose or elks which I have seen would
hardly have reached its shoulders. Presently it gave a
warning snort, and was off with its family among the
reeds, while the armadillos also scuttled for shelter.
A new-comer, a most monstrous animal, was coming
down the path.

The Lost World, London and New York, 1912

GENERAL ROMANCE
AND ADVENTURE

Travel literature – Exploration – Air travel – Channel Tunnel

Conan Doyle's approach to travel as romantic adventure was clear from some of his more general writings, such as *Through the Magic Door*, a series of essays about his favourite books. His references to the travel books on his own shelves confirm his love of romance and adventure.

Travel literature

I have been talking in the past tense of heroes and of knight-errants, but surely their day is not yet passed. When the earth has all been explored, when the last savage has been tamed, when the final cannon has been scrapped, and the world has settled down into unbroken virtue and unutterable dullness, men will cast their thoughts back to our age, and will idealise our romance and – our courage, even as we do that of our distant forbears. 'It is wonderful what these people did with their rude implements and their limited appliances!' That is what they will say when they read of our explorations, our voyages, and our wars.

Now, take that first book on my travel shelf. It is
Knight's 'Cruise of the Falcon'. Nature was guilty of
the pun which put this soul into a body so named. Read
this simple record and tell me if there is anything in
Hakluyt more wonderful. Two landsmen – solicitors,
if I remember right – go down to Southampton Quay.
They pick up a long-shore youth, and they embark in a
tiny boat in which they put to sea. Where do they turn
up? At Buenos Ayres. Thence they penetrate to Paraquay,
return to the West Indies, sell their little boat there, and
so home. What could the Elizabethan mariners have
done more? There are no Spanish galleons now to vary
the monotony of such a voyage, but had there been I am
very certain our adventurers would have had their share
of the doubloons. But surely it was the nobler when
done out of the pure lust of adventure and in answer
to the call of the sea, with no golden bait to draw them
on. The old spirit still lives, disguise it as you will with
top hats, frock coats, and all prosaic settings. Perhaps
even they also will seem romantic when centuries have
blurred them.

Another book which shows the romance and the
heroism which still linger upon earth is that large copy
of the 'Voyage of the Discovery in the Antarctic' by
Captain Scott. Written in plain sailor fashion with no
attempt at over-statement or colour, it none the less
(or perhaps all the more) leaves a deep impression
upon the mind. As one reads it, and reflects on what
one reads, one seems to get a clear view of just those
qualities which make the best kind of Briton. Every
nation produces brave men. Every nation has men

of energy. But there is a certain type which mixes its bravery and its energy with a gentle modesty and a boyish good-humour, and it is just this type which is the highest. Here the whole expedition seems to have been imbued with the spirit of their commander. No flinching, no grumbling, every discomfort taken as a jest, no thought of self, each working only for the success of the enterprise. When you have read of such privations so endured and so chronicled, it makes one ashamed to show emotion over the small annoyances of daily life. Read of Scott's blinded, scurvy-struck party staggering on to their goal, and then complain, if you can, of the heat of a northern sun, or the dust of a country road.

That is one of the weaknesses of modern life. We complain too much. We are not ashamed of complaining. Time was when it was otherwise – when it was thought effeminate to complain. The Gentleman should always be the Stoic, with his soul too great to be affected by the small troubles of life. 'You look cold, sir,' said an English sympathiser to a French émigré. The fallen noble drew himself up in his threadbare coat. 'Sir,' said he, 'a gentleman is never cold.' One's consideration for others as well as one's own self-respect should check the grumble. This self-suppression, and also the concealment of pain are two of the old noblesse oblige characteristics which are now little more than a tradition. Public opinion should be firmer on the matter. The man who must hop because his shin is hacked, or wring his hand because his knuckles are bruised should be made to feel that he is an object not of pity, but of contempt.

The tradition of Arctic exploration is a noble one among Americans as well as ourselves. The next book is a case in point. It is Greely's 'Arctic Service', and it is a worthy shelf-companion to Scott's 'Account of the Voyage of the Discovery'. There are incidents in this book which one can never forget. The episode of those twenty-odd men lying upon that horrible bluff, and dying one a day from cold and hunger and scurvy, is one which dwarfs all our puny tragedies of romance. And the gallant starving leader giving lectures on abstract science in an attempt to take the thoughts of the dying men away from their sufferings – what a picture! It is bad to suffer from cold and bad to suffer from hunger, and bad to live in the dark; but that men could do all these things for six months on end, and that some should live to tell the tale, is, indeed, a marvel. What a world of feeling lies in the exclamation of the poor dying lieutenant: 'Well, this is wretched,' he groaned, as he turned his face to the wall.

The Anglo-Celtic race has always run to individualism, and yet there is none which is capable of conceiving and carrying out a finer ideal of discipline. There is nothing in Roman or Grecian annals, not even the lava-baked sentry at Pompeii, which gives a more sternly fine object-lesson in duty than the young recruits of the British army who went down in their ranks on the Birkenhead. And this expedition of Greely's gave rise to another example which seems to me hardly less remarkable. You may remember, if you have read the book, that even when there were only about eight unfortunates still left, hardly able to move for weakness and hunger, the seven

took the odd man out upon the ice, and shot him dead
for breach of discipline. The whole grim proceeding
was carried out with as much method and signing of
papers, as if they were all within sight of the Capitol at
Washington. His offence had consisted, so far as I can
remember, of stealing and eating the thong which bound
two portions of the sledge together, something about as
appetising as a bootlace. It is only fair to the commander
to say, however, that it was one of a series of petty thefts,
and that the thong of a sledge might mean life or death
to the whole party.

Personally, I must confess that anything bearing
upon the Arctic Seas is always of the deepest interest to
me. He who has once been within the borders of that
mysterious region, which can be both the most lovely
and the most repellent upon earth, must always retain
something of its glamour. Standing on the confines
of known geography I have shot the southward flying
ducks, and have taken from their gizzards pebbles
which they have swallowed in some land whose
shores no human foot has trod. The memory of that
inexpressible air, of the great ice-girt lakes of deep blue
water, of the cloudless sky shading away into a light
green and then into a cold yellow at the horizon, of the
noisy companionable birds, of the huge, greasy-backed
water animals, of the slug-like seals, startlingly black
against the dazzling whiteness of the ice – all of it will
come back to a man in his dreams, and will seem little
more than some fantastic dream itself, so removed is
it from the main stream of his life. And then to play a
fish a hundred tons in weight, and worth two thousand

pounds – but what in the world has all this to do with my bookcase?

Yet it has its place in my main line of thought, for it leads me straight to the very next upon the shelf, Bullen's 'Cruise of the Cachelot', a book which is full of the glamour and the mystery of the sea, marred only by the brutality of those who go down to it in ships. This is the sperm-whale fishing, an open-sea affair, and very different from that Greenland ice groping in which I served a seven-months' apprenticeship. Both, I fear, are things of the past – certainly the northern fishing is so, for why should men risk their lives to get oil when one has but to sink a pipe in the ground. It is the more fortunate then that it should have been handled by one of the most virile writers who has described a sailor's life. Bullen's English at its best rises to a great height. If I wished to show how high, I would take that next book down, 'Sea Idylls'.

How is this, for example, if you have an ear for the music of prose? It is a simple paragraph out of the magnificent description of a long calm in the tropics.

'A change, unusual as unwholesome, came over the bright blue of the sea. No longer did it reflect, as in a limpid mirror, the splendour of the sun, the sweet silvery glow of the moon, or the coruscating clusters of countless stars. Like the ashen-grey hue that bedims the countenance of the dying, a filmy greasy skin appeared to overspread the recent loveliness of the ocean surface. The sea was sick, stagnant, and foul, from its turbid waters arose a miasmatic vapour like a breath of decay, which clung clammily to the palate and dulled all the senses. Drawn by some strange force, from the unfathomable depths below, eerie shapes sought the surface, blinking glassily at the unfamiliar glare they had exchanged for their native gloom – uncouth creatures bedight with tasselled fringes like weed-growths waving around them, fathom-long, medusae with coloured spots like eyes clustering all over their transparent substance, wriggling worm-like forms of such elusive matter that the smallest exposure to the sun melted them, and they were not. Lower down, vast pale shadows creep sluggishly along, happily undistinguishable as yet, but adding a half-familiar flavour to the strange, faint smell that hung about us.'

Take the whole of that essay which describes a calm in the Tropics, or take the other one 'Sunrise as seen from the Crow's-nest', and you must admit that there have been few finer pieces of descriptive English in our time. If I had to choose a sea library of only a dozen volumes I should certainly give Bullen two places. The others? Well, it is so much a matter of individual taste. 'Tom Cringle's Log' should have one for certain. I hope boys respond now as they once did to the sharks and the pirates, the planters, and all the rollicking high spirits of that splendid book. Then there is Dana's 'Two Years before the Mast'. I should find room also for Stevenson's 'Wrecker' and 'Ebb Tide'. Clark Russell deserves a whole shelf for himself, but anyhow you could not miss out 'The Wreck of the Grosvenor'. Marryat, of course, must be represented, and I should pick 'Midshipman Easy' and 'Peter Simple' as his samples. Then throw in one of Melville's Otaheite books – now far too completely forgotten – 'Typee' or 'Omoo', and as a quite modern flavour Kipling's 'Captains Courageous' and Jack London's 'Sea Wolf', with Conrad's 'Nigger of the Narcissus'. Then you will have enough to turn your study into a cabin and bring the wash and surge to your cars, if written words can do it. Oh, how one longs for it sometimes when life grows too artificial, and the old Viking blood begins to stir! Surely it must linger in all of us, for no man who dwells in an island but had an ancestor in longship or in coracle. Still more must the salt drop tingle in the blood of an American when you reflect that in all that broad continent there is not one whose forefather did not cross 3,000 miles of ocean. And yet there are in the Central States millions and millions of their descendants who have never seen the sea.

I have said that 'Omoo' and 'Typee', the books in which the sailor Melville describes his life among the Otaheitans, have sunk too rapidly into obscurity. What a charming and interesting task there is for some critic of catholic tastes and sympathetic judgment to undertake rescue work among the lost books which would repay salvage! A small volume setting forth their names and their claims to attention would be interesting in itself, and more interesting in the material to which it would serve as an introduction. I am sure there are many good books, possibly there are some great ones, which have been swept away for a time in the rush. What chance, for example, has any book by an unknown author which is published at a moment of great national excitement, when some public crisis arrests the popular mind? Hundreds have been still-born in this fashion, and are there none which should have lived among them? Now, there is a book, a modern one, and written by a youth under thirty. It is Snaith's 'Broke of Covenden', and it scarce attained a second edition. I do not say that it is a Classic – I should not like to be positive that it is not – but I am perfectly sure that the man who wrote it has the possibility of a Classic within him. Here is another novel – 'Eight Days', by Forrest. You can't buy it. You are lucky even if you can find it in a library. Yet nothing ever written will bring the Indian Mutiny home to you as this book will do. Here's another which I will warrant you never heard of. It is Powell's 'Animal Episodes'. No, it is not a collection of dog-and-cat anecdotes, but it is a series of very singularly told stories which deal with the animal side of the human, and which you will feel have an entirely new flavour if you have a discriminating palate. The book came out ten years ago, and is utterly unknown. If I can point to three in one small shelf, how many lost lights must be flitting in the outer darkness!

Let me hark back for a moment to the subject with which I began, the romance of travel and the frequent heroism of modern life. I have two books of Scientific Exploration here which exhibit both these qualities as strongly as any I know. I could not choose two better books to put into a young man's hands if you wished to train him first in a gentle and noble firmness of mind, and secondly in a great love for and interest in all that pertains to Nature. The one is Darwin's 'Journal of the Voyage of the Beagle'. Any discerning eye must have detected long before the 'Origin of Species' appeared, simply on the strength of this book of travel, that a brain of the first order, united with many rare qualities of character, had arisen. Never was there a more comprehensive mind. Nothing was too small and nothing too great for its alert observation. One page is occupied in the analysis of some peculiarity in the web of a minute spider, while the next deals with the evidence for the subsidence of a continent and the extinction of a myriad animals. And his sweep of knowledge was so great – botany, geology, zoology, each lending its corroborative aid to the other. How a youth of Darwin's age – he was only twenty-three when in the year 1831 he started round the world on the surveying ship *Beagle* – could have acquired such a mass of information fills one with the same wonder, and is perhaps of the same nature, as the boy musician who exhibits by instinct the touch of the master. Another quality which one would be less disposed to look for in the savant is a fine contempt for danger, which is veiled in such modesty that one reads between the lines in order to detect it. When he was in Argentina, the country outside the Settlements was covered with roving bands of horse Indians, who gave no quarter to any whites. Yet Darwin rode the four hundred miles between Bahia and Buenos Ayres, when even the hardy Gauchos refused to accompany him. Personal danger and a hideous death were small things to him compared to a new beetle or an undescribed fly.

The second book to which I alluded is Wallace's 'Malay Archipelago'. There is a strange similarity in the minds of the two men, the same courage, both moral and physical, the same gentle persistence, the same catholic knowledge and wide sweep of mind, the same passion for the observation of Nature. Wallace

by a flash of intuition understood and described in a
letter to Darwin the cause of the Origin of Species at
the very time when the latter was publishing a book
founded upon twenty years' labour to prove the same
thesis. What must have been his feelings when he read
that letter? And yet he had nothing to fear, for his book
found no more enthusiastic admirer than the man who
had in a sense anticipated it. Here also one sees that
Science has its heroes no less than Religion. One of
Wallace's missions in Papua was to examine the nature
and species of the Birds-of-Paradise; but in the course
of the years of his wanderings through those islands he
made a complete investigation of the whole fauna. A
footnote somewhere explains that the Papuans who
lived in the Bird-of-Paradise country were confirmed
cannibals. Fancy living for years with or near such
neighbours! Let a young fellow read these two books,
and he cannot fail to have both his mind and his spirit
strengthened by the reading.

Through the Magic Door,
London 1907 New York, 1908

Conan Doyle liked to suggest that his romantic view of
the world was being challenged because the black spaces
which once fed his imagination were being filled up by
the discoveries of the explorers of his age. However, he
admired these intrepid individuals, attending a luncheon
for Commander Ernest Shackleton, for example, and
helping to raise funding for Captain Robert Scott. On 3
May 1910 he gave a speech at the Royal Societies Club in
London for the American explorer Commander Robert

Peary, who recently claimed to have become the first person to reach the geographical North Pole. This talk was reported more or less verbatim in *The Times*.

Exploration

The writers of romance had always a certain amount of grievance that explorers were continually encroaching on the domain of the romance writer. (Laughter and cheers.) There had been a time when the world was full of blank spaces, and in which a man of imagination might be able to give free scope to his fancy. (Laughter.) But owing to the ill-directed energy of their guest and other gentlemen of similar tendencies these spaces were rapidly being filled up and the question was where the romance writer was to turn when he wanted to draw any vague and not too clearly-defined region. (Laughter.) Romance writers were a class of people who very much disliked being hampered by facts. (Laughter.) They liked places where they could splash about freely, and where no one was in a position to contradict them. There used to be in his younger days a place known as Tibet. (Laughter.) When they wanted a place in which to put a mysterious old gentleman who could foretell the future, Tibet was a useful spot. (Laughter.) In the last few years, however, a commonplace British army had passed through Tibet, and they had not found any Mahatmas. (Laughter.) One would as soon think now of placing an occult gentleman there as of placing him in Piccadilly-circus. (Laughter.) Then there was Central Africa, which his friend Mr. Rider Haggard as a young man had found to be a splendid hunting ground. There at least was a place where the romanced writer could do what he liked; but since those days they had the railway and the telegraph, and the question was when they came down to dinner whether they should wear a tail coat or whether a smoking jacket would do. (Laughter and cheers.) He had thought also that the Poles would last his time, but here was Commander Peary opening up the one and Captain Scott was going to open up the other. Really he did not know where romance writers would be able to send their characters in order that they might come back chastened and better men. (Laughter.) There were now no vast regions of the world unknown to them, and romance writers would have to be more precise in their writings. When he was young he remembered that he began a story by saying that there was a charming homestead at Nelson; 70 miles north-west of New Zealand. A wretched geographer wrote to him to say that 70 miles north-west of New Zealand was out at sea. (Laughter and cheers.) Even now he could not write about the open Polar sea, without Commander Peary's writing and contradicting him.

The Times, 4 May 1910

Conan Doyle's sense of adventure meant that he was also attracted by the possibilities of air travel. In May 1911 he took to the air from Hendon Airfield in a biplane. In November 1913 he published 'The Horror of the Heights' in *The Strand Magazine* – a story which mixed realism and fantasy about flying.

Air travel

Aeroplaning has been with us now for more than twenty years, and one might well ask: Why should this peril be only revealing itself in our day? The answer is obvious. In the old days of weak engines, when a hundred horse-power Gnome or Green was considered ample for every need, the flights were very restricted. Now that three hundred horse-power is the rule rather than the exception, visits to the upper layers have become easier and more common. Some of us can remember how, in our youth, Garros made a world-wide reputation by attaining nineteen thousand feet, and it was considered a remarkable achievement to fly over the Alps. Our standard now has been immeasurably raised, and there are twenty high flights for one in former years. Many of them have been undertaken with impunity. The thirty-thousand-foot level has been reached time after time with no discomfort beyond cold and asthma. What does this prove? A visitor might descend upon this planet a thousand times and never see a tiger. Yet tigers exist, and if he chanced to come down into a jungle he might be devoured. There are jungles of the upper air, and there are worse things than tigers which inhabit them. I believe in time they will map these jungles accurately out. Even at the present moment I could name two of them. One of them lies over the Pau-Biarritz district of France. Another is just over my head as I write here in my house in Wiltshire. I rather think there is a third in the Homburg-Wiesbaden district.

It was the disappearance of the airmen that first set me thinking. Of course, everyone said that they had fallen into the sea, but that did not satisfy me at all. First, there was Verrier in France; his machine was found near Bayonne, but they never got his body. There was the case of Baxter also, who vanished, though his engine and some of the iron fixings were found in a wood in Leicestershire. In that case, Dr. Middleton, of Amesbury, who was watching the flight with a telescope, declares that just before the clouds obscured the view he saw the machine, which was at an enormous height, suddenly rise perpendicularly upwards in a succession of jerks in a manner that he would have thought to be impossible. That was the last seen of Baxter. There was a correspondence in the papers, but it never led to anything. There were several other similar cases, and then there was the death of Hay Connor. What a cackle there was about an unsolved mystery of the air, and what columns in the halfpenny papers, and yet how little was ever done to get to the bottom of the business! He came down in a tremendous vol-plane from an unknown height. He never got off his machine and died in his pilot's seat. Died of what? 'Heart disease,' said the doctors. Rubbish! Hay Connor's heart was as sound as mine is. What did Venables say? Venables was the only man who was at his side when he died. He said that he was shivering and looked like a man who had been badly scared. 'Died of fright,' said Venables, but could not imagine what he was frightened about. Only said one word to Venables, which sounded like 'Monstrous'. They could make nothing of that at the inquest. But I could make something of it. Monsters! That was the last word of poor Harry Hay Connor. And he DID die of fright, just as Venables thought.

And then there was Myrtle's head. Do you really believe – does anybody really believe – that a man's head could be driven clean into his body by the force of a fall? Well, perhaps it may be possible, but I, for one, have never believed that it was so with Myrtle. And the grease upon his clothes – 'all slimy with grease,' said somebody at the inquest. Queer that nobody got thinking after that! I did – but, then, I had been thinking for a good long time. I've made three ascents – how Dangerfield used to chaff me about my shot-gun – but I've never been high enough. Now, with this new, light Paul Veroner machine and its one hundred and seventy-five Robur, I should easily touch the thirty thousand tomorrow. I'll have a shot at the record. Maybe I shall have a shot at something else as well. Of course, it's dangerous. If a fellow wants to avoid danger he had best keep out of flying altogether and subside finally into flannel slippers and a dressing-gown. But I'll visit the air-jungle tomorrow – and if there's anything there I shall know it. If I return, I'll find myself a bit of a celebrity. If I don't this note-book may explain what I am trying to do, and how I lost my life in doing it. But no drivel about accidents or mysteries, if YOU please.

I chose my Paul Veroner monoplane for the job. There's nothing like a monoplane when real work is to be done. Beaumont found that out in very early days. For one thing it doesn't mind damp, and the weather looks as if we should be in the clouds all the time. It's a bonny little model and answers my hand like a tender-mouthed horse. The engine is a ten-cylinder rotary

Robur working up to one hundred and seventy-five. It has all the modern improvements – enclosed fuselage, high-curved landing skids, brakes, gyroscopic steadiers, and three speeds, worked by an alteration of the angle of the planes upon the Venetian-blind principle. I took a shot-gun with me and a dozen cartridges filled with buck-shot. You should have seen the face of Perkins, my old mechanic, when I directed him to put them in. I was dressed like an Arctic explorer, with two jerseys under my overalls, thick socks inside my padded boots, a storm-cap with flaps, and my talc goggles. It was stifling outside the hangars, but I was going for the summit of the Himalayas, and had to dress for the part. Perkins knew there was something on and implored me to take him with me. Perhaps I should if I were using the biplane, but a monoplane is a one-man show – if you want to get the last foot of life out of it. Of course, I took an oxygen bag; the man who goes for the altitude record without one will either be frozen or smothered – or both.

I had a good look at the planes, the rudder-bar, and the elevating lever before I got in. Everything was in order so far as I could see. Then I switched on my engine and found that she was running sweetly. When they let her go she rose almost at once upon the lowest speed. I circled my home field once or twice just to warm her up, and then with a wave to Perkins and the others, I flattened out my planes and put her on her highest. She skimmed like a swallow downwind for eight or ten miles until I turned her nose up a little and she began to climb in a great spiral for the cloud-bank above me. It's all-important to rise slowly and adapt yourself to the pressure as you go.

It was a close, warm day for an English September, and there was the hush and heaviness of impending rain. Now and then there came sudden puffs of wind from the south-west – one of them so gusty and unexpected that it caught me napping and turned me half-round for an instant. I remember the time when gusts and whirls and air-pockets used to be things of danger – before we learned to put an overmastering power into our engines. Just as I reached the cloud-banks, with the altimeter marking three thousand, down came the rain. My word, how it poured! It drummed upon my wings and lashed against my face, blurring my glasses so that I could hardly see. I got down on to a low speed, for it was painful to travel against it. As I got higher it became hail, and I had to turn tail to it. One of my cylinders was out of action – a dirty plug, I should imagine, but still I was rising steadily with plenty of power. After a bit the trouble passed, whatever it was, and I heard the full, deep-throated purr – the ten singing as one. That's where the beauty of our modern silencers comes in. We can at last control our engines by ear. How they squeal and squeak and sob when they are in trouble! All those cries for help were wasted in the old days, when every sound was swallowed up by the monstrous racket of the machine. If only the early aviators could come back to see the beauty and perfection of the mechanism which have been bought at the cost of their lives!

About nine-thirty I was nearing the clouds. Down below me, all blurred and shadowed with rain, lay the vast expanse of Salisbury Plain. Half a dozen flying machines were doing hackwork at the thousand-foot level, looking like little black swallows against the green background. I dare say they were wondering what I was doing up in cloud-land. Suddenly a grey curtain drew across beneath me and the wet folds of vapours were swirling round my face. It was clammily cold and miserable. But I was above the hail-storm, and that was something gained. The cloud was as dark and thick as a London fog. In my anxiety to get clear, I cocked her nose up until the automatic alarm-bell rang, and I actually began to slide backwards. My sopped and dripping wings had made me heavier than I thought, but presently I was in lighter cloud, and soon had cleared the first layer. There was a second – opal-coloured and fleecy – at a great height above my head, a white, unbroken ceiling above, and a dark, unbroken floor below, with the monoplane labouring upwards upon a vast spiral between them. It is deadly lonely in these cloud-spaces. Once a great flight of some small water-birds went past me, flying very fast to the westwards. The quick whir of their wings and their musical cry were cheery to my ear. I fancy that they were teal, but I am a wretched zoologist. Now that we humans have become birds we must really learn to know our brethren by sight.

The wind down beneath me whirled and swayed the broad cloud-plain. Once a great eddy formed in it, a whirlpool of vapour, and through it, as down a funnel, I caught sight of the distant world. A large white biplane was passing at a vast depth beneath me. I fancy it was the morning mail service betwixt Bristol and London.

Then the drift swirled inwards again and the great solitude was unbroken.

Just after ten I touched the lower edge of the upper cloud-stratum. It consisted of fine diaphanous vapour drifting swiftly from the westwards. The wind had been steadily rising all this time and it was now blowing a sharp breeze – twenty-eight an hour by my gauge. Already it was very cold, though my altimeter only marked nine thousand. The engines were working beautifully, and we went droning steadily upwards. The cloud-bank was thicker than I had expected, but at last it thinned out into a golden mist before me, and then in an instant I had shot out from it, and there was an unclouded sky and a brilliant sun above my head – all blue and gold above, all shining silver below, one vast, glimmering plain as far as my eyes could reach. It was a quarter past ten o'clock, and the barograph needle pointed to twelve thousand eight hundred. Up I went and up, my ears concentrated upon the deep purring of my motor, my eyes busy always with the watch, the revolution indicator, the petrol lever, and the oil pump. No wonder aviators are said to be a fearless race. With so many things to think of there is no time to trouble about oneself. About this time I noted how unreliable is the compass when above a certain height from earth. At fifteen thousand feet mine was pointing east and a point south. The sun and the wind gave me my true bearings.

I had hoped to reach an eternal stillness in these high altitudes, but with every thousand feet of ascent the gale grew stronger. My machine groaned and trembled in every joint and rivet as she faced it, and swept away like a sheet of paper when I banked her on the turn, skimming downwind at a greater pace, perhaps, than ever mortal man has moved. Yet I had always to turn again and tack up in the wind's eye, for it was not merely a height record that I was after. By all my calculations it was above little Wiltshire that my air-jungle lay, and all my labour might be lost if I struck the outer layers at some farther point.

When I reached the nineteen-thousand-foot level, which was about midday, the wind was so severe that I looked with some anxiety to the stays of my wings, expecting momentarily to see them snap or slacken. I even cast loose the parachute behind me, and fastened its hook into the ring of my leathern belt, so as to be ready for the worst. Now was the time when a bit of scamped work by the mechanic is paid for by the life of the aeronaut. But she held together bravely. Every cord and strut was humming and vibrating like so many harp-strings, but it was glorious to see how, for all the beating and the buffeting, she was still the conqueror of Nature and the mistress of the sky. There is surely something divine in man himself that he should rise so superior to the limitations which Creation seemed to impose — rise, too, by such unselfish, heroic devotion as this air-conquest has shown. Talk of human degeneration! When has such a story as this been written in the annals of our race?

These were the thoughts in my head as I climbed that monstrous, inclined plane with the wind sometimes beating in my face and sometimes whistling behind

my ears, while the cloud-land beneath me fell away
to such a distance that the folds and hummocks of
silver had all smoothed out into one flat, shining plain.
But suddenly I had a horrible and unprecedented
experience. I have known before what it is to be in
what our neighbours have called a tourbillon, but
never on such a scale as this. That huge, sweeping river
of wind of which I have spoken had, as it appears,
whirlpools within it which were as monstrous as itself.
Without a moment's warning I was dragged suddenly
into the heart of one. I spun round for a minute or
two with such velocity that I almost lost my senses,
and then fell suddenly, left wing foremost, down the
vacuum funnel in the centre. I dropped like a stone,
and lost nearly a thousand feet. It was only my belt that
kept me in my seat, and the shock and breathlessness
left me hanging half-insensible over the side of the
fuselage. But I am always capable of a supreme effort
— it is my one great merit as an aviator. I was conscious
that the descent was slower. The whirlpool was a cone
rather than a funnel, and I had come to the apex. With
a terrific wrench, throwing my weight all to one side, I
levelled my planes and brought her head away from the
wind. In an instant I had shot out of the eddies and was
skimming down the sky. Then, shaken but victorious,
I turned her nose up and began once more my steady
grind on the upward spiral. I took a large sweep to
avoid the danger-spot of the whirlpool, and soon I was
safely above it. Just after one o'clock I was twenty-
one thousand feet above the sea-level. To my great joy
I had topped the gale, and with every hundred feet of

ascent the air grew stiller. On the other hand, it was very cold, and I was conscious of that peculiar nausea which goes with rarefaction of the air. For the first time I unscrewed the mouth of my oxygen bag and took an occasional whiff of the glorious gas. I could feel it running like a cordial through my veins, and I was exhilarated almost to the point of drunkenness. I shouted and sang as I soared upwards into the cold, still outer world.

It is very clear to me that the insensibility which came upon Glaisher, and in a lesser degree upon Coxwell, when, in 1862, they ascended in a balloon to the height of thirty thousand feet, was due to the extreme speed with which a perpendicular ascent is made. Doing it at an easy gradient and accustoming oneself to the lessened barometric pressure by slow degrees, there are no such dreadful symptoms. At the same great height I found that even without my oxygen inhaler I could breathe without undue distress. It was bitterly cold, however, and my thermometer was at zero, Fahrenheit. At one-thirty I was nearly seven miles above the surface of the earth, and still ascending steadily. I found, however, that the rarefied air was giving markedly less support to my planes, and that my angle of ascent had to be considerably lowered in consequence. It was already clear that even with my light weight and strong engine-power there was a point in front of me where I should be held. To make matters worse, one of my sparking-plugs was in trouble again and there was intermittent misfiring in the engine. My heart was heavy with the fear of failure.

It was about that time that I had a most extraordinary experience. Something whizzed past me in a trail of smoke and exploded with a loud, hissing sound, sending forth a cloud of steam. For the instant I could not imagine what had happened. Then I remembered that the earth is for ever being bombarded by meteor stones, and would be hardly inhabitable were they not in nearly every case turned to vapour in the outer layers of the atmosphere. Here is a new danger for the high-altitude man, for two others passed me when I was nearing the forty-thousand-foot mark. I cannot doubt that at the edge of the earth's envelope the risk would be a very real one.

'The Horror of the Heights', *The Strand Magazine*, November 1913. Collected in *Danger! And Other Stories*, London 1918, New York 1919

As well as flying, Conan Doyle was interested in most things related to travel. He was a great advocate of a tunnel under the English Channel, between England and France, for example, as he argued in this letter to *The Times*.

Channel Tunnel

TO THE EDITOR OF THE TIMES.

Sir, – I welcome General Sir R. Talbot's letter dealing with the Channel Tunnel which appeared in your issue to-day. The matter seems to me of such importance that I grudge every day that passes without something having been done to bring it to realisation. Built from national fund, it would in peace be a most valuable asset, while in war with any nation but France it would vastly increase our strength both for offensive and defensive purposes. The advantages which I see for a national tunnel are briefly as follows:—

1. If constructed by the nation for anything like the estimate advanced by capable engineers it should be a source of great profit to the country.
2. It should stimulate our trade with the Continent, since bulk need not be broken.
3. It should bring to England very many thousands of Continental travellers every year who are at present deterred by the crossing.
4. Should we ever be forced to send troops to the Continent, it provides a safe line of communication besides ensuring an unopposed transit.
5. It enables food to be introduced into the country in war time, and would help us to hold out, even after a naval defeat. All the supplies of the Mediterranean are available via Marseilles.
6. It passes out some of our exports in war time, and to that extent relieves the Fleet of the duty of convoying them.

These six reasons seem to me to be weighty ones. Against them there is only one that I have ever heard, the fear of invasion. This can of course only mean invasion by France, which cannot surely be regarded as a serious danger, although I admit that every defensive precaution should be taken. As to invasion, by any other country, it means that they have first to win and to hold both ends of the tunnel. Such a contingency is, I hold, beyond all bounds of common sense.

Yours faithfully,

ARTHUR CONAN DOYLE.
Athenaeum Club, March 10.

The Times, 11 March 1913

These final passages show Conan Doyle continuing to be excited by the potential of travel, pushing its boundaries into the skies and beneath the oceans. He remained true to his childhood enthusiasm for exploration in an age when he was also becoming painfully aware that the number of truly unknown areas in the world was diminishing. The contradiction between the questing spirit of the modern world and a nobler ideal of discovery and adventure was one Conan Doyle wrestled with throughout his life. It is reflected in his Sherlock Holmes stories where the romantic detective calls on the latest scientific advances to solve his mysteries. And it goes to the heart of Conan Doyle himself – the split between his scientifically trained doctor's quest for knowledge and his innate sense of something deeper, more elemental and more spiritual.

Conan Doyle's travel writing is at its best when he was trying to convey something of the complex interplay between people, their history and their environment. This was particularly apparent in his accounts of the deserts of both Egypt and Southern Africa. He was fascinated by wide open spaces in North America, Australia and of

course the sea. And he was always aware of the discipline
and hardships that accompany real travel. This was as true
in his youthful excursions to the Arctic and Africa as in his
later journeys in Canada and Australia where his concerns
about the economic potential of these British dominions
sprang just as much from his enduring curiosity about man
and his surroundings.

ACKNOWLEDGEMENTS

I am grateful to Michael Gunton, senior archivist at Portsmouth Library and Archive Service, and to his colleagues at the city's Arthur Conan Doyle Collection. The majority of the photographs come from the Arthur Conan Doyle Collection, part of the Richard Lancelyn Green bequest held by Portsmouth City Council. In addition photographic images were provided by Georgina Doyle (Lady Wilson) and Alamy. I am grateful to them all for permission to reproduce these items.

Thank you to Richard Pooley and Jon Lellenberg from the Conan Doyle Estate for providing permissions and advice.

Many thanks also to Tatiana Wilde, who commissioned this book at I.B. Tauris, and to my editor, Jayne Parsons, who took it on at Bloomsbury and guided it to publication with great energy, enthusiasm and expertise. I am also grateful to Claire Browne for her oversight and to Tom Parker for his expert work on the maps.

SELECT BIBLIOGRAPHY

The standard editions of the Sherlock Holmes stories are as follows:

A Study in Scarlet (1888)
The Sign of Four (1890)
The Adventures of Sherlock Holmes (1892)
The Memoirs of Sherlock Holmes (1893)
The Hound of the Baskervilles (1902)
The Return of Sherlock Holmes (1905)
The Valley of Fear (1915)
His Last Bow (1917)
The Casebook of Sherlock Holmes (1927)

In addition the following works by Arthur Conan Doyle have been consulted for this book:

Fiction:
Micah Clarke (1889)
The Captain of the Pole-Star and Other Tales (1890)
The Firm of Girdlestone (1890)
The White Company (1891)
The Exploits of Brigadier Gerard (1896)
The Tragedy of the Korosko (1898)
The Adventures of Gerard (1903)
Sir Nigel (1906)
The Lost World (1912)
The Poems of Arthur Conan Doyle – Collected Edition (1922)

Non-Fiction:
The Great Boer War (1900)
Through the Magic Door (1907)

The Crime of the Congo (1909)
Western Wanderings (1915)
A Visit to Three Fronts (1916)
The Wanderings of a Spiritualist (1921)
Our American Adventure (1923)
Our Second American Adventure (1924)
Memories and Adventures (1924)
Our African Winter (1929)

Other books which have proved useful in compiling this anthology include:

Conan Doyle, Arthur, *Dangerous Work: Diary of an Arctic Adventure*, edited by Jon Lellenberg and Daniel Stashower (British Library, London, 2012)

Conan Doyle, Arthur, *Essays on Photography*, edited by John Michael Gibson and Richard Lancelyn Green (Martin Secker & Warburg, London, 1982)

Conan Doyle, Arthur, *Letters to the Press*, edited by John Michael Gibson and Richard Lancelyn Green (Martin Secker & Warburg, London, 1986)

Doyle, Georgina, *Out of the Shadows: The Untold Story of Arthur Conan Doyle's First Family* (Calabash Press, Ashcroft, B.C., 2004)

Lellenberg, Jon, Stashower, Dan and Foley, Charles, *Conan Doyle: A Life in Letters* (HarperPress, London, 2007)

Lycett, Andrew, *Conan Doyle: The Man Who Created Sherlock Holmes* (Weidenfeld & Nicolson, London, 2007)

Pugh, Brian, *A Chronology of Arthur Conan Doyle* (MX Publishing, London, 2012)

Redmond, Christopher, *Welcome to America, Mr Sherlock Holmes* (Simon & Pierre, Toronto, 1987)

Stavert, Geoffrey, *A Study in Southsea* (Milestone Publications, Portsmouth, 1987)

A NOTE ON THE AUTHOR

Andrew Lycett is a writer and broadcaster who has written acclaimed biographies of Ian Fleming, Rudyard Kipling, Dylan Thomas, Wilkie Collins and Arthur Conan Doyle. As a journalist, Lycett has contributed regularly to *The Times*, *Sunday Times* and many other newspapers and magazines. He is a Fellow of both the Royal Society of Literature and the Royal Geographical Society.

INDEX